# SECULAR
# BUDDHISM

ALSO BY STEPHEN BATCHELOR

*Alone with Others: An Existential Approach to Buddhism* (1983)
*The Tibet Guide: Central and Western Tibet* (1988)
*The Faith to Doubt: Glimpses of Buddhist Uncertainty* (1990)
*The Awakening of the West: Encounters between*
*Buddhism and Western Culture* (1994)
*Buddhism without Beliefs: A Contemporary Guide*
*to Awakening* (1997)
*Verses from the Center: A Buddhist Vision of the Sublime* (2000)
*Living with the Devil: A Meditation on Good and Evil* (2004)
*Confession of a Buddhist Atheist* (2010)
*After Buddhism: Rethinking the Dharma for a Secular Age* (2015)

# SECULAR
# BUDDHISM

IMAGINING
THE DHARMA IN AN
UNCERTAIN WORLD

*Stephen Batchelor*

Yale UNIVERSITY PRESS/NEW HAVEN & LONDON

Published with assistance from the Louis Stern Memorial Fund.

Yale University Press books may be purchased in quantity for
educational, business, or promotional use. For information, please
e-mail sales.press@yale.edu (U.S. office) or sales@yaleup.co.uk
(U.K. office).

Designed by Mary Valencia.
Set in Scala type by Integrated Publishing Solutions.
Printed in the United States of America.

Library of Congress Control Number: 2016948566
ISBN 978-0-300-22323-1 (hardcover : alk. paper)

A catalogue record for this book is available
from the British Library.

This paper meets the requirements of ANSI/NISO
Z39.48-1992 (Permanence of Paper).

10 9 8 7 6 5 4 3 2 1

*For Helen Tworkov*

It should be borne in mind that there is nothing more difficult to arrange, more doubtful of success, and more dangerous to carry through than initiating change.

The innovator makes enemies of all those who prospered under the old order, and only lukewarm support is forthcoming from those who would prosper under the new.

—Niccolò Machiavelli, *The Prince*

# CONTENTS

# PREFACE

As the practice of mindfulness finds its way into mainstream Western culture, more and more people today find themselves engaging in a form of Buddhist meditation. Such men and women may have little or no interest in Buddhism as a religion; their adoption of meditation occurs entirely within secular contexts such as healthcare, education, or the workplace.

The very fact that a core practice of an ancient world religion can be shown through clinical trials to be effective irrespective of whether one is a Buddhist raises fundamental questions about the nature of Buddhism itself. Is this tradition best characterized as a religion? Or did it start out as a practical philosophy and mutate into a religion? Might we still be able to recover from the teachings of the Buddha a vision of human flourishing that is secular rather than religious in orientation yet without compromising the integrity of the dharma?

Such questions have given rise to a phenomenon that is now being called "secular Buddhism." This book traces how my own understanding and practice of the dharma has evolved in an increasingly secular direction over the past twenty-five years. The writings collected here date to the early 1990s, when I started writing for *Tricycle: The Buddhist Review.* I regard the work that began in this period as what eventually resulted in my coming to advocate a fully fledged secular practice of Buddhism. A key moment in this process was the publication of *Buddhism without Beliefs,* which was commissioned by *Tricycle,* in 1997.

The introductory essay ("In Search of a Voice") and the concluding essay ("An Aesthetics of Emptiness") were written for this volume. One other piece ("A Much Younger Man, but No Less Charming") is published here for the first time. The other essays and interviews have appeared in a broad range of journals, anthologies, magazines, and newspapers (for publishing details, see Acknowledgments). I have left these pieces in the form in which they originally appeared, deleting passages only if they repeat what has already been said elsewhere in the collection. Occasionally I have rewritten a sentence if I judge it to be factually incorrect, misleading, ambiguous, or poorly crafted. Otherwise, the reader will notice how through the course of these writings I struggle to settle on the meaning of such terms as "spiritual," "religious," "secular," "agnostic," "skeptical," "non-self," and "emptiness."

# INTRODUCTION

# In Search of a Voice

My quest over the past four decades to understand how the Buddha's teachings—the dharma—might speak to our condition today has pursued two primary strands: a search for foundational Buddhist texts that address universal human concerns, on the one hand, and an attempt to articulate the message of those texts in a contemporary idiom, on the other. Without differentiating between teachings that address issues specific to the beliefs of the ancient world and those that address what it means to be fully human irrespective of cultural or historical context, one will lack a solid basis on which to develop a Buddhist vision for our times. Yet even if one were to identify clearly such teachings, without also finding an appropriate voice in which to express them, they would risk remaining the preserve of specialists and fail to speak to the concerns of a broader public.

Such a quest is nothing new. Each time Buddhism has entered into a new cultural sphere, it has faced the same challenge. As a result, every tradition that has come down to us from Asia is founded on a different set of foundational Buddhist texts and over time has constructed its own canon. Moreover, each tradition speaks to us in a distinctive voice inflected by the cultural and religious concerns of Indians, Chinese, Tibetans, Japanese, and so on. In some cases, this has led Buddhists to compose apocryphal sutras that are attributed to the Buddha in order to grant them authority. Elsewhere, the writings of founding figures in those traditions, such as Buddhaghosa, Huineng, and Tsongkhapa, have themselves acquired canonical status. This creative vitality that has characterized all historical Buddhist schools will probably continue as long as the dharma remains a living tradition. Exactly how it will manifest in the context of modernity is, of course, impossible to foresee. For this reason, the reflections that follow should be treated with caution as part of a tentative work-in-progress.

In my own case, this ongoing process of cultural adaptation has occurred through dialogue and conversation with a wide range of figures from both Buddhist and non-Buddhist traditions. Moreover, for me, as a scholar-practitioner, such dialogues have addressed not only questions of textual interpretation but existential concerns about what it means to be fully human. To illustrate this, I will provide examples of four conversations that I have held over the years with (1) the Mahayana Buddhist author Śāntideva, (2) the Christian church father Augustine of Hippo, (3) Gotama, the Buddha, and (4) the German philosopher Ludwig Feuerbach.

## ( 1 )

I can still picture a key moment in my conversation with the Indian Buddhist monk-poet Śāntideva (eighth century CE). It took place in 1975 on a wooded hillside above the Himalayan town of Dharamsala when I was a recently ordained Tibetan Buddhist novice monk. I can only describe it as a dumbstruck epiphany concerning what it felt like to translate a text from a foreign tongue (Tibetan) into my own (English).

To be struck "dumb" might seem an odd way of expressing an insight into the linguistic act of translation. I can find no better way to capture the momentary suspension of thought and words as I marveled in what was happening. I was seated cross-legged in a focused reverie, beneath a canopy of dark green leaves, with a red, plastic bound *Shakti* PRODUCT notebook on my lap and a fountain pen in one hand, pondering how to translate verse 35 from chapter 2 of Śāntideva's *Bodhicaryāvatāra:*

> *mi mdza' rnams kyang med 'gyur zhing*
> *mdza' ba rnams kyang med par 'gyur*
> *bdag kyang med par 'gyur ba ste*
> *de bzhin thams cad med par 'gyur*

At some point I found myself writing these lines:

> My foes will become nothing,
> My friends will become nothing,
> I too will become nothing,
> Likewise all will become nothing.[1]

The exercise of translating a Buddhist text is a double act. The first part has to do with making sense of the vocabulary, grammar, and syntax, then rendering it into an English that also respects the verse form and meter of the original. The second part has to do with listening to what the author is trying to communicate to someone else with similar concerns, then finding a phrasing in English that will allow readers to hear what Śāntideva is saying with the same existential urgency as it spoke to me in Tibetan.

With this verse, I found myself challenged to sense my own mortality as acutely as the author expressed his. I could have noted how strongly Buddhist monks in eighth-century India were influenced by the concept of impermanence or how Śāntideva achieves his rhetorical effect by insistent repetition of the phrase "become nothing." Rather than retreat from the text in these ways, I drank in the words as if to quench a wordless thirst. Trusting the author, I looked to him for guidance. In assenting to his ideas, I sought to be changed by what he said: to feel in my bones that I will disappear, just as everyone and everything else will disappear.

Such silent epiphanies reveal how translation involves more than just substituting a sentence in one language with a sentence in another. It requires that one convey a peculiar configuration of sense, feeling, perception, anguish, desire, and understanding from one world and resurrect it in another. The resultant translation can be neither quite the same as nor entirely different from what has been "carried over" (Latin: *trans-latus*). The translator is but a conduit through which a minor miracle occurs. The translation is inscribed in one's flesh: in the pulsing of blood, sweat on the brow, spasms of dread or rapture that course through the nerves.

During the following summer of 1976 I fought my way through brambles and creepers into an isolated stretch of woodland near the Swiss village of Rikon. I carried a sleeping bag, four days' supply of muesli, a pot for making tea, the Tibetan text of Śāntideva's *Bodhicaryāvatāra*, Thogs med bZang po's thirteenth-century commentary to it, and Sarat Chandra Das's *A Tibetan-English Dictionary*. My goal was to translate the seventy-six verses of chapter 7 of the work, which concerns *brtson 'grus* (*vīrya*), variously translated as "effort," "energy," "enthusiasm."

Following the principle of conditionality ("if this is, that arises; if this is not, that does not arise"), Śāntideva understands how effort is not a matter of gritting one's teeth and willfully forcing oneself to act. Effort arises naturally once you establish the conditions that generate it. Again, this starts by refining one's intuition of mortality:

> Having blocked off every path,
> Death is on the prowl.
> How can you enjoy food?
> Or delight in falling asleep?[2]

The precarious nature of each moment leads you to reconsider what matters most for you, letting it crystallize into the question "What do I do?" For Śāntideva the only meaningful answer is to wake up, to become optimally human in each moment, not just for your own fulfillment but as an illustration of what a flourishing life can be. To realize such a vision may require an almost arrogant degree of self-confidence—to regard oneself, in Śāntideva's words, "as a lion among jackals."[3]

This leonine attitude has nothing to do with proclaiming one's achievements in order to raise oneself in others' esteem. It is an inner, psychological confidence. It entails transforming the way you see yourself rather than the image of yourself that you project to the world. In taking the vow of a bodhisattva, Śāntideva has already affirmed that he aspires to sacrifice himself for others: to become "a protector for those without one, a guide for travelers on the way," even "a slave for all who want a slave."[4] His self-confidence concerns his ability to overcome the forces of greed, hatred, egoism, and self-doubt that prevent him from realizing his altruistic aspirations. For

> When crows finding a dying snake,
> They behave as if they were eagles.
> When I see myself as a victim,
> I am hurt by trifling failures.[5]

By comparing one who is crushed by these forces to a dying snake, Śāntideva recognizes how low self-esteem magnifies the power of what assails that person, thereby rendering him or her impotent. For the scavenging crows of reactivity appear as mighty eagles to such a victim. And the pain they inflict, though trivial, becomes unbearable.

In the solitude of the Swiss forest, "among the deer, the birds and trees that say nothing unpleasant and are delightful companions,"[6] I succeeded in translating Śāntideva's seventy-six verses on effort almost effortlessly. Rarely have I experienced such a sustained, ecstatic convergence between the content of a text and the act of translating it. The aspiration to complete the task and the self-confidence that animated it were complemented by the two other conditions that Śāntideva regards as integral to effort: joy and relaxation. At the opening of the chapter, he defines effort as "finding joy in what is good."[7] Perhaps "enthusiasm," with its etymological echo of being divinely inspired, would be a better term. Śāntideva compares such effort to how a child would feel in running outside to play[8] or how "an elephant tormented by the midday sun" would feel on "plunging into a cool lake."[9] And, crucially, this effort also depends on knowing when to put the work aside and relax in order to restore oneself.[10]

Translating this text as a *practitioner* rather than a scholar involved interfusing different strands of my own life with that of the author. The linguistic strands, of course, were crucial. For all that remains of Śāntideva are his words. Apart from dubious fragments of legend, we know nothing else about him. Yet reading Śāntideva means to converse with Śāntideva: to agree and sympathize with him but also to argue and dispute. In this way, I slowly came to know him. And what mattered most in forging this acquaintance with an invisible stranger were the threads of shared concern, which bound us together as practitioners of the dharma across the twelve hundred years that separated us in time.

As a sympathetic reader, I absorbed his understanding in a way that changed me: I came to share his spiritual and literary aspirations, I assumed a similar stance to my own life and death, my yearnings were affirmed and strengthened by his, even my delight in the natural world was enhanced by his praising the opportunities it afforded for contemplative solitude. Like other key relationships in my life, getting to know Śāntideva transformed me.

Śāntideva, however, wrote in Sanskrit, and I read him in Tibetan. My English translation, which was published in 1979, was thus a translation of a translation. From the standpoint of modern scholarship this would be regarded as a serious weakness in understanding Śāntideva's text. Unlike many other Sanskrit works translated into Tibetan, the Sanskrit of the *Bodhicaryāvatāra* has been preserved. Why then, were I genuinely interested in what Śāntideva had to say, did I not learn Sanskrit and read his work in the language that he himself had used? Surely many of the same difficulties I faced in rendering the text from Tibetan into English would have been faced by the translators who rendered it from Sanskrit into Tibetan. They too would have been forced to choose one word among many possible options to translate a Sanskrit term just as I had to make similar judgments in translating a Tibetan term. They too were fallible human beings. How can I be sure that my resultant English translation did not incorporate distortions or errors made by the Tibetans who translated it from Sanskrit?

These are valid objections. In an ideal world, I would have learned Sanskrit. But in the world we inhabit, I have no regrets about not having done so. In the end, such decisions are made according to one's priorities and the limited availability of time in which to realize them. As a practitioner, my priorities are not the same as those of a scholar. Many of the greatest monks and yogins of Tibet were inspired by Śāntideva's work and composed insightful commentaries on it without knowing a word of Sanskrit. Would they have gained deeper insights into the *Bodhicaryāvatāra* had they been able to read it in the original? Perhaps, but I fear this is to miss a crucial point.

A living tradition is one in which people today are engaged in an ongoing conversation with the past about the core questions of what it means to be human. While the accuracy of the translation of a text may play a role in this conversation, for a practitioner it will always be subordinate to the existential, ethical, and philosophical issues addressed by the text. When a text functions as a vital reference within a living community extended over time, it becomes far more than a philological object stored in a library for the scrutiny of scholars.

( 2 )

If Śāntideva changed me, Augustine (354–430 CE) showed me who "I" was. After years of studying Buddhist texts, to read Augustine's *Confessions* was like peering into a mirror and seeing my own face staring back. However much I aspired to be a Buddhist, I could not discard my European and Christian heritage as though it were an article of clothing that could be shed at will. Augustine showed me the extent to which a Western sensibility informed me through and through: not in any particular belief or opinion I hold but in the very way in which I inhabit and negotiate the world. I did not need to spend years poring over the writings of Augustine to understand this. All I had to do was read a few pages of the *Confessions* in an English translation. The theology did not engage me. It was in the very granularity of the world he evoked that I recognized myself as a fellow citizen.

Take the famous passage in which Augustine recalls the time he stole some pears.

> There was a pear-tree near our vineyard, loaded with fruit that was attractive neither to look at nor taste. Late one night a band of ruffians, myself included, went off to shake down the fruit and carry it away, for we had continued our games after dark, as was our pernicious habit. We took away an enormous quantity of pears, not to eat them ourselves, but

simply to throw them to the pigs. Perhaps we ate some of them, but our real pleasure consisted in doing something that was forbidden.[11]

Now, you will not find in any classical Indian Buddhist writings a passage remotely like this. Buddhist texts certainly encourage one not to steal, but they do so in a way that is abstracted from any particular act of theft. Augustine focuses on the "pear-tree near our vineyard," "a band of ruffians, myself included," "shaking down the fruit," "throwing it to the pigs," and the uncertain "perhaps we ate some" before acknowledging the deeper, shameful motive that drove him to behave as he did. Such language reflects Augustine's own Greco-Roman background as much as it foreshadows what we would find today in a work of literary fiction. Augustine helped me see how deeply and intuitively embedded I am in this cultural sphere.

In hindsight, I suspect Śāntideva appealed to me because of all the Indian Buddhist writers I had encountered, he came closest to expressing such a sensibility. There is something engagingly personal about Śāntideva's work. Unlike other Indian authors, he does not conceal himself behind the words of his text. He openly declares his motives, berates himself for his weaknesses, and shares his heartfelt aspirations to improve himself. Yet while employing himself as a psychological example of a fallible Buddhist practitioner, he does not disclose a single autobiographic detail. His apparent readiness to expose himself fails to reveal the kind of conflicted, all too human person whom I discovered in Augustine.

Getting to know Śāntideva through his *Bodhicaryāvatāra* was like getting to know an eminent professor or priest who speaks eloquently and persuasively in public but shies away from any further intimacy. Encountering Augustine, by contrast, plunges one headlong into the innermost world of his thoughts, feelings, and anxieties. As a Westerner I am primed to identify with Augustine precisely because of the influence he has already exerted on the formation of the Western sensibility in which I have been raised. As much as I may identify with Śāntideva's passions and ideas, he remains culturally foreign to me and, to that extent, a stranger.

I likewise identify with Augustine as a fellow convert. The *Confessions* tell the story of an intelligent but tormented young man in search of salvation. He is educated in the Hellenistic philosophies of his day, embraces the Gnostic creed of Manichaeism for several years, then finally is converted to Christianity through his encounter with Ambrose, bishop of Milan, at the age of thirty-three. He knew nothing about Buddhism since it had not penetrated into the Roman world. Being closer in many respects to the Gnosticism, Stoicism, and Skepticism he rejected, I doubt that Gotama's teachings would have held any great appeal for him. In any case, I do not identify with Augustine because I suspect he was an "anonymous Buddhist" (to paraphrase Karl Rahner's "anonymous Christian"). I understand the urgency of his quest; I am moved by its resolution when he accepts Christ as his savior; and I admire his courage to embark on a career within a church that was still marginal, and whose members were subject to suspicion and ridicule. These are the parallels in which I recognize the course of my own life.

Moreover, while Augustine was fluent in Latin, his Greek was poor and his Hebrew almost nonexistent. This meant that he had to rely largely on Latin translations of primary biblical texts as the basis for his voluminous writings, which were to have a profound influence in the development of Christian thought over the following centuries. Aware that his Greek was insufficient to read the original texts of Paul and others, he did not exert himself to improve it. His priorities were those of a practicing Christian in search of God, not of a linguist in search of philological precision. Given the limitations of time, the constant threat of death, and the urgency of his mission, he chose to persevere in refining and articulating his philosophical understanding even though it meant basing it on texts that in some cases were Latin translations of Greek translations of Hebrew. Conscious of the shortcomings of this approach, he commented in *The Trinity*:

> Anyone reading this should travel on with me where we agree; search with me where we are unsure; rejoin me if he finds me astray; call me back if I am astray. In this way we may jointly proceed along the path opened up by love, venturing toward the one of whom we are told, "Search always for his countenance."[12]

Understanding the truths of Christianity, he realizes, is the work of a community over time, not the task of one mind, however brilliant, working in isolation.

The French classicist Pierre Hadot has observed how in the process of translating biblical texts from Hebrew and Greek into Latin "many slippages of meaning, if not misinterpretations" occurred.[13] As an example he cites how Augustine interprets the Latin *in idipsum* from Psalm 4:9 to be a name of God, "the selfsame," whereas the original Hebrew simply meant "at this very moment."[14] On the basis of this misreading, which was further colored by his Neoplatonist leanings, Augustine then develops a metaphysical theory of God as "one who is identical with himself." Rather than dismiss this doctrine as invalid because it is founded on a linguistic error, Hadot recognizes how such "creative mistakes" have sometimes brought about "important evolutions in the history of philosophy."[15] Or to put it more playfully and ironically, "sometimes the wrong train will get you to the right station."[16]

## ( 3 )

My conversation with Buddhist tradition has taken me on a circuitous route from Śāntideva back to the Buddha (c. 480–c. 400 BCE), the man we simply know as Gotama (the forename "Siddhattha"—"the one who has realized his goal"—is an epithet not mentioned in the discourses). Along the way I became acquainted with the Tibetan lama Tsongkhapa (1357–1419), Zen masters Linji Yixuan (d. 866) and Bojo Chinul (1158–1210), and the Indian philosopher Nāgārjuna (second century CE). Many years would pass before I began to focus my attention on the person of Gotama, but it now strikes me as inevitable that this is where the conversation would lead.

I have long been puzzled why Buddhists of all traditions unhesitatingly describe themselves as followers of the Buddha yet ignore or disparage the discourses that are most likely to go back to him, put into his mouth sayings and views that emerged centuries after his death, regard a mythic account of his life as biography, and accept a comically idealized picture of what he looked like. In the late 1970s, while still a Tibetan Buddhist monk in Switzerland, I read two books that overturned the traditional view of the Buddha that I had been taught: Trevor Ling's *The Buddha* and Bhikkhu Ñāṇamoli's *The Life of the Buddha*. Whereas the former sought to understand Gotama and his teaching in the context of the social, economic, and religious conditions of fifth century BCE India, the latter recounted the story of his life entirely on the basis of texts within the Pali Canon. Together, these works introduced me for the first time to a human being, rather than a quasi-god, who had lived and died on this same earth on which I also walked.

Scholars disagree as to whether the earliest textual materials in Pali and other classical languages provide a sufficient basis on which to be able to make any historical assertions about Gotama.

Although few today would question that such a person existed, many would consider the account of his life given in these texts to be hagiography rather than biography.[17] At this distance in time and with such a paucity of data, they insist that the historical Buddha will remain forever beyond our reach. I do not accept this judgment.

As a practitioner, to read these early texts means to enter into a potentially life-transforming dialogue with their author. To pursue this conversation requires the presence of an interlocutor with whom I share common concerns and goals. As with Śāntideva, Gotama starts to come alive for me through the power of his ideas and metaphors, as well as through the extraordinary coherence of his vision. Unlike Śāntideva, Gotama's teaching is largely dialogical: the discourses introduce a wide range of consistently portrayed characters with whom he interacts. Also unlike Śāntideva, Gotama's teaching takes place in a highly detailed world peopled by family members, kings and generals, disciples from different social backgrounds, wandering ascetics, and priests, merchants, officials, and doctors. The more I immerse myself in this world, the more I am convinced that it is not a theatrical backdrop for an inspiring hagiography. It is an utterly human world, shot through with the quirks, vanity, and tawdriness of life. Without reaching the same degree of granularity, it is more like the world that emerges from the *Confessions* of Augustine than, for example, the make-believe world depicted in the later Mahayana Sūtras of Buddhism. And when you suspend the idealistic picture of Gotama as the perfectly enlightened one who cannot put a foot wrong, you discover that his life ended not in glory but in tragedy.[18]

It took me a long time to differentiate the myth of the Buddha from the story of the man called Gotama. The Buddhist religion has succeeded in propagating the myth of the prince-in-the-palace-who-renounces-the-world-and-attains-spiritual-perfection because of its potent archetypal appeal. In speaking directly to the universal human condition of birth, sickness, aging, and death, it can be understood by the educated and uneducated alike, irrespective of time, place, and culture. The problem lies not in the myth itself but in mistaking the myth for historical fact. (It would be just as mistaken to reject the myth on the grounds that it is historically inaccurate.) The mythic and historical narratives are both legitimate in their respective spheres. One does not need to choose between them. As Buddhism encounters modernity with its heightened sense of historical consciousness, the time has come to highlight the story of the man, which tradition has largely ignored. This allows a dialogic relation to develop with another human person, which is a crucial if not defining feature of so-called secular Buddhism.

Here, once again, the issue of language and translation looms large. Unlike Augustine and Śāntideva, Gotama wrote nothing, making him comparable in this regard to his contemporary Socrates in Athens. In contrast to Socrates, Gotama did not have a Plato, Xenophon, or Aristophanes to inscribe his sayings and episodes of his life on clay tablets or papyrus. His teachings were memorized and passed down orally for four centuries before they were written down on *ola* leaves in Sri Lanka around 80 BCE.

Modern scholars are highly suspicious of oral tradition. Their legitimate concern has, however, been exaggerated. Behind the unwillingness to confer legitimacy on oral tradition often lie the prejudices of those raised in a culture that venerates the written word. An even more troubling bias is the unstated belief that people in oral cultures do not take the preservation of their traditions seriously. As a result, oral tradition is regarded as little more than a game of Chinese whispers. Yet were this the case, it would follow that if two groups of monks were entrusted with the memorization of a large body of discourses and then had no contact with each other over many centuries, the result would be two quite different canons. This is not just a thought experiment; it actually happened. One group of monks charged with this task migrated from northeast India over a few generations to Sri Lanka, while the other remained in the northern parts of the subcontinent. Today, by comparing the discourses in Pali preserved in Sri Lanka with a Chinese translation (the *Āgamas*) of the now lost Sanskrit original preserved in northern India, we find an extraordinary degree of concordance. They are indisputably versions of the same original material. It is here, among these texts, that I engage in dialogue with Gotama. And I do so with a degree of confidence that something close to the words I read were initially spoken by this man or one of his immediate followers.

My Pali, which I started to learn only in my fifties, is not nearly as proficient as my classical Tibetan, which I learned when I was in my early twenties. I have poor retention of vocabulary and case endings and an imperfect grasp of grammar and syntax. I am acutely aware of the deficiencies of my linguistic skills, yet I have not made it a priority to master the Pali language (assuming my aging brain could still do it). My primary concerns remain existential, philosophical, and ethical. I continue to depend on English translations, but whenever I encounter a passage that I wish to study in depth, I turn to the Pali and analyze it with the help of dictionaries and grammars. This approach may not be ideal, but it enables me to get as close to the person and words of Gotama as I am ever likely to.

One passage that I have pondered at length is Gotama's account of his awakening in the *Ariyapariyesana Sutta*. This is my translation:

This dharma I have reached is deep, hard to see, difficult to awaken to, quiet and excellent, not confined by thought,

subtle, sensed by the wise. But people love their place [ālaya]:
they delight and revel in their place. It is hard for people
who love, delight and revel in their place to see this ground
[ṭhāna]: "because-of-this" conditionality [idappaccayatā], conditioned arising [paṭiccasamuppāda]. And also hard to see
this ground: the stilling of inclinations, the relinquishing of
bases, the fading away of reactivity, desirelessness, ceasing,
nirvana.[19]

What strikes me here is how Gotama presents his awakening as
a radical, existential shift in perspective rather than a privileged,
mystical insight into the nature of "reality." This shift entails moving from a perspective on life governed by one's identification with
a "place"—be it a physical, social, religious, political, or psychological "place"—to one founded upon one's "ground"—in this case,
the sheer contingency of one's existence, on the one hand, and the
immanent, nonreactive space of nirvana, on the other. These two
dimensions of one's "ground" are equally fundamental and primordial. While conditioned arising discloses the causal unfolding
of life, nirvana discloses the possibility of a life no longer determined by one's reactivity or habitual inclinations.

This passage has provided me with a basis on which to elaborate an entirely pragmatic understanding of the dharma. As a practitioner, the task is to stabilize attention on the fluid, unpredictable,
and contingent nature of experience as the ground that enables
one to take ethical choices that are not conditioned by habitual reactive patterns of greed, hatred, and self-centeredness. I take this to
be the core of Gotama's awakening, which he subsequently develops into a series of four tasks: to comprehend dukkha, to let go of
reactivity, to behold the stopping of reactivity (i.e., nirvana), and to
cultivate the eightfold path. Together, these two doctrines serve as
the framework for what I have come to call "a secular Buddhism."

However, my rendering of *ālaya* as "place" and *ṭhāna* as "ground" has been criticized as a misreading of the Pali terms.[20] *Ālaya*, it is claimed, here means something like "attachment," while *ṭhāna* functions as little more than a linguistic placeholder, which should be rendered as "fact" or "state." There may, therefore, be no *philological* justification for my claim that Gotama's awakening constituted a radical shift of perspective from his "place" to his "ground." Nonetheless, this criticism does not affect my broader interpretation of the passage. However one translates these particular terms, it remains the case that by seeing conditioned arising and nirvana, Gotama was liberated from his prior attachments to embark on a way of life that was no longer determined by them. Even if the place/ground distinction is not explicit in the text, it serves as an effective way to highlight this shift in perspective from a life governed by attachments to one founded on a vision of contingency and nonreactivity.

So is this an instance of incompetent scholarship that has led to inexcusable error, or is it one of Pierre Hadot's "creative mistakes" that has led to a valuable insight? If one's primary relation to the text is that of a detached philologist, then one's concern will be to judge the literal accuracy of the translation; but if it is that of a practitioner engaged in an existential dialogue with Gotama, then one will seek a reading that helps one flourish as a person. As a practitioner, my reading of any specific passage cannot be taken in isolation. For it is part of an ongoing conversation—with Buddhist tradition in general and the *suttas* of the Pali Canon in particular—that over many years has changed me. Such changes do not remain quarantined in the privacy of my mind; they actively inform how I make sense of the world, which includes, of course, the very passages that have contributed to making those changes. A dialogical relation with tradition, therefore, transforms not only the reader but also the texts that are being read.

I also consider myself an artist. From an aesthetic perspective, I try to hear how these scriptures sing. I pay attention to the vocabulary, grammar, and syntax of a given sentence, but I am just as concerned to hear how that sentence sounds as a melodic line within the emerging symphony of the canon. Over time, those passages that resonate for me at the same key and pitch have coalesced into the body of primary sources on which I build my understanding of what Gotama teaches. Through continuous reflection upon and conversation with such source texts have I slowly and tentatively begun to find my own voice.

# ( 4 )

The first Buddhist meditation I practiced entailed visualizing a seated figure of Śākyamuni Buddha on a bejeweled throne in the space before me. To his right was Avalokiteśvara, the bodhisattva of compassion, to his left Mañjuśrī, the bodhisattva of wisdom, while in front of his throne stood the wrathful figure of Vajrapāṇi, the bodhisattva of power. After creating this image, I was instructed to recite the mantras of these figures while imagining beams of light and nectar emanating from their hearts and entering mine.

For the Tibetan lamas who taught me this practice, these visualized figures were not understood as mere symbols or archetypes. Despite being "empty of inherent existence," they were regarded as possessing both an agency that was independent of mine as well as the power to intervene in human affairs by granting blessings and answering prayers. In other words, they functioned as gods, which happens to be the very term (hla) by which they are known in Tibetan.[21] In Tibetan Buddhist philosophy to be "empty of inherent existence" is the ultimate nature of all things. Gods, therefore, are no different from humans in terms of how they operate as agents in the conventional or relative world.

As hard as I tried over the years, I found it very difficult to "speak" with these Buddhas and bodhisattvas as though they were quasi-persons with agency. I could not dispel a gnawing suspicion of bad faith when, in the course of reciting a tantric *sādhanā* like the one described above, I heard myself requesting insights or blessings from them. To interpret these figures as symbols or archetypes only made matters worse. For the idea of conducting a meaningful conversation with a symbol struck me as even more absurd. In the end, while still a Tibetan Buddhist monk, I abandoned these practices altogether. And it was around this time that I first came across the work of Ludwig Feuerbach (1804–72).

Feuerbach was a student of Hegel who came to reject his teacher's emphasis on the primacy of Spirit in the unfolding of history and advocated instead a liberal, materialist, and atheist view of the world. He is perhaps best known for serving as a bridge between the ideas of Hegel and those of Karl Marx and Friedrich Engels. Trained as a theologian, he launched a critique against religion in general and Christianity in particular.

Feuerbach's basic idea is simple. "Religion," he wrote in the preface to his most famous book, *The Essence of Christianity* (1841), "is the dream of the human mind. But even while dreaming we are not in heaven or in the realm of Nothingness. We are right here on earth."[22] Feuerbach argued that the function of religion was to project the essential human qualities of reason, love, and will onto the nonhuman and transcendent figure of God, who then becomes an object of worship. As a result of this transference: "In proportion as God becomes more ideally human, the greater becomes the apparent difference between God and man. To enrich God, man must become poor; that God may be all, man must become nothing."[23] Since God is merely "the projected essence of man,"[24] if people are to recover their true humanity, Feuerbach maintains that they need to reclaim their essential nature from the God onto whom they have projected it. In the words of Karl Marx: "[Feuerbach's] work consists in the dissolution of the religious world into its secular basis. . . . Feuerbach resolves the religious essence into the human."[25]

While an echo of Buddhism may be detected in his phrase "in the realm of Nothingness," the primary target of Feuerbach's critique was Christianity. The visualization practice that I described above, however, fits Feuerbach's thesis to the letter. As the dharma evolved into another Indian religion, Gotama lost his humanity and turned into the godlike figure of Śākyamuni Buddha. At the same time the human qualities of reason, love, and will were projected, respectively, onto the godlike bodhisattvas Mañjuśrī, Avalokiteśvara, and Vajrapāṇi. The practitioner thus finds herself supplicating these "gods" to grant her in the form of blessings the very qualities she gave away to them in the first place. In both theism and Buddhism, as the tradition crystallizes into orthodoxies and hierarchical institutions, a similar gap opens up between the ordinary person and her essential humanity.

By the time of Śāntideva, Buddhism had come to function as a polytheistic religion. The *Bodhicaryāvatāra* includes confession of sins, threats of hellish punishment, and supplicatory prayers such as this one:

> To the Guardian Avalokiteśvara
> Who infallibly acts with compassion,
> I utter a mournful cry:
> "Please protect this evil doer!"[26]

By reflecting on how one is always "in the presence of Buddhas and bodhisattvas endowed with unobstructed vision," one is encouraged to "develop a sense of shame, respect and fear."[27] Śāntideva's world is a far cry from that of Gotama's. These kinds of practices are unimaginable in the discourses of the Pali Canon.

Gotama's ironic atheism and emphasis on self-reliance have given way to the kind of devotion and dependency that Feuerbach regards as the essence of religious behavior.

This process waxes and wanes over time. Feuerbach approvingly quotes Augustine as saying, "God is nearer, more closely related to us, and therefore more easily known by us than sensible corporeal things."[28] Christian mystics such as Meister Eckhart and Protestant reformers such as Luther likewise understood the experience of God to be a profoundly intimate one. In Buddhism this emphasis is even more explicit since the aim of the practice is for each person to become fully awakened. Yet the history of both traditions is marked by critical moments when the gap between the ordinary person and her religious ideal becomes so vast that it can no longer be sustained. There then follows a collapse of the old order, which allows the possibility of something new being born. A good example of this in Buddhism occurs with the emergence of Chan (Zen) in China, where we find teachers such as Mazu Daoyi (709–88) repeatedly insisting that the Buddha is nothing other than one's own mind.

No matter how radical the reform of a religious tradition, over time the new and vibrant school tends to coalesce into yet another orthodoxy and hierarchic institution. As power becomes concentrated into the hands of an elite body of priests, the gap between the unenlightened and the enlightened starts opening up again, thus repeating the old pattern of disempowerment and alienation. Whenever a religion becomes an instrument of state power, thereby further enhancing the authority of its priests, it becomes even more difficult to challenge its dogmas, particularly if they become enshrined in law.

An established religion exercises its power most keenly by controlling the interpretation of its canonical texts. In religious studies departments of universities today a similar role is assumed by experts who decree what the languages and doctrines of a particular religion "really" mean. Those with a vested interest in preserving the correct interpretation of texts cannot tolerate the idea that "ordinary" people might enter into a living dialogue with the authors of those texts. They will actively discourage them by emphasizing the difficulty of such writings and the need for arduous study to acquire the linguistic and interpretive tools required to understand them correctly. There is some legitimacy to this concern, but it can be used illegitimately to justify a blanket condemnation of any attempt to question orthodox beliefs.

A Feuerbachian approach to Buddhism would entail a recovery of the historical Gotama as a human conversation partner as well as an uncompromisingly secular reading of his teaching.[29] Discarding all elements of supernaturalism and magical thinking, one returns to the mystery and tragedy of the everyday sublime.[30] Instead of nirvana being located in a transcendent realm beyond the human condition, it would be restored to its rightful place at the heart of what it means each moment to be fully human. Rather than devoutly repeating what has been said many times before, you risk expressing your understanding in your own stammering voice.

# ( 5 )

The writings included in the five parts of this book can be seen in two ways. On the one hand, they trace the development of my ideas over the past twenty-five years. On the other, they illustrate the finding of an increasingly secular voice during the same period. I understand these two processes to be part of a single conversation with (and between) the Buddhist and Western traditions that have formed me.

The essay "A Secular Buddhism" (Part 2) is the result of forty years of study and reflection. During this period, which started in the early 1970s, I moved from being a Tibetan Buddhist "believer" into being a Sŏn (Zen) Buddhist "skeptic," then an "agnostic" Buddhist, before coming out as a "secular" Buddhist primarily informed by the texts of the Pali Canon. This process is described in the essays found in Part 3 and the interviews in Part 4. I am reluctant to consider where I have currently arrived as the end point of my journey. I continue to be more interested in the ongoing conversation than with defining and defending a position.

On occasion, the conversation recorded here involves specific people who have played a role in the formation of my ideas and voice. In particular I need to mention the British Theravāda monk Ñāṇavīra Thera (Harold Musson), and the Anglican theologian Don Cupitt. Ñāṇavīra's life and thought are explored in Part 1, and an interview with Don Cupitt is found in Part 4.

I am also grateful to my conversation partners Jeff Hardin and Chris Talbott, whose interviews with me for *Sati Journal* and *Insight Journal*, respectively, appear below in Part 4. For the most part, though, my interlocutors are implied rather than stated. These would include my primary Buddhist teachers Geshe Ngawang Dhargyey, Geshe Tamdrin Rabten, and Pangjang Kusan Sunim, as well as figures from the Western tradition such as Martin Heidegger, Paul Tillich, Dietrich Bonhoeffer, and Richard Rorty. In addition, I am grateful to numerous friends, colleagues, and critics, who, unbeknown to themselves, have influenced the way my ideas and voice have developed over the years.

In parallel with my writing, I make art, which is the broad theme of Part 5. My primary mediums are photography and collage. These creative activities provide an ongoing, nonverbal counterpoint to my work as a writer. My conversation with tradition, therefore, takes place not only in words but in images. I have been inspired by many works of Asian Buddhist art, particularly those of China, Korea, and Japan. More recently, I have been deeply moved by the pre-iconic, rock-cut temples that have survived in India, specifically those of Kārla, Bhājā, Bedsā, Ajaṇṭā, and Ellora, as well as the magnificent stupa at Sāñcī. The Western artistic tradition—from Fra Angelico to Damien Hirst—has likewise exerted and continues to exert a formative influence on my work. In this area of my life, my brother David has been a constant source of insight and guidance.

Thus have I organized the essays and conversations included in this book into five parts. I have presented those parts in a sequence. And within each part, I have arranged the pieces in the chronological order in which they were written. By doing this, I have transformed them. Each piece of writing now stands in a relationship to the other pieces in a way that could not have been foreseen when it was first composed. I realize that some readers may choose to read only one essay and ignore the rest, in which case the piece will retain a degree of its original autonomy. But the implied reader I have had in mind while composing this book will start with the Introduction and end up reading the final essay, "An Aesthetics of Emptiness." I have created this book as a work in its own right. It is more than just the sum of its parts. The organization of the material is not arbitrary. I have imposed and followed certain formal rules. I have designed the work to be conceptually coherent and aesthetically pleasing. *Secular Buddhism*, therefore, is like one of my collages of found materials.

# 1

# LOOKING FOR ÑĀṆAVĪRA

# Existence, Enlightenment, and Suicide

> The Buddha's Teaching is quite alien to the European tradi-
> tion, and a European who adopts it is a rebel.
> —Ñāṇavīra Thera (1964)

## ( 1 )

In the early 1960s Somerset Maugham encouraged his nephew Robin to expand his horizons and go to Ceylon: "Find that rich Englishman who is living in a jungle hut there as a Buddhist monk," he suggested.[1] An aged and somewhat embittered man living alone in a luxurious villa on the Riviera, Maugham was fascinated by a privileged Westerner who had renounced a life of comfort to live as a hermit in Asia. This interest echoed an earlier fascination with the American Larry Darrell, the fictional hero of his novel *The Razor's Edge*.

Traumatized by his experiences of active service in the First World War, the young Larry Darrell returns home to an affluent and privileged society now rendered hollow and futile. The subsequent events of the novel unfold through the urbane and jaded eyes of Maugham himself, a narrator who assumes a haughty indifference to Larry's existential plight while at the same time being drawn to him by an anguished curiosity.

Late one night in a café Larry tells Maugham how the shock of seeing a dead fellow airman, a few years older than himself, had brought him to his impasse. The sight, he recalls, "filled me with shame." Maugham is puzzled by this. He too had seen corpses in the war but had been dismayed by "how trifling they looked. There was no dignity in them. Marionettes that the showman had thrown into the discard."[2]

Having renounced a career and marriage, Larry goes to Paris, where he lives austerely and immerses himself in literature and philosophy. When asked by his uncomprehending fiancée why he refuses to come home to Chicago, he answers, "I couldn't go back now. I'm on the threshold. I see vast lands of the spirit stretching out before me, beckoning, and I'm eager to travel them."[3]

After an unsatisfying spell in a Christian monastery Larry finds work as a deckhand on a liner, jumps ship in Bombay, and ends up at an ashram in a remote area of South India at the feet of an Indian swami. Here, during a retreat in a nearby forest, he sits beneath a tree at dawn and experiences enlightenment. "I had a sense," he tells Maugham, "that a knowledge more than human possessed me, so that everything that had been confused was clear and everything that had perplexed me was explained. I was so happy that it was pain and I struggled to release myself from it, for I felt that if it lasted a moment longer I should die."[4]

The final glimpse we have of Larry is as he prepares to board ship for America, where he plans to vanish among the crowds of New York as a cabdriver. "My taxi," he explains, "[will] be merely the instrument of my labour . . . an equivalent to the staff and begging-bowl of the wandering mendicant."[5]

Maugham's story works insofar as it reflects an actual phenomenon: Western engagement with Eastern traditions in the wake of the First World War. Larry's anonymous return to America likewise bears a prophetic ring. But the novel fails in the author's inability to imagine spiritual experience as anything other than a prolonged mystical orgasm. The sincerity and urgency of Larry's quest is trivialized, and his final resolve fails to carry conviction.

The handful of Westerners who actually traveled to Asia in the first half of the twentieth century in search of another wisdom had to leave behind not only the security of their traditions but also the noncommital romanticism of Somerset Maugham. For the first time in nearly two thousand years, they were preparing to embrace something else. And this step was of another order than either the intellectual enthusiasms of a Schopenhauer or the muddled fantasies of a Blavatsky.

( 2 )

So, at his uncle's behest, Robin Maugham, an investigative journalist, novelist, travel writer, and defiantly outspoken homosexual, set off on what he would later describe as his "search for nirvana." Six weeks later, around New Year 1965, he arrived in Ceylon. At the Island Hermitage, founded in Dodanduwa in 1911 by the German Nyanatiloka, the doyen of Western Buddhist monks, he was directed to the town of Matara in the extreme south. From Matara Maugham was driven by jeep to the village of Būndala, where the farmers led him to a path that disappeared into the forest. "It was very hot," he recalled. "I could feel the sweat dripping down me. The path became narrower and darker as it led further into the dense jungle." He came to a clearing in which stood a small hut. As he approached, "a tall figure in a saffron robe glided out on to the verandah."

> The gaunt man stared at me in silence. He was tall and lean with a short beard and sunken blue eyes. His face was very pale. He stood there, motionless, gazing at me.
> "Would you care to come in?" he asked.

His voice was clear with a pleasantly cultured intonation about it; it was calm and cool yet full of authority. He might have been inviting me in for a glass of sherry in his rooms at Cambridge.[6]

Harold Edward Musson was born in Aldershot barracks in 1920. From the age of seven to nine he had lived in Burma, where his father commanded a battalion. He remembered asking someone, "Who was the Buddha?" and being told, "The Buddha was a man who sat under a tree and was enlightened."[7] From that moment he decided that this was what he wanted to do. He was educated at Wellington College and went up to Magdalene College, Cambridge, in 1938, where he read mathematics and then modern languages. It was during this time that he "slowly began to realise that . . . I would certainly end my days as a Buddhist monk."[8] He nonetheless volunteered for the army in 1940 and became an officer in Field Security, first in Algiers and later in Italy. His task was to interrogate prisoners of war. In 1945 he was hospitalized in Sorrento and became absorbed in a book on Buddhism called *La Dottrina del Risveglio* (*The Doctrine of Awakening*) by the Italian Julius Evola.

## ( 3 )

Julius Cesare Andrea Evola was born to a devout Catholic family in Rome in 1898. Having served in a mountain artillery regiment during the First World War, he found himself (like his fictional counterpart Larry Darrell) incapable of returning to normal life. He was overcome with "feelings of the inconsistency and vanity of the aims that usually engage human activities."[9] In response, he became an abstract painter involved in the Dadaist movement and a friend of its founding figure, the Rumanian Tristan Tzara. But by 1921 he became disillusioned with the Dadaist project of "over-throwing all logical, ethical and aesthetic categories by means of producing paradoxical and disconcerting images in order to achieve absolute liberation."[10] He finally rejected the arts as inadequate to the task of resolving his spiritual unrest, and after 1922 he produced no further poems or paintings.

A further response to his inner crisis was to experiment with drugs through which he attained "states of consciousness partially detached from the physical senses, . . . frequently approaching close to the sphere of visionary hallucinations and perhaps also madness."[11] But such experiences only aggravated his dilemma by intensifying his sense of personal disintegration and confusion to the point where he decided, at the age of twenty-three, to commit suicide.

He was dissuaded from carrying this out only when he came across a passage from the *Middle Length Discourses* in the Pali Canon where the Buddha spoke of those things with which the disciple committed to awakening must avoid identifying. Having listed the body, feelings, the elements, and so on, he concludes: "Whoever regards extinction as extinction, who thinks of extinction, who reflects about extinction, who thinks: 'Extinction is mine,' and rejoices in extinction, such a person, I declare, does not know extinction."[12] For Evola this was "like a sudden illumination. I realised that this desire to end it all, to dissolve myself, was a bond—'ignorance' as opposed to true freedom."[13]

During the early 1920s Evola's interests turned to the study of philosophy and Eastern religion. During this time he came into contact with Arturo Reghini, a high-ranking Mason and mathematician who believed himself to be a member of the Scuola Italica, an esoteric order that claimed to have survived the fall of ancient Rome. Through Reghini, Evola was introduced to René Guénon, whose concept of "Tradition" came to serve as "the basic theme that would finally integrate the system of my ideas."[14]

Evola distinguishes two aspects of this concept. First, it refers to "a primordial tradition of which all particular, historical, pre-modern traditions have been emanations." Second, and more important, Tradition

> has nothing to do with conformity or routine; it is the fundamental structure of a kind of civilisation that is organic, differentiated and hierarchic in which all its domains and human activities have an orientation from above and towards what is above.

Such civilizations of the past had as their natural center an elite or a leader who embodied "an authority as unconditional as it was legitimate and impersonal."[15]

It comes as no great surprise, therefore, that Evola strongly identified with the Right and supported the rise of Fascism in both Italy and Germany. Following Reghini he denounced the church as the religion of a spiritual proletariat and attacked it ferociously in his book *Pagan Imperialism* (1927). Around the same time he published such titles as *Man as Potency* and *Revolt against the Modern World*, revealing his indebtedness to Nietzsche and Spengler. He did not, however, join the Fascist Party and looked down upon Mussolini with aristocratic disdain. (Toward the end of his life he declared that he had never belonged to any political party or voted in an election.)

After Hitler came to power, Evola was feted by high-ranking Nazis, his books were translated into German, and he was invited to the country to explain his ideas to select aristocratic and military circles. But, as with many of his German admirers, he kept aloof from what he considered the nationalist, populist, and fanatic elements of National Socialism. He claims in his autobiography that because of his position as a foreigner from a friendly nation, he was free to present ideas which had they been voiced by a German might have led to imprisonment in a concentration camp. Nonetheless, when Mussolini was overthrown in 1943, Evola was invited to Vienna by a branch of the SS to translate proscribed texts of Masonic and other secret societies.

In the same year *The Doctrine of Awakening*, Evola's study of Buddhism, was published in Italy. He regarded the writing of this book as repayment of the "debt" he owed to the doctrine of the Buddha for saving him from suicide. The declared aim of the book was to "illuminate the true nature of original Buddhism, which had been weakened to the point of unrecognisability in most of its subsequent forms." The essential spirit of Buddhist doctrine was, for Evola, "determined by a will for the unconditioned, affirmed in its most radical form, and by investigation into that which leads to mastery over life as much as death."[16]

As its subtitle ("A Study on the Buddhist Ascesis") suggests, Evola's aim was to emphasize the primacy of spiritual discipline and practice as the core of tradition as represented by Buddhism. He condemns the loss of such ascesis in Europe and deplores the pejorative sense the term has assumed. Even Nietzsche, he notes with surprise, shared this anti-ascetic prejudice. Today, he argues, the ascetic path appears with the greatest clarity in Buddhism.

Evola bases his arguments on the Italian translations of the Pali Canon by Neumann and de Lorenzo published between 1916 and 1927. As for many of his generation, the Pali texts represented the only true and original source of the Buddha's teaching. He was nonetheless critical of a large body of accepted opinion that had grown up around them.

Renunciation, for example, does not, for Evola, arise from a sense of despair with the world; he maintains that the four encounters of Prince Siddhartha should be "taken with great reserve." For true Aryan renunciation "is based on 'knowledge' and is accompanied by a gesture of disdain and a feeling of transcen-

dental dignity; it is qualified by the superior man's will for the unconditioned, by the will . . . of a man of quite a special 'race of the
spirit.'"[17] The bearing of such a person is "essentially aristocratic,"
"anti-mystical," "anti-evolutionist," upright and "manly." This race
of the spirit is united with the "blood . . . of the white races who
created the greatest civilisations both of the East and the West"—
in particular males of warrior stock. The Aryan tradition has been
largely lost in the West through the "influence on European faiths
of concepts of Semitic and Asiatic-Mediterranean origin."[18] Yet in
the East, too, Buddhism has degenerated into Mahayana univer-
salism that wrongly considers *all* beings to have the potentiality
to become a Buddha. As for Buddhism being "a doctrine of universal compassion encouraging humanitarianism and democratic
equality," this is merely one of many "Western misconceptions."[19]

Evola considers the world of his time to be perverse and dys-
functional. "If normal conditions were to return," he sighs, "few
civilisations would seem as odd as the present one."[20] He deplores
the craving for material things, which causes man entirely to overlook mastery over his own mind. Nonetheless,

> one who is still an "aryan" spirit in a large European or
> American city, with its skyscrapers and asphalt, with its pol-
> itics and sport, with its crowds who dance and shout, with
> its exponents of secular culture and of soulless science and
> so on—amongst all this he may feel himself more alone and
> detached and nomad than he would have done in the time
> of the Buddha.[21]

Evola believed that the original Buddhism disclosed through
his study revealed the essence of the Aryan tradition that had become lost and corrupted in the West. For him "Aryan" means more
than "noble" or "sublime," as it was frequently rendered in translations of Buddhist texts. "They are all later meanings of the word,"

he explains, "and do not convey the fullness of the original nor the spiritual, aristocratic and racial significance which, nevertheless, is preserved in Buddhism."[22] Other "innate attributes of the aryan soul" that are described in Buddhist texts are an absence of "any sign of departure from consciousness, of sentimentalism or devout effusion, or of semi-intimate conversation with a God."[23] Only among some of the German mystics, such as Eckhart, Tauler, and Silesius, does he find examples of this spirit in the Western tradition, "where Christianity has been rectified by a transfusion of aryan blood."[24]

Not only does Buddhism display an Aryan spirit but, for Evola, it also endorses the superiority of the warrior caste. Brushing aside the Buddha's well-known denunciation of the caste system, Evola notes that "it was generally held that the *bodhisatta* . . . are never born into a peasant or servile caste but into a warrior or brahmin caste." He cites several examples where the Buddha makes analogies between "the qualities of an ascetic and the virtues of a warrior."[25] Of all the Mahayana schools the only one he admired was that of Zen, on account of its having been adopted in Japan as the doctrine of the Samurai class.

# ( 4 )

What appeal could this book have had for an officer of the Allied forces advancing through Italy as part of a campaign to overthrow a regime based on notions of Aryan supremacy? Yet Captain Musson immediately set about translating *The Doctrine of Awakening* into English, a task he completed three years later. In his brief foreword he offers no apology for the author's extreme views but simply asserts that Evola had "recaptured the spirit of Buddhism in its original form." The book cleared away "some of the woolly ideas that have gathered around . . . Prince Siddhartha and the doctrine he disclosed." But its "real significance" was to be found in "its encouragement of a practical application of the doctrine it discusses."[26]

If one ignores Evola's supremacist and militaristic views, *The Doctrine of Awakening* offers a clear and often thoughtful account of early Buddhist doctrine. Evola proudly recalls that the English edition "received the official approbation of the Pali [Text] Society," through their "recognition of the value of my study."[27] It is nonetheless curious that in 1951, so shortly after the war, the book would be published in London by a reputable Orientalist publisher (Luzac) without any reference to the author's extreme right-wing views.

By the time *The Doctrine of Awakening* appeared in print, Musson had followed the book's advice and was already a *bhikkhu* in Ceylon. "I think the war hastened my decision," he later told Robin Maugham in the course of their conversation. "Though it was inevitable, I think, in any case. But the war forced maturity on me."[28] Since Harold Musson, like Larry Darrell (and probably Julius Evola), had a private income, he did not have to seek work upon leaving the army. He settled in London. With time and money on his hands, he leisurely worked on his translation of Evola and "tried to get as much pleasure out of life as I could."[29] Then one evening, in a bar, he ran into Osbert Moore, an old army friend who had shared his enthusiasm for *The Doctrine of Awakening* while in Italy. They began comparing notes. "Gradually we came to the conclusion that the lives we were leading at present were utterly pointless. We shared the belief that the whole of this existence as we saw it was a farce."[30] By the time the bar closed, they had resolved to go to Ceylon and become *bhikkhus*.

They left England in November 1948 and were ordained as novices in an open glade at the Island Hermitage by Nyanatiloka, then an old man of seventy-one, on April 24, 1949. Moore was given the name "Ñāṇamoli," and Musson "Ñāṇavīra." In 1950 they both received *bhikkhu* ordination in Colombo.

For the next year Ñāṇavīra devoted himself "fairly continuously" to the practice of meditative absorption (*jhāna, samādhi*), the attainment of which, he later declared, had been his motive in coming to Ceylon. A few months before Maugham's visit he had explained to a Singhalese friend that it was "the desire for some definite non-mystical form of practice that first turned my thoughts to the East. Western thinking . . . seemed to me to oscillate between the extremes of mysticism and rationalism, both of which were distasteful to me, and the yoga practices—in a general sense—of India offered themselves as a possible solution."[31] This is what he had seen as the "real significance" of Evola's book and, as he confirmed sixteen years later, the point on which "Eastern thought is at its greatest distance from Western."[32] But after a year's practice he contracted typhoid, which left him with chronic indigestion so severe that at times he would "roll about on [his] bed with the pain."[33] It also prevented him from attaining anything more than the "low-level results of [the] practice."[34]

Unable to pursue the *jhānas* he turned his linguistic skills to the study of Pali, which he soon mastered, and set about reading the Buddha's discourses and their Singhalese commentaries. His analytical bent led him to assume that "it was possible to include all that the [Buddha] said in a single system—preferably portrayed diagrammatically on one very large sheet of paper."[35] But the more he read, the more he realized that this approach was "sterile" and incapable of leading to understanding. And the more he probed the discourses, the more he came to doubt the validity of the commentaries, which, "in those innocent days," he had accepted as authoritative. His friend Ñāṇamoli, meanwhile, had likewise mastered Pali and was preparing to translate the greatest

Theravāda commentary of them all: Buddhaghosa's *The Path of Purification* (*Visuddhi Magga*).

Over the following months and years Ñāṇavīra became increasingly independent in his views, both challenging the accepted orthodoxy and refining his own understanding. Temperamentally, he acknowledged a tendency to stand apart from others. "I am quite unable," he wrote in 1963, "to identify myself with any organised body or cause (even if it is a body of opposition or a lost cause). I am a born blackleg."[36] Having renounced a life of comfort in England and all the values it stood for, he now rejected the prevailing orthodoxy of Singhalese Buddhism. But he did not turn against the Buddha's word: "It was, and is, my attitude towards the [Buddha's discourses] that, if I find anything in them that is against my own view, *they are right,* and I am *wrong.*"[37] He came to view only two of the three "baskets" (*piṭaka*) of the canon as authentic: those containing the discourses and the monastic rule. "No other Pali books whatsoever," he insisted, "should be taken as authoritative; and ignorance of them (and particularly of the traditional Commentaries) may be counted a positive advantage, as leaving less to be unlearned."[38]

This radical tendency toward isolation led him in 1954 to leave the Island Hermitage for the physical solitude of his hut in the jungle. "Aren't you lonely?" inquired Maugham. "After a bit," he replied, "you find you simply don't *want* other people. You've got your centre of gravity within yourself. . . . You become self-contained."[39] Two years earlier he had confessed: "I am one of those people who think of other people as 'they,' not as 'we.'"[40] Despite persistent ill health, his study and practice of mindfulness continued with increasing intensity.

Then, on the evening of June 27, 1959, something happened that radically changed the course of his life. He recorded the event in Pali in a private journal:

HOMAGE TO THE AUSPICIOUS ONE, WORTHY, FULLY AWAKENED.

—At one time the monk Ñāṇavīra was staying in a forest hut near Būndala village. It was during that time, as he was walking up and down in the first watch of the night, that the monk Ñāṇavīra made his mind quite pure of constraining things, and kept thinking and pondering and reflexively observing the Dhamma as he had heard and learnt it, the clear and stainless Eye of the Dhamma arose in him: "Whatever has the nature of arising, all that has the nature of ceasing."

Having been a teaching-follower for a month, he became one attained to right view.[41]

Thus he claimed to have "entered the stream" (sotāpatti), glimpsed the unconditioned (nirvana), and become, thereby, a "noble one" (ariya).

The Buddha used the term ariya to refer to those who had achieved a direct experiential insight into the nature of the four truths (suffering, its origins, its cessation, and the way to its cessation). For such people these truths are no longer beliefs or theories but realities. When someone comes to know them as such, he or she is said to have "entered the stream," which culminates, within a maximum of seven further lifetimes either as a human or a god, in arahant-hood, that is, the final attainment of nirvana. While the Buddha used this term in a purely spiritual sense, he maintained a distinction between an ariya and an "ordinary person" (puthujjana), that is, one who had not yet had the experience of stream entry. The experience, however, is available to anyone, irrespective of their social position, sex, or racial origins. By offering this radical redefinition of "nobility," the Buddha introduced into caste-bound India a spiritual tradition able to transcend the limits of the indigenous culture. Yet in the final analysis, concluded Ñāṇavīra, "the Buddha's Teaching is for a privileged class—those who are fortunate enough to have the intelligence to grasp it . . . , and they are most certainly not the majority!"[42]

Up to this point Ñāṇavīra had maintained a continuous correspondence with his friend Ñāṇamoli (Moore). Now he stopped it, because "there was no longer anything for me to discuss *with* him, since the former relationship of parity between us regarding the Dhamma had suddenly come to an end."[43] And it was never to be resumed, for eight months later, on March 8, 1960, Ñāṇamoli Thera died suddenly of a heart attack in a remote village while on a walking tour. He left behind some of the finest English translations from Pali of key Theravāda texts. Added to this loss had been the death three years earlier of Ñāṇavīra's first preceptor, Nyanatiloka, on May 28, 1957.

( 5 )

In the year following his stream entry (1960) Ñāṇavīra began writing a series of "notes" on Pali technical terms. By the summer of 1961 he had finished two such notes, one on *paṭiccasamuppāda* (conditionality) and one on *paramattha sacca* (ultimate truth). In July of the same year, a German Buddhist nun called Vajira (Hannelore Wolf), who had been in Ceylon since 1955 and since 1959 had been living as a hermit, called on Ñāṇavīra for advice. He subsequently sent her a copy of the two notes he had just finished typing. These had a tremendous impact on her. "Your notes on *viññāṇa-nāmarūpa* [consciousness-name/form]," she wrote, "have led me away from the abyss into which I have been staring for more than twelve years." And added, "I do not know . . . by what miraculous skill you have guided me to a safe place where at last I can breathe freely."[44] The correspondence and one further day-long meeting resulted in Vajira likewise "entering the stream," in late January 1962. Vajira underwent an ecstatic but turbulent transformation from an ordinary person (*puthujjana*) to an *ariya,* the validity of which Ñāṇavīra did "not see any reason to doubt." Vajira, from her side, now regarded Ñāṇavīra as an *arahant*. But the rapidity and intensity of the change provoked a kind of nervous breakdown, and the Ceylonese authorities deported her to Germany (on February 22, 1962). On her return she ceased to have any contact with her former Buddhist friends in Hamburg. This, commented Ñāṇavīra, was "a good sign, not a bad one—when one has got what one wants, one stops making a fuss about it and sits down quietly."[45]

Four months after Vajira's departure, Ñāṇavīra's chronic indigestion (amoebiasis) was further aggravated by satyriasis—a devastatingly inappropriate malady for a celibate hermit. Satyriasis— "the overpowering need on the part of a man to seduce a never-ending succession of women" (Britannica)—is the male equivalent to nymphomania in women. "Under the pressure of this affliction," he noted on December 11, "I am oscillating between two poles. If I indulge the sensual images that offer themselves, my thought turns towards the state of a layman; if I resist them, my thought turns towards suicide. Wife or knife, one might say."[46] In fact, the previous month he had already made an unsuccessful attempt to end his life. Although he realized that the erotic stimulation could be overcome by meditative absorption, such practice was prevented by his chronic indigestion. By November 1963, he had "given up all hope of making any further progress for myself in this life"[47] and had also resolved not to disrobe. It was simply a question of how long he could "stand the strain."[48]

While for the ordinary person (*puthujjana*) suicide is ethically equivalent to murder, for an *ariya* it is acceptable under circumstances that prevent further spiritual practice. For the *ariya* is no longer bound to the craving that drives the endless cycle of death and rebirth, his or her liberation being guaranteed within a finite period of time. Ñāṇavīra cites instances from the canon of *ariya bhikkhus* at the time of the Buddha who had taken their lives and become *arahants* in the process. He does not seem to have been driven by the conventional motives for suicide: resentment, remorse, despair, grief. He writes openly of his dilemma to friends with droll understatement and black humor:

> All the melancholy farewell letters are written (they have to be amended and brought up to date from time to time, as the weeks pass and my throat is still uncut); the note for the coroner is prepared (carefully refraining from any witty remarks that might spoil the solemn moment at the inquest when the note is read out aloud); and the mind is peaceful and concentrated.49

His friends responded with a mixture of concern, bewilderment and alarm. "People want their Dhamma on easier terms," he reflected, "and they dislike it when they are shown that they must pay a heavier price—and they are frightened, too, when they see something they don't understand: they regard it as morbid and their concern (unconscious, no doubt) is to bring things back to healthy, reassuring, normality."50

Most of 1963 was taken up with preparing his notes for publication, something he would have considered "an intolerable disturbance"51 had his health not prevented him from practice. Despite such disclaimers, one has the strong impression that he wished to communicate his vision of the Dhamma to a wider public. (Maugham records him as saying, "I'm hoping to find an English publisher for [them].")52 Through the help of the Ceylonese judge Lionel Samaratunga a limited edition of 250 cyclostyled copies of *Notes on Dhamma, 1960–1963* was produced toward the end of the year and distributed to leading Buddhist figures of the time and various libraries and institutions. The response was largely one of polite incomprehension.

## ( 6 )

When Robin Maugham entered the tiny hut at the beginning of 1965, Ñāṇavīra had largely completed the revisions to his *Notes on Dhamma*. "I looked round the room with its faded blue walls," Maugham recalls. "There was a table made from a packing-case with an oil-lamp on it, a chair, a chest and a bookcase. There were two straw brooms and two umbrellas—and his plank bed and the straw mat I was sitting on."[53] But he was quite unaware of Ñāṇavīra's work. The questions he asked as he squatted uncomfortably on the floor were typical of those a sympathetic but uninformed European would make today. Maugham's principal interest was to understand Ñāṇavīra's character. To this end he asked at length about his relations with his family, the reasons why he became a monk, if he felt lonely, and whether he missed the West.

Maugham left the first meeting with a positive impression. "I liked his diffident smile and I admired his courage," he reflected. "But I still wondered if he was completely sincere."[54] During the second meeting his doubts were put to rest. Ñāṇavīra explained how his mother had come out to Ceylon and tried to persuade her only child to return home. When he refused she suffered a heart attack. As soon as she recovered she went back to England and died. "His voice was quite impassive as he spoke," explained Maugham. "I find it hard to describe the tone of his voice. Yet if I don't I shall miss the whole point of the man I'd travelled so far to see. There was no harshness in his tone. There was no coldness. There was understanding and gentleness. And it was only these two qualities that made his next remark bearable."

> "My mother's death didn't worry me," he said. "Even now, during this life, every moment we are born and die. But we continue. We take some other shape or form in another life."

Ñāṇavīra fell silent. He was visibly tired. Then he added: "The whole point of Buddhism is to bring an end to this farcical existence. The whole point of our present existence is to reach Nirvana—complete understanding of natural phenomena— thereby ending the chain of re-birth."[55]

In Ñāṇavīra's account of the meeting, however, it is Robin Maugham's sincerity that is put into question. "The visitors I spoke of in my postcard," he wrote in a letter two days later,

> came and talked and took photographs and notes for sev- eral hours on the afternoon of the eighth. The older one is Robin Maugham, a nephew of the celebrated Somerset Maugham. He is a novelist (third-rate, I suspect) and a writer of travel books. Although they both seemed interested in the Dhamma, I rather think that their principal reason for vis- iting me was to obtain material for their writings. I had a slightly uncomfortable feeling of being exploited; but, unfor- tunately, once I start talking, I like going on, without proper regard for the repercussions later on. So probably, in about a year's time, there will be a new travel book with a chapter (complete with photographs) devoted to yours truly, and the romantic life he is leading in the jungle.[56]

Contrary to his own version, Maugham was not alone. Thus the dramatic encounter between two tormented souls—the man of the world and the hermit—is compromised by the presence of a third man—probably Maugham's secretary and assistant. Ñāṇavīra's prediction about the outcome of the visit proved entirely accurate except in the timing. Maugham's sensational account of the meet- ing was published in the *People* newspaper of September 26, 1965, but it took ten years before the travel book (*Search for Nirvana*, 1975) appeared with a chapter (complete with photographs) on his encounter with Ñāṇavīra.

At root, though, Maugham seems sincere. As they were parting, he had the strong impression that Ñāṇavīra still wanted to tell him something "of such importance that it would change my whole life." But the monk abruptly averted his "mellow gaze" and simply said goodbye. Maugham and his companion walked away toward the path that led from the jungle glade to the village. Then he turned back: "His lean gaunt figure in a saffron robe was standing motionless on the verandah. Perhaps he knew a truth that would make the existence of millions of men a happier thing. Perhaps he knew the answer. Perhaps he had found the secret of life. But I would never know."[57]

The revision of his *Notes on Dhamma* completed, Ñāṇavīra returned to his simple routine of meditation, correspondence, and daily chores. His chronic indigestion continued to be aggravated by satyriasis. Six months (Maugham, presumably for dramatic effect, says two weeks) after their meeting, on the afternoon of July 7, 1965, Ñāṇavīra ended his life by putting his head into a cellophane bag containing drops of chloroform. Only a month earlier his letters had been exploring the meaning of humor.

The memory of the English monk from Aldershot continued to haunt Robin Maugham. In 1968 he published *The Second Window*, an autobiographical novel about a journalist who becomes entangled in a child sex-abuse scandal in Kenya. As a digression from the main theme, the protagonist visits Ceylon to track down a certain Leslie Edwin Fletcher who is rumored to be living there as a Buddhist hermit. While clearly based on Maugham's encounter with Ñāṇavīra, the fictionalized version turns him into a gloomy, confused, and pathetic figure. A radio play (*A Question of Retreat*) followed in a similar vein.

Shortly afterward, in 1972, Julius Evola published his autobiography. Toward the end of the war Evola had been injured by a bomb in Vienna and for the remainder of his life was partially paralyzed. He returned to Italy and became a focal figure for the far right, receiving in his apartment a steady trickle of those who still admired the values he espoused. Although he died in 1974, he has been resurrected recently as a hero of resurgent neo-fascist groups in Italy.

Recalling *The Doctrine of Awakening*, he wrote in his autobiography: "The person who translated the work [into English], a certain Mutton [*sic*], found in it an incitant to leave Europe and withdraw to the Orient in the hope of finding there a center where one still cultivated the disciplines that I recommended; unfortunately, I have had no further news of him."[58] Evola also confessed that he himself was not a Buddhist and his study was intended to balance his earlier work on the Hindu tantras. He saw Buddhism as the "'dry' and intellectual path of pure detachment" as opposed to that of the tantras which taught "affirmation, engagement, the utilisation and transformation of immanent forces liberated through the awakening of the Shakti, i.e., the root power of all vital energy, particularly that of sex."[59] The only other work of Evola's to have been translated into English was *The Metaphysics of Sex* (London, 1983).

## ( 7 )

In 1987 a book was published by Path Press, Colombo, with the title *Clearing the Path: Writings of Ñāṇavīra Thera, 1960–1965*. This hardcover book of nearly six hundred pages contains the text of Ñāṇavīra's revised *Notes on Dhamma, 1960–1965* together with 149 letters of varying lengths written by Ñāṇavīra to nine correspondents, which serve (as the author himself stated) as a commentary on the *Notes*. The texts are scrupulously edited, extensively annotated, and cross-referenced by means of a comprehensive index. The compilation, editing, and publication of this book was a labor of love performed (anonymously) by Ven. Bodhesako (Robert Smith), an American *sāmaṇera* from Chicago, who died suddenly of gangrene of the intestines in Nepal in 1989, shortly after completing the work.

*Clearing the Path* is presented by Bodhesako as a "work book. Its purpose is to help the user to acquire a point of view that is different from his customary frame of reference, and also more satisfactory."[60] As such it is to be used as a tool for inner change. This supports Ñāṇavīra's own contention in his preface to the *Notes* that "the reader is presumed to be subjectively engaged with an anxious problem, the problem of his existence, which is also the problem of his suffering." He adds:

> There is therefore nothing in these pages to interest the professional scholar, for whom the question of personal existence does not arise; for the scholar's whole concern is to eliminate or ignore the individual point of view in an effort to establish the objective truth—a would-be impersonal synthesis of public facts.[61]

He later remarked that the *Notes* "were not written to pander to people's tastes" and were made "as unattractive, academically speaking, as possible."[62] He declared that he would be satisfied if only one person were ever to benefit from them.

In their final version, *Notes on Dhamma* consist of the two essays on *paṭiccasamuppāda* (conditionality) and *paramattha sacca* (ultimate truth) and twenty shorter notes on a range of key Pali terms, such as *attā* (self), *citta* (mind), *rūpa* (form), and so on. They are all written in a dense, exact style in numbered sections, most of the key terms remaining in Pali. Ñāṇavīra composed them as an explicit critique of the orthodox Theravāda position "with the purpose of clearing away a mass of dead matter which is choking the [Buddha's discourses]."[63]

In keeping with Ñāṇavīra's wishes, the *Notes* have not been indexed. This, he felt, would turn the book into a "work of reference," whereas "it is actually intended to be read and digested as a single whole, with each separate note simply presenting a different facet of the same central theme."[64] Elsewhere he describes his *Notes* as being like "so many beads inter-connected with numbers of threads, in a kind of three-dimensional network."[65]

This holomorphic character of the *Notes* is reflected most explicitly in the fourth and final section entitled "Fundamental Structure," which consists of two parts, "Static Aspect" and "Dynamic Aspect." In his usual ironic manner, Ñāṇavīra describes this section as "really a remarkably elegant piece of work, almost entirely original, and also quite possibly correct. I am obliged to say this myself, since it is improbable that anybody else will. It is most unlikely that anyone will make anything of it."[66] This is certainly true for the present writer.

"Fundamental Structure" attempts to describe by means of terse philosophical language and symbolic diagrams the "inherent structure governing the selectivity of consciousness,"[67] which is common to both the enlightened and unenlightened person alike. Ñāṇavīra compares this fundamental structure to a chessboard on which both "passionate chess," that is, a game following the rules but complicated by the influence of passion, and its opposite, "dispassionate chess," can both be played. But he admits that these ideas are "only indirectly connected to the Buddha's Teaching proper."[68] He sees them as a possible corrective to certain tendencies in abstract, scientific thinking to distance oneself from a sense of concrete existential location. For someone who does not suffer from this problem, however, he acknowledges that it will serve no purpose to study "Fundamental Structure."

Ñāṇavīra recognizes a yawning gulf between the worldview of the average Western person and the teaching of the Buddha. For those not inclined to the somewhat dry and technical approach of "Fundamental Structure," he recommends prior study of existentialist philosophy, as found in the writings of Kierkegaard, Sartre, Camus, and, in particular, Martin Heidegger's *Being and Time*. For these thinkers had also discarded the detached, rationalist approach to philosophy and emphasized immediate questions of personal existence. He also speaks highly of James Joyce's *Ulysses*, the early novels of Aldous Huxley, and the writings of Franz Kafka, all of which had a strong influence on him as a young man. Ñāṇavīra nonetheless warned against confusing existentialism with Buddhism. For "one who has understood the Buddha's Teaching no longer asks these questions; he is *ariya* 'noble,' and no more a *puthujjana*, and he is beyond the range of the existential philosophies." The Dhamma does not offer answers; it shows "the way leading to the final cessation of all questions about self and the world."[69]

Ñāṇavīra also found the very positivism he so deplored in the West infecting the writings of some of the most respected Sri Lankan authorities on Buddhism. K. N. Jayatilleke, O. H. de A. Wijesekera, and G. P. Malalasekera are all taken to task on this point. Despite their being professed Buddhists, Ñāṇavīra compares the former two unfavorably with the Christian thinker Kierkegaard. He criticizes Jayatilleke, for example, for presenting the four noble truths as though they were propositions of fact, thus obscuring their character as imperatives for action. He compares them to the bottle in *Alice's Adventures in Wonderland* labeled "Drink Me!" From this perspective (also that of the *Dhammacakkappavattana Sutta*),

the Four Noble Truths are the ultimate tasks for a man's performance—Suffering commands "Know me absolutely!", Arising commands "Abandon Me!", Cessation commands "Realize me!", and the Path commands "Develop me!"[70]

Startling images of this kind abound throughout Ñāṇavīra's letters, which reveal him both as a rigorous analytical thinker and also a literary stylist of a high order. By reflecting, in addition, the radical seriousness and renunciation he adopted toward the personal realization of the Buddha's teaching, Ñāṇavīra's writings stand out as one of the most original and important contributions to Buddhist literature of the twentieth century.

But why then, if this is true, does Ñāṇavīra Thera remain such an obscure figure? The short answer is because he singularly fails to fit the popular stereotype of what a contemporary Buddhist should be.

## ( 8 )

It is frequently assumed in the West that Buddhists are mystically inclined, liberal, ecologically sensitive, democratic, pacifist, tolerant, life-affirming, compassionate, and spiritual. After reading *Clearing the Path*, however, such are not the qualities one would readily ascribe to Ñāṇavīra Thera. Since the image he presents is at odds with this stereotype, he is liable to appear to many Western (and modern Asian) Buddhists as instinctively unattractive. What validity then does the stereotype have? Could it be that it is no more than a romantic reinvention of Buddhism, which presents a model of "spirituality" that embodies those values the "materialistic" West feels it has lost? Is the real reason for Ñāṇavīra's unattractiveness the challenge he presents to the assumptions on which the stereotype is based? Or, alternatively, is the stereotype valid and Ñāṇavīra Thera deluded and misguided?

As the first step in unraveling Ñāṇavīra's motives, it is helpful to consider his relation to the book that inspired him to become a *bhikkhu* and its author, Julius Evola. In only one of his published letters (February 21, 1964) does he mention (in passing) Evola's

*The Doctrine of Awakening.* He adds in parenthesis, "which, however, I cannot now recommend to you without considerable reserves."[71] But nowhere does he state what those reserves are.

There is no evidence in Ñāṇavīra's writings that he subscribed to Evola's political or racist views, but there are a number of threads that forge a link between the spiritual outlooks of the two men. One of these threads would be Ñāṇavīra's privileged military background and somewhat aristocratic bearing, which would have been endorsed by Evola's ideas on the superiority of the warrior caste and the aristocratic nature of Buddhism. While nothing in the content of his writings suggests any conscious promotion of such values, his capacity for self-discipline and his wry, detached tone of voice reflect a person who assumed authority as a right rather than a privilege.

Perhaps the strongest thread is the fact that Harold Musson's foreword to *The Doctrine of Awakening* could, with minor adjustments, have served as a foreword fifteen years later to Ñāṇavīra Thera's *Notes on Dhamma*. For the aim of the two works is essentially the same. To summarize Musson's foreword, these are: (1) "to recapture the spirit of Buddhism in its essential form"; (2) "to clear away some of the woolly ideas" (the preface to *Notes on Dhamma* says "dead matter") that have gathered around the Buddha's teaching; and (3), and most important, the "encouragement of a practical application of the doctrine."[72]

While Ñāṇavīra makes no reference to, and could well have been unfamiliar with, Evola's Guénonist conception of tradition, he certainly is a traditionalist, though in a narrower sense than Guénon. He says at one point that there is nothing he dislikes more than someone who declares that the aim of all religions is the same. Whereas Guénon, who spent the last twenty years of his life as a convert to Islam in Cairo, eventually came to include Buddhism as part of the revelation that lies at the heart of all religions, Ñāṇavīra came to regard any view that did not accord with his reading of the early Buddhist canon as deficient. He is dismissive of theistic belief and religion in general and Christianity in particular.

Ñāṇavīra likewise shares Evola's contempt for the modern world. He is scathing about evolutionary and relativist conceptions of ethics and regards the Buddha's ethical code as an absolute and invariable truth. He also has little sympathy for the Western devotion to democracy, which he describes as "a general inadequacy in modern European thought—the growing view that the majority must be right, that truth is to be decided by appeal to the ballot-box."[73] For Ñāṇavīra the majority are simply a majority in delusion and therefore unlikely to arrive at the kinds of conclusions which would be reached by an enlightened minority of *ariyas*. He would disagree with Evola, though, in the value of pursuing *any* course of political action. For Ñāṇavīra it is not the modern world that is flawed, but existence as such.

A real but rarely acknowledged problem lies in the Buddhist conception of an *ariya*, the "superior" person who has gained privileged insight into the nature of existence. This view is held in common by all Buddhist schools and is pivotal to the oft-repeated argument that Buddhism, unlike other traditions, offers a practical way of personal transformation through spiritual practice. As Evola was aware, this doctrine plays into the hands of the political right. This principle was the basis for the government of old Tibet, which believed that the best way to run a country was by an enlightened elite, particularly an elite motivated by boundless compassion for all beings.

As soon as one seriously introduces Buddhist values into the arena of politics, one will encounter difficulties in reconciling them not only with capitalism and consumerism but also with liberal democracy. While it may be fashionable to draw on Buddhist doctrines, such as interconnectedness, to support a Green political ideology, for example, one needs to be aware that the body of doctrine that enshrines such a notion could also be used to support a Green totalitarianism, a society governed by an enlightened minority who would compassionately dictate what would be best for the survival of the planet.

Not that any of these questions would have been of concern to Ñāṇavīra. For in many ways Ñāṇavīra represents the kind of Theravāda Buddhist monk that Mahayana Buddhists would criticize as self-centered and uncaring. (It comes as no surprise that he vehemently asserts that the "Mahāyāna is *not* the Buddha's teaching.")[74] Only once in his writings does he mention the traditional Theravāda meditation of loving kindness (*mettabhāvanā*), and then only to say that he has never formally practiced it. His tendency to physical isolation could arguably reflect a philosophical tendency to solipsism; in one letter he describes the appearance of another person as merely "a certain modification of my experience that requires elaborate description."[75] And elsewhere he writes, "I am far more strongly moved by episodes in books than by those in real life, which usually leave me cold."[76] He is quite unequivocal about nirvana being the cessation of existence in any form. "There *is* a way out," he insists, "there is a way to put a stop to existence, if only we have the courage to let go of our cherished humanity."[77]

Nor should Ñāṇavīra's experience be judged negatively according to Mahayana Buddhist standards. A so-called Hīnayāna *ariya* is considered even in the Mahayana traditions as part of the Buddhist sangha and, as such, an object of respect and refuge. Ñāṇavīra may not have been motivated by great compassion, but he did claim to have experienced directly the unconditioned reality of nirvana, which is the central truth of all Buddhist traditions.

Is a right-wing misogynist with uncontrollable lusts and a penchant for suicide thereby automatically disqualified from experienc-

ing nirvana? Ñāṇavīra points to passages in the Pali Canon where
the stream entrant is shown to be capable of anger, jealousy, deceit,
and drunkenness, transgressing the lesser monastic rules, even
disrobing on account of sensual desire, and, as a layman, break-
ing the five precepts. "Unless you bring the [practitioner] down to
earth," he writes, "the Buddha's Teaching can never be a reality
for you. So long as you are content to put the *sotāpanna* (stream
entrant) on a pedestal well out of reach, it can never possibly occur
to you that it is your duty to become *sotāpanna* yourself . . . here
and now in this very life."[78]

For Ñāṇavīra, Buddhism offers a radical and uncompromising
praxis as a response to the deepest questions of human existence.
As such it avoids the extremes of rationalism and romanticism. A
scholar of Buddhism, he comments, can only feel safe as long as his
subject "is not one day going to get up and look him between the
eyes. . . . (Quite the last thing that a professor of Buddhism would
dream of doing is to profess Buddhism—*that* is left to mere ama-
teurs like myself.)"[79] He is likewise aware of how his solitary life in
the Ceylonese jungle is liable to be interpreted romantically: "The
British public wants romance," he complains, "and I am *not* a romantic figure, and have no desire to be portrayed as one."[80] As in
the Buddha's famous parable of the raft, Buddhism is a means to
an end and *not* an end in itself. For Ñāṇavīra even the terms "Buddhism" and "Buddhist" carry "a slightly displeasing air about them
—they are too much like labels one sticks on the outside of packages regardless of what the packages contain."[81]

Toward the end of his life Ñāṇavīra was convinced that the
Dhamma was "very far from being understood in the West."[82] For
whether aware of it or not, Europeans were still fundamentally
preoccupied with the question of God, the very idea of a "moral
but Godless universe"[83] being utterly alien. Yet behind the belief in
God lies the even more deeply entrenched sense that the universe

has a meaning or purpose. He approvingly quotes Nietzsche: "*Has existence then a significance at all?*—the question that will require a couple of centuries even to be heard in all its profundity."[84]

Nietzsche's question disturbs in the same way as Ñāṇavīra's suicide. For such statements challenge those collectively held, Christian-based views about the nature of life which still dominate our instinctive moral sense of good and evil. For Buddhism to penetrate deeply into the European psyche it will have to reach such pre-articulate strata of experience. Otherwise it is liable to become merely a consoling set of beliefs and views still founded on a theistic ethos. Enlightenment is not a transcendent mystical rapture but an ethical experience that reveals the nature of the existential dilemma and the way to its resolution.

Ñāṇavīra firmly challenges the idea that the Buddha's teaching is in any way life-affirming. He condemns the fairly common practice at his time among Buddhists to call upon the good authority of notable non-Buddhists to attest to the Buddha's good character. He finds it particularly galling that a certain Sri Lankan professor would recruit Albert Schweitzer to this purpose. For "Schweitzer's philosophy is 'Reverence for Life,' whereas the Buddha has said that just as even the smallest piece of excrement has a foul smell so even the smallest piece of existence is not to be commended."[85]

This scatological view of existence is for many Western people very difficult to swallow. Yet Ñāṇavīra feels justified in making such statements not merely on the basis of canonical authority, but on the authority of his own enlightenment, his stream entry. And it is this authority that he likewise calls upon to justify his final act of suicide.

The debate over the validity of Ñāṇavīra's claim to be a stream entrant had already begun in Sri Lanka before he died. It is an offense deserving expulsion from the order for a *bhikkhu* to declare himself to have a spiritual attainment that he in fact does not have.

Even if he does have the attainment, he is forbidden to tell of it to anyone except a fellow *bhikkhu*. Ñāṇavīra's claim to stream entry was recorded in a letter in a sealed envelope that was to be opened only by the senior *bhikkhu* of the Island Hermitage in the event of his death. For some reason (perhaps a rumor of suicide?), the letter was opened in 1964 and the contents became known. To defuse the matter, Ñāṇavīra spoke openly about it for the first time to a fellow *bhikkhu* in Colombo, thus letting "this rather awkward cat . . . out of the bag."[86]

How does one decide whether another person really is a stream entrant or whether they are deluding themselves? According to tradition, only an *ariya* can recognize another *ariya*. It would follow, therefore, that only a bona fide *ariya* would have the authority to deny Ñāṇavīra's claim. But then the same questions would arise with regard to *that* person, which would require the authority of yet another bona fide *ariya,* and so on ad infinitum.

Subjectively, however, the attainment of stream entry can be validated by a discernible and definitive psychological change. For upon attaining stream entry three "fetters" (*saṃyojana*) disappear for good: (1) views that a self abides either in or apart from the psycho-physical aggregates (*sakkāya diṭṭhi*); (2) doubts about the validity of the Buddha, the dhamma, the sangha, the training, conditionality, and other key doctrines (*vicikicchā*); and (3) attachment to the efficacity of mere rules and rituals (*sīlabbata parāmāsa*). For Ñāṇavīra to have made the claim he did implies that he actually experienced the disappearance of these tendencies from his own mind. But only he (or another clairvoyant *ariya*) would have been able to know this. Although his writings bear no trace of these attitudes, that alone would be insufficient evidence to conclude anything about the degree of the author's attainment, for it could reflect merely a commitment to doctrinal orthodoxy.

One also cannot rule out the possibility that Ñāṇavīra Thera was suffering from a delusion, that he was driven to suicide by unconscious fears and desires over which he had no awareness or control. The clearest statement of his own views on the matter appears in a letter of May 16, 1963. "Do not think," he writes,

> that I regard suicide as praiseworthy—that there can easily be an element of weakness in it, I am the first to admit . . . —, but I certainly regard it as preferable to a number of other possibilities. (I would a hundred times rather have it said of the Notes that the author killed himself as a *bhikkhu* than that he disrobed; for *bhikkhus* have become *arahants* in the act of suicide, but it is not recorded that anyone became *arahant* in the act of disrobing.)[87]

It might help overcome the unease about the stigma of suicide if one described Ñāṇavīra's act as one of "enlightened euthanasia."

The greatest irony of this story is how a passage from a *sutta* saved an Italian fascist from committing suicide, in gratitude for which he wrote a book that impelled an English army officer to become a *bhikkhu,* who eventually committed suicide with the conviction that it was fully justified by the *suttas.*

The value of Ñāṇavīra Thera's life lies not so much in the answers it gives but in the questions it raises about what it means for a European to be a practicing Buddhist. His writings clear away many woolly ideas about the Buddha's teaching (at least as found in the Pali Canon) and force one to address uncomfortable questions that are usually ignored. Are either Evola's fascist or Ñāṇavīra's life-denying interpretations of the Buddha's teaching any more or less tenable than the liberal-democratic and life-affirming readings of the tradition that abound in the West today? Even if Ñāṇavīra's work only forces us to recognize the subconscious and culturally biased assumptions we project onto Buddhism, then it will have provided an important service. This does not mean that we would then have to adopt his (or, heaven forbid, Evola's) views rather than our own, but simply that we would have stepped free of one more "thicket of views," thus enabling a clearer vision of how to proceed along a path whose ultimate destination we cannot know.

Whatever reservations one may have about Ñāṇavīra Thera, one has to acknowledge that he was the first European to have left such a vivid and rigorous account of a life dedicated to realizing the truths disclosed by the Dhamma. Of course, it is impossible to say whether other Western Buddhists have not accomplished the same or more. But their published writings tend not to discuss these matters. Ñāṇavīra's uniqueness lies in his having embraced the Dhamma with wholehearted confidence, having sought to clear away with reason much of the confusion surrounding its orthodox interpretation, having practiced it relentlessly, having recorded his experience of it in detail, and ultimately having sacrificed his life for it.

# "A Much Younger Man, but No Less Charming"

## Stephen Batchelor talks to Peter Maddock

The visitors I spoke of in my postcard came and talked and took photographs and notes for several hours on the afternoon of the 8th [January 1965]. The older one is Robin Maugham, a nephew of the celebrated Somerset Maugham. He is a novelist (third-rate, I suspect) and a writer of travel books. Although they both seemed interested in the Dhamma, I rather think that their principal reason for visiting me was to obtain material for their writings. I had a slightly uncomfortable feeling of being exploited; but, unfortunately, once I start talking, I like going on, without proper regard for the repercussions later on. So probably, in perhaps a year's time, there will be a new travel book with a chapter (complete with photographs) devoted to yours truly, with the romantic life he is leading in the jungle.

Whether or not this would (or will) be a bad thing or not, I really can't say. I thoroughly dislike the idea myself, but people are already so much misinformed about the Dhamma in the West (particularly in England) that—if Robin Maugham gives a reasonably accurate account of his visit—it is possible that some good might come of it. Not to me, of course, since it will be a source of disturbance; but that no longer matters so very much. If only he doesn't go and give the impression that I am seeking publicity by building me up into a kind of

character in a novel! But it is so difficult to know what to say
and what not to say to people who come and see me.

Maugham was at Eton and Cambridge (he went down
the year before I went up) and was in the Middle East during
the war; so, since we have much the same sort of background,
we were quite at ease with one another. His friend, a much
younger man, but no less charming, gave a rupee to one
of the villagers because of his poverty-stricken appearance.
Unfortunately, the man in question is the second-wealthiest
person in the village, owning a tractor, a house, and about
twenty-five thousand rupees in cash. They roared with laugh-
ter when I told them, and I still find myself chuckling when
I think about it. Delicious irony!

—ÑĀṆAVĪRA THERA (1965)

Two Englishmen—Robin Maugham and his friend—visited
me. I rather fear that they are proposing to write me up and
present me in print and picture to the British Public—let us
hope not too grotesquely. I dislike this sort of thing; but I also
dislike being disagreeable to people—and, besides, I am fond
of talking. The British Public wants romance—and I am
not a romantic figure, and have no desire to be portrayed as
one. "The World Well Lost for Love" is something the public
can understand, and they can perhaps also understand "The
World Well Lost for Love of God"; but what they can not understand is "The World Well Lost" tout court.

—ÑĀṆAVĪRA THERA (1965)

**Peter, could you first give me some background as to how you
came to know Robin Maugham?**

I was articled to a lawyer called David Jacobs and Robin was
a client of his. In 1964, Robin asked me: "Do you want to come

to Ceylon for three months?" I said, "Sure." I was eighteen at the time. I asked David if I could be let off my articles and David agreed. So I went with Robin.

**What was Robin Maugham's interest in going to Ceylon?**

I think he had been there before. Robin's uncle [W. Somerset Maugham] had for many years traveled, first with Gerald Haxton and then Alan Searle, and written on board cargo boats. Robin did the same from quite an early age. When he wanted to write, he would get on the Blue Star and would be at sea for eight weeks, creating a very organized and disciplined capsule, which enabled him to write. It was his preferred way of doing it. I think it was the Maugham tradition.

**What was his specific interest in going to Ceylon this time?**

I don't think he had one. He was just traveling. I don't recall that he had any specific motive in going to Ceylon. I think he was doing a novel at the time and he was proposing to spend the winter there. He had friends coming out, I remember Hector Bolitho, who was one of those strange writers, whose claim to fame was a biography of Queen Victoria. And a group of other writers. Robin tended to travel those winter months.

**In his book *Search for Nirvana*, which appeared some years later and records this visit to Ceylon, Robin gives the impression that he was on some sort of spiritual quest.**

I don't think so. Robin was in the Western Desert as a tank commander and saw a lot of violence and the ugliness of war at an early age—he was born in 1916 so would have been twenty-three, twenty-four—and I discussed with him spirituality on a number of occasions. Robin was the generation before flower power—as was Harold Musson. Remember I was talking about spirituality with a man who had been talking with someone, then thirty seconds later he'd turn round and the person'd be lying there dead with his head blown off. And that was the sort of reality that Robin faced at a young age after having had a relatively protected life. I remember we were having dinner together, at the Ivy as a matter of fact, and I said, "Basically, you are into a very narrow frame and what you should do is take acid." And he said, "Well I think there is only that much experience [Peter Maddock spreads his hands about a foot apart], that much knowledge and information you are ever going to have." And I think that was very much geared by his having seen the underbelly of the beast.

**Did he take any acid?**

No, no, he wouldn't. Robin's tipple was alcohol. Robin was an alcoholic, not a drug addict.

**So you left England on the boat. Did you go in any capacity other than just a friend of Robin's?**

Well, yes, as a friend. He was desperately in love with me at the time. And I also had helped him write a book called *The Green Shade* [published 1966]. Robin was somebody very much in need of ideas. A good friend of his, Sandy Pratt—who ran Sandy's Bar in Ibiza—he's still alive, must be eighty or ninety, said to me, "The problem with Robin was that he hated writing." But Robin wrote some wonderful stuff. *Come to Dust* [1945], his memoir of the war, is absolutely fantastic, staggering. *The Servant* [1948] is amazing. *Line on Ginger* [1949] was good. His early stuff was brilliant. Well worth reading. Robin was a very complex character. He came from a very privileged background, his father was Lord Chancellor. We once drove past a house in Cadogan Square, and we were talking about the leisure class and staffing and he said, "I remember when we lived there"—the house we were passing—"we had thirty-three indoor staff." Times change.

**So you set off by boat . . .**

Yes, we went by boat with Messageries Maritimes, a line that no longer exists, from Marseille. I think the Suez Canal was closed at the time and we went all the way around Africa and it took forever. It stopped at Aden, Karachi, somewhere in Egypt—a six-week voyage before we arrived in Ceylon.

We stayed at the Galle Face Hotel [in Colombo]. Robin was someone important—Joseph Losey had just finished [the film of] *The Servant* in 1963. He was also a peer of the realm, which meant a lot in those days, and a celebrated journalist. He was very well connected. Mrs. Bandaranaike was the PM at the time, and the ex-PM, Sir John Kotalawela, was the person who set up the reception committee for Robin. So when Robin arrived he was basically very well taken care of.

**Do you remember how and when Robin first came to hear of Harold Musson, Ñāṇavīra Thera?**

There was this journalist, Nalin Fernando—I think his uncle had a newspaper—and Robin said to him, "I'm looking for a human-interest story." And Harold Musson's name came up somehow. He had to be located, which took some time, and then he had to agree to do the interview. I went once, I think Robin went back to reinterview him. Ceylon was still pretty rough in those days, it was relatively undeveloped. There was a mixture of connections, but Nalin Fernando was the main one and he came with us—he may still be alive now.

**So you set off with Robin for Būndala. How do you remember that journey?**

We went to Dodanduwa [Island Hermitage] first. To get to Dodanduwa you have to go across on a catamaran, it takes about forty-five minutes. I think there were maybe half a dozen Europeans or Americans there. The head *bhikkhu* brought out a young American [possibly Nyanasumana], he was a trainee. He was quite young and terribly earnest. I remember talking to him and being amazed that someone could be that earnest. If I remember correctly, his being there was in some way connected to the Vietnam War, with not being in America, and thus rejecting those values.

I was eighteen at the time, and I remember discussing with him what it meant to fall victim to the thing you most try to flee, and the flight not really being the answer to your problem.

R. D. Laing also visited this island and spent some time there when he visited Ceylon. The head *bhikkhu* told somebody—I forget who, a journalist friend of mine—that [Laing] was the only person who had ever come to the island who was able to meditate for sixteen hours a day as soon as he got there. He had an absolutely total ability to move into it. I think he spent some time on the island.

The journey to Būndala was a nightmare, very difficult in those days, and took forever.

I was interested to learn recently that Ñāṇavīra was forty-five when he died. But then he certainly looked ageless, timeless. And we spent a lot of time there, hours with him in his hut, in lotus position, talking about Theravāda Buddhism. Robin and he certainly came from very similar backgrounds. They had both been in the army during the war. So he too had seen the underbelly of the beast. Very much the same generation, who saw the Second World War that everybody had said could never happen. Giving meaning to life can be difficult after that. This is clearly what happened with Ñāṇavīra.

**What was his place at Būndala like?**

It was terribly primitive, immensely primitive, quite isolated too. Although his tone of voice was very much that of the *English oblique,* that is to say, he was not earnest in any way and saw things through the prism of the English upper classes, he was an Edwardian product and viewed the world in that way. He was very, very clear about his teaching, about what he believed. One of the things he told us at that time was of his experience of *sotāpatti,* stream entry, reaching that point at which the end of the tunnel was in sight.[1] Both Robin and I asked him if he were there. But as I said, [he spoke] obliquely, with a sense of humor but a totally different way of seeing things.

**Do you remember the way in which Ñāṇavīra told you of his attainments?**

You get people who go to an ashram in India and become gurus. But Ñāṇavīra was very much an emaciated Edwardian gentleman. In a dhoti but still exactly who he was before. I don't think there had been a change in personality, like some people who become British gurus and set up ashrams. For them there is a massive personality shift, they become earnest about their beliefs. I remember there wasn't anything of that about him. I think Robin asked him if he had any regrets. . . . It was a very frank conversation.

But if you are on a path, you don't worry about how other people might interpret you, you take it as any experience that passes in front of your door, you experience it for the sake of experiencing it. And that may have been why he agreed to see Robin. Whether there was a class thing in there whereby he received him because he was a viscount, a peer of the realm, who knows? I very much doubt it. With hindsight, I would say that he was bored to death. I would guess there was an element of boredom in Ñāṇavīra, because it was only a theory and he had gone as far as he could go with it and there was really nowhere else to take it.

He was very calm but not happy. Happiness was not an element there. Nor was there any despair—I suspect it was probably boredom that killed him, and illness, obviously, what with having amoebic dysentery on a daily basis, the sort of thing that would take the quality of life to a point where one would say, "Why bother?" As a man he was immensely engaging. He was clearly way up there in what he was doing. It seemed as though to talk to us was an immense relief from his boredom, to have some entertainment, some distraction—something not quite so serious as staying on the path.

Robin and Ñāṇavīra had a very easy conversation, an easy flow. Robin was a charming person. One has the feeling that Robin sensationalized his account of the meeting when he wrote it up. I don't think Robin said anything that wasn't true, but, yes, it was probably sensationalized—*The People* is a terrible Sunday rag.

**In *The People* article it says that Robin was inspired to seek out "that rich Englishman who is living in a jungle hut there as a Buddhist monk" by his uncle Somerset Maugham.**

Well if he was, then I didn't know anything about it. It was never mentioned to me, and I'd be surprised. In 1964 Somerset Maugham was not a well man, he died the following year. I stayed myself at the Villa Mauresque for a couple of weeks in the summer of '64, and I would say that he was in an advanced stage of senile dementia. If he had given Robin a clue, it would have been several years before that. But it is possible. These things come about, but I certainly do not recall Robin ever saying to me, "Well, there is this guy I want to interview in Ceylon." In a sense, Robin used *The People* when he was traveling because he knew that when he found a human interest story he could sell it and it would help pay for Robin's extremely expensive lifestyle.

**After your meeting with Ñāṇavīra Thera that day, what do you recall of its effect on Robin Maugham?**

As a journalist, he was getting a story that he wanted. On a personal level, I don't think Robin felt that there was any reality in this theory. I don't think Robin had any belief in reincarnation or any belief in Buddhism, as a matter of fact. As I said before, Robin had seen such horrors in his early youth that he never engaged. . . . I think that's maybe what they had in common—Musson and Maugham—they'd seen the underbelly of the beast, the true horror, how things can turn.

**Yet Robin Maugham kept coming back to this encounter with Ñāṇavīra. He dramatized it in his novel *The Second Window* [1968]**

and later in a play, *A Question of Retreat*. **Don't you think it was more than just a fascination with a very good story?**

It was about a paucity of ideas. Robin did reuse material all the time. He had a very good play called *The Two Wise Virgins of Hove* [1960], which he transmuted several times. Robin, as Sandy said, was not somebody who enjoyed writing, and his output as he got into his fifties declined abruptly. He was a young writer. He went back to ideas that were familiar. A lot of his stuff goes back to the same themes.

**So you don't think the meeting affected him spiritually?**

No, I don't think Robin had a spiritual side. I think it had been extinguished in him. He was a very moral person. There was a writer called Michael Davidson, who wrote a wonderful book called *The World, the Flesh and Myself*, absolutely brilliant in its use of English. He was a very old friend of Robin's and he'd fallen on hard times, so Robin bought him this boat in Littlehampton for £3,000. And I said to Robin—there was then some bill to be paid, "Why are you paying Michael's bills when he's said such terrible things about you?" And he said, "Well, he's an old friend, my dear. One doesn't want to become ungenerous just because somebody is having a hard time and turns on you." I saw this with Robin many, many times, this generosity of spirit, not just with money, but time. A moral person, someone who didn't lie, for example. But in terms of a spiritual side, in terms of seeking something, being a seeker or a believer. . . . It's like when I asked him that question, when I suggested he drop acid with me, and he said that was as far as he thought it goes—perhaps he was right.

**What was the effect of meeting Ñāṇavīra on you as a young man at that time?**

I was very interested. I went to a Jesuit boarding school when I was six years old. So I had heavy indoctrination, then I went on to a Benedictine school where I stayed 'til I was in my mid-teens.

So I was interested in asking questions and finding answers at that time. I was probably asking more questions [to Ñāṇavīra] than Robin.

**Were you particularly interested in Buddhism?**

No. It was something that was relatively new to me, it was the first time I'd experienced it, and it was very strong at that time in Ceylon. [Ñāṇavīra] explained everything about it that was to be explained. He was definitely a teacher by nature. He was someone who enjoyed teaching.

**Did your recollection of him lead to any further interest in what he said?**

Yes, it did. It was part of an ongoing study I was making in my life, which was obviously a searching for answers. I later saw R. D. Laing and asked him very much the same questions—the sort of ashram clichés that were asked at the time: *Who am I? Where am I going?*—those sort of questions that people were asking in the 1960s. And I think these were very much the sort of questions [Ñāṇavīra] was asking, but the generation before, who had experienced horror.

Did he have a profound effect on me? Absolutely. It was a day in my life, forty-five years ago now, that is still very vivid to me: where he was living—this sort of hovel—what he looked like, how he was in the world, and, looking back on it with my own life experience, reaching conclusions about what he was doing and whether he was on the right track.

**Did you keep in contact with Robin Maugham in his later years?**

I became a great admirer of Robin, he was an extraordinary person, flawed in some ways but had enormous qualities. I saw him on his deathbed. I was in Brazil and my secretary called me and said that Robin was in hospital. I flew back to London and went straight down to the hospital in Brighton to see him. He had

had a stroke and was lying unconscious. I said to him, "Robin, I'm going to take hold of your hand and if you would rather be alone squeeze it." And he squeezed it, so I left. And that was the end of Robin.

## POSTSCRIPT

Since the first publication of "Existence, Enlightenment, and Suicide" in 1996, a great deal more material by and about Ñāṇavīra Thera has come to light and been published. Path Press Publications has been revived and makes available the following books:

Ñāṇavīra Thera, *Seeking the Path: Early Writings, 1954–1960* (2010)
Ñāṇavīra Thera, *Notes on Dhamma* (2009)
Ñāṇavīra Thera, *Clearing the Path, 1960–1965* (2010)
Ñāṇavīra Thera, *The Letters of Sister Vajirā* (2010)
Bhikkhu Hiriko Ñāṇasuci, *The Hermit of Būndala: Biography of Ñāṇavīra Thera and Reflections on His Life and Work* (2014)

For further information, go to www.nanavira.org, where all these books can be purchased as hard copies or downloaded without charge as PDF files.

Chapter 11 of my book *Confession of a Buddhist Atheist* is likewise devoted to the life and thought of Ñāṇavīra Thera.

# 2

# BUDDHISM 2.0

# A SECULAR BUDDHISM

## ( 1 )

I will be using the term "secular" in three overlapping senses. The first of these is the popular way the word is used in contemporary media; that is, "secular" is what stands in contrast or opposition to whatever is called "religious." When, during a panel discussion on some topic, such as the existence of God, the moderator says, "And now I would like to invite X to offer a secular perspective on this question," we know what is meant without having to define with any precision either "secular" or "religious." Second, I will also be using the term in full consciousness of its etymological roots in the Latin *saeculum,* which means "this age," "this *siècle* [century]," "this generation." I thus take "secular" to refer to those concerns we have about *this* world, that is, everything that has to do with the quality of our personal, social, and environmental experience of living on this planet. Third, I likewise understand the term in its Western, historical-political sense as referring to (in Don Cupitt's definition) "the transfer of authority over a certain area of life from the Church to the 'temporal power' of the State." Cupitt points out how over the past two to three hundred years "a large-scale and long-term process of secularization is gradually transforming the whole of our culture, as the religious realm slowly contracts until eventually the majority of the population can and do live almost their entire lives without giving religion a thought."¹

I intend to show what might happen when "Buddhism" or "dharma" is rigorously qualified by these three senses of the term "secular." What, in other words, would a nonreligious, this-worldly, secularized Buddhism look like? To what extent can we see this process of secularization as being already underway? Can Buddhism—as it is traditionally understood—survive the process intact? Or are we witnessing the end of Buddhism, at least as we know it, and the beginning of something else?

## ( 2 )

> Birth is *dukkha*, ageing is *dukkha*, sickness is *dukkha*, death is *dukkha*, encountering what is not dear is *dukkha*, separation from what is dear is *dukkha*, not getting what one wants is *dukkha*. In brief, these five bundles of clinging are *dukkha*.
>
> —THE FIRST DISCOURSE
> (DHAMMACAKKAPPAVATTANA SUTTA)

I was recently teaching a group of students in a Buddhist studies program affiliated with a Vipassana meditation center in England. Since it was the first module of the course, the students introduced themselves as a way of explaining how and why they had enrolled. One young woman, "Jane," recounted how she had gone to her doctor to seek treatment for the pain produced by the scars left by severe burns. The doctor referred her to a pain clinic in London that offered her two choices: a series of steroid injections or an eight-week course in mindfulness meditation. Jane opted for the mindfulness and, having completed the course, found that it worked.

This did not mean that the pain miraculously vanished but that Jane was able to deal with it in a way that dramatically reduced the distress it caused, enabling her to lead a more fulfilled and active life. No doubt most patients would have left it at that and simply employed the mindfulness as an effective technique of pain management. Others, like Jane, seem to realize that the skill they had been taught had implications beyond that of simple pain relief. Although doctors and therapists who employ mindfulness in a medical setting deliberately avoid any reference to Buddhism, you do not have to be a rocket scientist to figure out where it comes from. A Google search will tell you that mindfulness is a form of Buddhist meditation.

Jane is not the only person I have met whose practice of Buddhism started with exposure to mindfulness as a medical treatment. In every Buddhist meditation course I lead these days, there will usually be one or two participants who have been drawn to the retreat because they want to deepen their practice of "secular mindfulness" (as it is now being called) in a setting that provides a richer contemplative, philosophical, and ethical context. For certain people, an unintended consequence of such mindfulness practice is the experience of a still, vivid, and detached awareness that does more than just deal with a specific pain; it opens a new perspective on how to come to terms with the totality of one's existence, that is, birth, sickness, aging, death, and everything else that falls under the broad heading of what the Buddha called *dukkha*. The simple (though not necessarily easy) step of standing back and mindfully attending to one's experience rather than being uncritically overwhelmed with the imperatives of habitual thoughts and emotions can allow a glimpse of an inner freedom *not* to react to what one's mind is insisting that one do. The experience of such inner freedom, I would argue, is a taste of nirvana itself.

This story illustrates well the three uses of the word "secular" outlined above. Here we have a practice of mindfulness that (1) is presented and undertaken without any reference at all to religion,

(2) is concerned entirely with the quality of one's life in this world, this age, this *saeculum,* and (3) is an example of how the "state," in Jane's case the British National Health Service, has taken over a certain area of life that was traditionally the preserve of a "church," that is Theravāda Buddhism. However, as with Jane and others, their practice of secular mindfulness did not stop here but opened unexpected doors into other areas of their life, some of which might be regarded as the traditional domains of religion. Perhaps the penetration of mindfulness into health care is like that of a Buddhist Trojan horse. For once mindfulness has been implanted into the mind/brain of a sympathetic host, dharmic memes are able to spread virally, rapidly, and unpredictably.

## ( 3 )

The kind of Buddhism sought out by Jane and others on the basis of their practice of mindfulness may have little if anything to do with Buddhism as it is traditionally understood and presented. By "traditional Buddhism" I mean any school or doctrinal system that operates within the soteriological worldview of ancient India. Whether Theravāda or Mahayana in orientation, all such forms of Buddhism regard the ultimate goal of their practice to be the attainment of nirvana, that is, the complete cessation of the craving (*taṇhā*) that drives the relentless cycle of birth, death, and rebirth. Such craving is at the root of greed, hatred, and bewilderment that prompt one to commit acts that cause one to be reborn after death in more or less favorable conditions in *saṃsāra.* Although I have presented this formulation of the existential dilemma and its resolution in Buddhist terms, the same soteriological framework is shared by Hindus and Jains. In each of these Indian traditions, adepts achieve salvation or liberation by bringing to an end the mechanism that perpetuates the cycle of birth and death, whereby one achieves the "deathless" (Buddhism) or "immortality" (Hinduism)—though both terms are a translation of the same word in Pali/Sanskrit: *amata/amṛta*. Buddhism, Hinduism, and Jainism differ only in the doctrinal, meditative, and ethical strategies they employ to achieve the same goal.

So embedded is this Indian soteriological framework in Buddhism that Buddhists might find it unintelligible that one would even consider questioning it. For to dispense with such key doctrines as rebirth, the law of karma, and liberation from the cycle of birth and death would surely undermine the entire edifice of Buddhism itself. Yet for those who have grown up outside of Indian culture, who feel at home in a modernity informed by the natural sciences, to then be told that one cannot "really" practice the dharma unless one adheres to the tenets of ancient Indian soteriology makes little sense. The reason people can no longer accept these beliefs need not be because they reject them as false, but because such views are too much at variance with everything else they know and believe about the nature of themselves and the world. For some, they simply don't work anymore, and the intellectual gymnastics one needs to perform to make them work seem casuistic and, for many, unpersuasive. They are *metaphysical* beliefs, in that (like belief in God) they can neither be convincingly demonstrated nor refuted. One has to take them on trust, albeit with as much reason and empirical evidence as one can muster to back them up.

To use an analogy from the world of computers, the traditional forms of Buddhism are like software programs that run on the same operating system. Despite their apparent differences, Theravāda, Zen, Shin, Nichiren, and Tibetan Buddhism share the same underlying soteriology, that of ancient India outlined above. These diverse forms of Buddhism are like "programs" (e.g., word processing, spreadsheets, Photoshop, etc.) that run on an "operating system" (a soteriology), which I will call "Buddhism 1.0." At first sight, it would seem that the challenge facing the dharma as it enters modernity would be to write another software program, for example, "Vipassana," "Soka Gakkai," or "Shambhala Buddhism," that would modify a traditional form of Buddhism in order to address more adequately the needs of contemporary practitioners. However, the cultural divide that separates traditional Buddhism from modernity is so great that this may not be enough. It might well be necessary to rewrite the operating system itself, resulting in what we could call "Buddhism 2.0."

# ( 4 )

On what grounds would such a Buddhism 2.0 be able to claim that it is "Buddhism" rather than something else altogether? Clearly, it would need to be founded upon canonical source texts, be able to offer a coherent interpretation of key practices, doctrines, and ethical precepts, and to provide a sufficiently rich and integrated theoretical model of the dharma to serve as the basis for a flourishing human existence. To design a Buddhism 2.0 is, admittedly, an ambitious project, and what follows will be no more than a tentative sketch. But without making such an effort, I believe the dharma might find itself condemned to an increasingly marginal existence in mainstream culture, catering only to those who are willing to embrace the worldview of ancient India. Whatever potential the teachings of the Buddha could have for making positive contributions to many of the pressing issues of our *saeculum* may thereby be minimized if not realized at all.

The history of Buddhism is the history of its own ongoing interpretation and representation of itself. Each Buddhist tradition maintains that it alone possesses the "true" interpretation of the dharma, whereas all the other schools either fall short of this truth or have succumbed to "wrong views." Today, from a historical-critical perspective, these kinds of claims appear strident and hollow. For we recognize that every historical form of Buddhism is contingent upon the wide array of particular and unique circumstances out of which it arose. The idea that one such school has somehow succeeded in preserving intact what the Buddha taught whereas all the others have failed is no longer credible. Whether we like it or not, Buddhism has become irrevocably plural. There exists no independent Buddhist judiciary that can pass judgment as to whose views are right and whose wrong.

In terms of my own theory of Buddhism 2.0, I need to be alert to the tendency of falling into the very trap that I am critiquing. The more I am seduced by the force of my own arguments, the more I am tempted to imagine that my secular version of Buddhism is what the Buddha originally taught, which the traditional schools have either lost sight of or distorted. This would be a mistake, for it is impossible to read the historical Buddha's mind in order to know what he "really" meant or intended. At the same time, each generation has the right and duty to reinterpret the teachings that it has inherited. In doing so, we may discover meanings in these texts that speak lucidly to our own *saeculum* but of which the original authors and their successors may have been unaware. As the term itself suggests, "Buddhism 2.0" contains a touch of irony. I take what I am saying with utmost seriousness, but I recognize that it too is as contingent and imperfect as any other interpretation of the dharma.

( 5 )

If any doctrine can be regarded as seminal to the Buddha's dispensation it would be that of the four noble truths as enunciated in *The First Discourse*, believed to have been delivered in the Deer

Park at Isipatana (Sarnath) not long after his awakening in Uru-velā (Bodh Gaya). Yet when we first read this text in the form it has come down to us in (there are seventeen versions in Pali, San-skrit, Chinese, and Tibetan), it would appear to be firmly rooted in the soteriology of Buddhism 1.0. The suffering of birth, sick-ness, aging, and death (the first noble truth) originates in craving (the second noble truth). Only by bringing this craving to a stop through the experience of nirvana (the third noble truth) will the suffering that craving causes likewise come to an end. And the only way to realize this final deliverance from suffering is by prac-ticing the noble eightfold path (the fourth noble truth). The end of suffering, therefore, is only attainable by ending the craving that drives the cycle of rebirth. Indeed, the Buddha declares toward the conclusion of the sermon that "this is the last birth." As long as one remains in this world as an embodied creature, the most one can achieve is a certain mitigation of suffering. For suffering truly to cease one must stop the process of rebirth altogether.

Such a reading of the discourse would seem to leave little if any room for a secular interpretation of the text. For this world of birth, sickness, aging, and death that constitutes our *saeculum* is precisely what needs to be brought to an end if we are ever to achieve a genuine salvation or liberation. Orthodox Buddhism shows itself here to be thoroughly committed to the Indian ascetic tradition, which regards life in this world as beyond salvation and to be renounced. The principal virtue of human existence is that in the course of the interminable round of rebirths it is the most favorable state in which to be born because it provides the best conditions for escaping rebirth altogether. And this is not just the view of Theravāda Buddhism. The Mahayana traditions say exactly the same, the only difference being that the compassionate bodhi-sattva renounces his or her final liberation from rebirth until all other sentient beings have achieved it first.

On a closer analysis of this discourse, however, certain incongruities appear in the fabric of the text. *The First Discourse* cannot be treated as a verbatim transcript of what the Buddha taught in the Deer Park, but as a document that has evolved over an unspecified period of time until it reached the form in which it is found today in the canons of the different Buddhist schools. At this point, modern historical-critical scholarship comes to our aid as a means of upsetting some of the time-honored views of Buddhist orthodoxy.

( 6 )

The British philologist K. R. Norman is one of the world's foremost experts on what are called "mid Indo-Āryan Prakrits," that is, those spoken languages (Prakrits) which were used after the classical and before the modern period in India. Included among these is Pali, the language in which the discourses attributed to the Buddha in the Theravāda school are preserved. In a 1982 paper entitled "The Four Noble Truths," Norman offers a detailed, philological analysis of *The First Discourse* and arrives at the startling conclusion that "the earliest form of this *sutta* did not include the word *ariyasaccaṃ* [noble truth]."[2] On grammatical and syntactical grounds, he shows how the expression "noble truth" was inexpertly interpolated into the text at a later date than its original composition. But since no such original text has come down to us, we cannot know what it *did* say. All that can reasonably be deduced is that instead of talking of four noble truths, the text spoke merely of "four."

The term "noble truth" is so much taken for granted that we fail to notice its polemical, sectarian, and superior tone. All religions maintain that what they and they alone teach is both "noble" and "true." This is the kind of rhetoric used in the business of religion. It is easy to imagine how over the centuries after the

Buddha's death his followers, as part of the intersectarian one-upmanship of ancient India, made increasingly elevated claims about the superiority of their teacher's doctrines, which resulted in the adoption of the expression "noble truth" to privilege and set apart the dharma from what their competitors taught.

One implication of Norman's discovery is that the Buddha may not have been concerned with questions of "truth" at all. His awakening may have had little to do with gaining a veridical cognition of "reality," a privileged understanding that corresponds to the way things actually *are*. Numerous passages in the canon attest to how the Buddha refused to address the big metaphysical questions: Is the world eternal, not eternal, finite, infinite? Are the body and mind the same or different? Does one exist after death or not, or neither or both?[3] Instead of getting bogged down in these arguments, he insisted on revealing a therapeutic and pragmatic path that addressed the core issue of human suffering. He recognized that one could endlessly debate the truth or falsity of metaphysical propositions without ever reaching a final conclusion and, meanwhile, fail to come to terms with the far more pressing matter of one's own and others' birth and death.

As soon as the seductive notion of "truth" begins to permeate the discourse of the dharma, the pragmatic emphasis of the teaching risks being replaced by speculative metaphysics, and awakening comes to be seen as achieving an inner state of mind that somehow accords with an objective metaphysical "reality." This tendency becomes even more pronounced when "truth" is further qualified as being either an "ultimate" (*paramattha*) or a merely "conventional" (*samutti*) truth. Although this two-truth doctrine is central to the thinking of all Buddhist orthodoxies, the terms "ultimate truth" and "conventional truth" do not occur a single time in the *Sutta* or *Vinaya Piṭaka*s (baskets) of the Pali Canon. Yet for most Buddhist schools today—including the Theravāda—

enlightenment is understood as gaining direct insight into the nature of some ultimate truth.

This privileging of "truth," I would argue, is one of the key indicators of how the dharma was gradually transformed from a liberative praxis of awakening into the religious belief system called Buddhism.

## ( 7 )

Open any introductory book on Buddhism and you will find, usually within the first few pages, an account of the four noble truths. Invariably, they will be presented in the form of four propositions, something like this:

1. Existence is suffering.
2. The origin of suffering is craving.
3. The cessation of suffering is nirvana.
4. The noble eightfold path is the way that leads to the cessation of suffering.

By the very way in which this information is presented, the reader is challenged to consider whether these propositions are true or false. From the very outset of one's engagement with the dharma, one finds oneself playing the language game "In Search of Truth." The unstated presumption is that if you believe these propositions to be true, then you qualify to be a Buddhist, whereas if you regard them as false, you do not. One is thus tacitly encouraged to take the further step of affirming a division between "believers" and "nonbelievers," between those who have gained access to the truth and those who have not. This establishes the kind of separation that can lead to cultish solidarity as well as hatred for others who fail to share one's views. "When the word 'truth' is uttered," remarked the Italian philosopher Gianni Vattimo, "a shadow of violence is cast as well."[4] Yet if Mr. Norman is correct, the Buddha may not have presented his ideas in terms of "truth" at all.

Each of these propositions is a metaphysical statement, no different in kind from "God is love," "creation arose from the breath of the One," "bliss is eternal union with Brahman," or "you will only come to the Father through Me." Perhaps because of Buddhism's more psychological-sounding and nontheistic terminology (not to mention the widespread perception of Buddhism as "rational" and "scientific"), you may not notice the blatantly metaphysical nature of the claims of the four noble truths until you start trying either to prove or refute them.

"Craving is the origin of suffering." How then is craving the origin of old age? How is craving the origin of the pain of a baby born with cystic fibrosis? How is craving the origin of being accidentally run over by a truck? I have noticed how contemporary Buddhist teachers, uncomfortable perhaps with the metaphysics of karma and rebirth, will often try to explain this psychologically. "Craving does not cause the physical pain of old age or being squashed beneath the wheels of a 3.5-ton vehicle," they will say. "But it is by craving for these things not to be happening, by failing to accept life as it presents itself to us, that we thereby cause ourselves unnecessary mental anguish in addition to the physical pain." It is self-evident that we frequently cause ourselves unnecessary mental anguish in this way, and a number of passages in the Pali Canon can be cited to support such a reading. However, when the Buddha defines what he means by *dukkha* in *The First Discourse*, he does not describe it as "unnecessary mental anguish" but as birth, sickness, aging, and death as well as the "five bundles of clinging" (materiality, feelings, perceptions, inclinations, consciousness) *themselves*. In other words, the totality of our existential condition in this world. If we take the text as it stands, the only reasonable interpretation of the proposition "craving is the origin of suffering" is the traditional one: craving is the origin of suffering because craving is what causes you to commit actions that lead to your being born, getting sick, growing old, and dying. But this, of course, is metaphysics: a truth claim that can be neither convincingly demonstrated nor refuted.

In my book *Buddhism without Beliefs* (1997) I also made the mistake of interpreting *dukkha* in terms of the craving that is said to cause it. I reasoned that if *dukkha* originated from craving, then it must refer to the mental anguish that is produced when in the grip of craving. I therefore translated *dukkha* as "anguish." Irrespective of whether or not craving gives rise to such anguish, this is not how *dukkha* is presented in *The First Discourse*. As a result of this kind of interpretation, *dukkha* comes to be seen as a purely subjective problem that can be "solved" by correct application of the techniques of mindfulness and meditation. For *dukkha* is just the suffering unnecessarily added on to the inevitable pains and frustrations of life. This psychological reading turns the practice of the dharma increasingly inward, away from a concern with the pervasive *dukkha* of life and the world and toward an exclusive, even narcissistic, concern with subjective feelings of lack and anguish.

## ( 8 )

The notion of "truth" is so entrenched in our discourse about religion, and further reinforced by Buddhism's own account of its teaching, that you might find it hard, even threatening, to "unlearn" thinking and speaking about the dharma in this way. Yet this unlearning is precisely what needs to be done if we are to make the shift from a belief-based Buddhism (version 1.0) to a praxis-based Buddhism (version 2.0). We have to train ourselves to the point where on hearing or reading a text from the canon our initial response is no longer "Is that true?" but "Does this work?"

At the same time, we also need to undertake a critical analysis of the texts themselves in order to uncover, as best we can at this distance in time, the core terms and narrative strategies that inform a particular passage or discourse. If we subtract the words "noble truth" from the phrase "four noble truths," we are simply left with "four." And the most economic formulation of the Four, to be found throughout Buddhist traditions, is this:

Suffering (*dukkha*)
Arising (*samudaya*)
Ceasing (*nirodha*)
Path (*magga*)

Once deprived of the epithet "noble truth" and no longer phrased in propositional language, we arrive at the four keystones on which both Buddhism 1.0 and Buddhism 2.0 are erected. Just as there are four nucleobases (cytosine, guanine, adenine, and thymine) that make up DNA, the nucleic acid that contains the genetic instructions for all living organisms, one might say that suffering, arising, ceasing, and path are the four nucleobases that make up the dharma, the body of instructive ideas, values, and practices that give rise to all forms of Buddhism.

# ( 9 )

Craving is repetitive, it wallows in attachment and greed, obsessively indulging in this and that: the craving of sensory desire, craving for being, craving for non-being.
—*THE FIRST DISCOURSE*

Following Carol S. Anderson (1999), I translate *samudaya* as "arising" rather than the more familiar "origin." I also note that I. B. Horner (1951) renders it as "uprising" in her translation of

*The First Discourse.* While it is undeniable that from an early period Buddhist orthodoxy has understood *samudaya* to mean "origin" or "cause" (of *dukkha*), on closer analysis this seems a rather forced interpretation. While the proposition "craving is the origin of suffering" at least makes logical sense (whether or not you believe it), to say "craving is the *arising* of suffering" is clumsy and unclear. In *The First Discourse,* craving (*taṇhā*) is identified as *samudaya:* "arising." Yet in ordinary speech to say something "arises" suggests that it *follows* from something else, as in "smoke arises from fire." In the traditional formulation of the four noble truths, however, this common-sense understanding is inverted: craving, identified as *samudaya,* is not *what arises* from *dukkha* but *that which gives rise* to *dukkha*.

That craving is *what arises,* however, is central to another classical Buddhist doctrine: that of the twelve links of conditioned arising (*paṭiccasamuppāda*). Craving, it is said, is what arises from feelings (*vedanā*), which in turn arise from contact, the six senses, *nāmarūpa,* and consciousness. Together, the chain of causes that culminates in the arising of craving describes in linear sequence the totality of the human existential condition, commonly summarized in Buddhism by the "five bundles of clinging" (materiality, feelings, perceptions, inclinations, and consciousness). Now since *The First Discourse* regards these five bundles as shorthand for what is meant by *dukkha,* then, according to the twelve links theory, it is clear that craving is what arises from *dukkha* rather than the other way round. "Craving" describes all our habitual and instinctive reactions to the fleeting, tragic, unreliable, and impersonal conditions of life that confront us. If something is pleasant, we crave to possess it; if something is unpleasant, we crave to be rid of it. The practice of mindfulness trains us to notice how this reactive pattern *arises from* our felt encounter with the world in such a way that we cease to be in thrall to its imperatives and are thereby liberated to think and act otherwise.

The twelve links, of course, do not stop here: craving is said to give rise to clinging (*upādāna*), which in turn gives rise to becoming (*bhava*), which leads to birth, and aging, and death, thus completing the sequence. This theory thus validates the orthodox belief that craving is the origin of birth, sickness, aging, and death, that is, *dukkha*. While it is not difficult to see how craving would lead to clinging, I have never understood how clinging gives rise to *becoming*, which then gives rise to *birth*.[5] How do emotions such as craving and clinging give rise to an existential state of becoming, which then somehow serves as the condition for finding oneself inside a fertilized ovum again? The empirical precision that characterizes the links from "consciousness" and *nāmarūpa* to "craving" is replaced in the later links by what seems to be metaphysical speculation.

Why were the early Buddhists so concerned to insist that craving is the cause of birth, sickness, aging, and death? One answer would be: in order that Buddhist thought could provide a convincing account of creation that would fit with the worldview of ancient India and the consolatory schemes implicit within it.[6] To say "craving is the cause of suffering" is simply a reiteration of the prevalent Indian understanding of the origin of the world found in the Vedas and Upaniṣads. In the Rig Veda we find an account of creation that describes how "in the beginning there was desire (*kāma*)."[7] The pre-Buddhist *Brhad-āranyaka Upaniṣad* expands on this to explain how a person's desires (*kāma*) lead to actions (*karma*) that result in being reborn in the world, whereas "one who is freed from desire" becomes one with Brahman and after death "goes to Brahman."[8] The Buddhist twelve-link model provides a nontheistic account of the same process: craving leads to rebirth and the stopping of craving results in liberation from rebirth. Although Buddhists use the term *taṇhā* (craving) rather than *kāma* (desire), *kāma* is nonetheless one of the three kinds of *taṇhā* described in *The First Discourse*. *Kāmataṇhā* refers to the cravings of sensual desire, while *bhavataṇhā* has to do with the narcissistic longing to persist, and *vibhavataṇhā*, the self-disgusted longing for oblivion.

Yet if we consider what is probably an earlier version of the link theory of conditioned arising, found in the *Sutta-Nipāta* (verses 862–74), we are presented not with twelve but *six* links. Rather than seeking to explain how aging and death arise, this version more modestly sets out to describe how "quarrels, disputes, lamentations and grief, together with avarice, pride, arrogance and slander" arise. It offers nothing more than an empirical analysis of human conflict. The Buddha notes that conflicts arise from what is held dear, that holding things dear arises from longing (*chanda*), that longing arises from "what is pleasant and unpleasant in the world," which arise from contact, which in turn arises from *nāmarūpa*, that is, being-in-the-world.[9] Given that religious doctrines tend to become longer rather than shorter over time, this six-link version is likely to be closer to what was originally taught. It provides a this-worldly examination of the origins of conflict with no appeal to any metaphysical notions like *bhava* or rebirth. It is also worth noting that instead of "craving" (*taṇhā*), the *Sutta-Nipāta* uses the more neutral term *chanda*—the simple "longing," "wish," or "desire" for something.

( 10 )

*Yaṃ kiñci samudayadhammaṃ sabbaṃ taṃ nirodhadhamman.* These are the final words of *The First Discourse,* uttered by Kondañña, one of the five ascetics to whom the discourse was delivered, as an expression of his insight into what the Buddha said. It means, literally, "whatever is an arising *dhamma,* that is a ceasing *dhamma,*" or, more succinctly and colloquially, "whatever arises ceases." Sāriputta, who became the Buddha's foremost disciple, is also said to have uttered this phrase as an expression of his insight on first hearing a summary of Gotama's teaching.[10]

You will notice that the phrase contains two terms of the Four, namely the second and third elements: arising (*samudaya*) and ceasing (*nirodha*). In the context of the *sutta*, it is clear that Kondañña is not uttering a banal generalization along the lines of "whatever goes up must come down." He is describing the core shift, one might even say the "hinge" on which the Four turn, which he has just experienced for himself ("the dispassionate, stainless dharma eye arose in Kondañña").

*The First Discourse* defines ceasing as "the traceless fading away and ceasing of that craving, the letting go and abandoning of it, freedom and independence from it." Since *what ceases* is explicitly stated to be craving, then it is clear that *what arises* must also be craving. Kondañña's utterance provides the strongest evidence that *samudaya* refers to the arising of craving, *not* to the arising of *dukkha* as is traditionally taught. Since craving is something that arises, craving is something that ceases—this is Kondañña's insight, the "opening of his dharma eye," which is the first glimpse of the freedom of nirvana: the ceasing, even momentarily, of craving.

In the *Discourse to Kaccānagotta* we again find the two terms *samudaya* and *nirodha*, now employed as part of the Buddha's account of what constitutes "complete view" (*sammā diṭṭhi*):

> This world, Kaccāna, for the most part depends on a duality —upon the notion of "it is" [*atthita*] and the notion of "it is not" [*natthita*]. But for one who sees the arising [*samudaya*] of the world as it occurs with complete understanding [*sammā paññā*], there is no notion of "it is not" in regard to the world. And for one who sees the ceasing [*nirodha*] of the world as it occurs with complete understanding, there is no notion of "it

is" in regard to the world. . . . "Everything is," Kaccāna, this
is one dead end. "Everything is not," Kaccāna, this is another
dead end. Without veering towards either of these dead ends,
the Tathāgata teaches the dharma by the middle.[11]

This passage, which would later serve as the only explicit canonical basis for Nāgārjuna's philosophy of the middle way,[12] expands the usage of *samudaya* and *nirodha* beyond the arising and
ceasing of craving to include the arising and ceasing of the world.
Such a vision liberates one from what lies at the root of craving,
namely, the reification, entrenched in language-users, of the notions "is" and "is not." For one who understands the contingent,
fluid, and processual nature of life realizes that the categories of
"is" and "is not" are incapable of adequately representing a world that
is endlessly arising and ceasing, forever eluding one's conceptual
grasp. This is what Nāgārjuna and his followers mean when they say
that persons and things are "empty of own-being" (*svabhāvaśūnya*).

To gain such insight is to arrive at a "complete view," also
known as an "opening of the dharma eye," which is the first element of the eightfold path. And the eightfold path, or the middle
way, is how *The First Discourse* defines the fourth term of the Four:
path (*magga*). We are now in a position to see how the Four describe a trajectory: suffering (*dukkha*) is what leads to the arising
(*samudaya*) of craving, upon the ceasing (*nirodha*) of which the
possibility of a path (*magga*) emerges.

( 11 )

The narrative structure of the text of *The First Discourse* provides
further support for this reading of the Four as the outline of a trajectory of practice rather the conceptual foundations for a system of
belief. The text breaks down into four principal stages:

1. The declaration of a middle way that avoids dead ends.
2. The definitions of the Four.
3. The presentation of the Four as tasks to be recognized, performed, and accomplished.
4. The declaration that peerless awakening is achieved by the recognition, performance, and accomplishment of these tasks.

The key to understanding *The First Discourse* lies in seeing how each stage of the text is the precondition for the next stage, and how the practice of each element of the Four is the precondition for the practice of the next element of the Four. This narrative strategy is a *demonstration* of the core principle of conditioned arising (*paṭiccasamuppāda*) itself, that is, "when this is, that comes to be; when this is not, that does not come to be."[13] Seen in this light, the text is not explicating a theory of "four truths" but is showing us how to perform "four tasks."

So how do the Four become four tasks to be recognized, performed, and accomplished? This is what the (bare bone) text of *The First Discourse* says:

"Such is *dukkha*. It can be fully known. It has been fully known.
"Such is the arising. It can be let go of. It has been let go of.
"Such is the ceasing. It can be experienced. It has been experienced.
"Such is the path. It can be cultivated. It has been cultivated."

Each element of the Four is (1) to be recognized as such, then (2) acted on in a certain way until (3) that action is accomplished. Thus each becomes a specific task to be performed in a certain way. While *dukkha* is to be fully known (*pariññā*), the arising (of craving) is to be let go of (*pahāna*), its ceasing is to be experienced, literally, "seen with one's own eyes" (*sacchikāta*), and the path is to be cultivated, literally, "brought into being" (*bhāvanā*).

We need look no further than the text of *The First Discourse* itself to discover how the Four constitute the core practices of the dharma: embracing *dukkha*, letting go of the craving that arises in reaction to it, experiencing the fading away and ceasing of that craving, which allows the eightfold path to be created and cultivated. According to this text, the Buddha's awakening too is to be understood in terms of his having recognized, performed, and accomplished these four tasks. Rather than describing his experience beneath the tree at Uruvelā as a transcendent insight into ultimate truth or the deathless, the Buddha says in *The First Discourse:*

> As long as my knowledge and vision were not entirely clear about these twelve aspects of the Four, I did not claim to have had a peerless awakening in this world.

Awakening is not a singular insight into the absolute, comparable to the transcendent experiences reported by mystics of theistic traditions, but a complex sequence of interrelated achievements gained through reconfiguring one's core relationship with *dukkha*, arising, ceasing, and the path.

This reading of *The First Discourse* also answers a question that has puzzled many: why are the four noble truths presented in the sequence we find them? Why does the text first present suffering (an effect), then go back to present its cause (craving)? And then why does it present the end of suffering (an effect), and then go back to present its cause (the eightfold path)? This sequence of "effect, cause, effect, cause" is commonly interpreted as an example of the Buddha's "therapeutic" approach. First you need to recognize you are ill, then you go to a doctor who diagnoses the cause of the illness, then the doctor assures you that there is a cure for the illness, and finally proceeds to provide a remedy.

This metaphor, however, is nowhere to be found in the discourses or monastic training texts of the Pali Canon. It is a later—and, to my mind, strained—commentarial device with authoritarian undertones, introduced to justify the incongruous ordering of the propositional "truths." But if one understands the Four as tasks rather than truths, the puzzle is solved. The Four are presented in that order *because that is the order in which they occur* as tasks to be performed: fully knowing suffering leads to the letting go of craving, which leads to experiencing its cessation, which leads to the cultivation of the path.

( 12 )

This gestalt switch (like "switching" an image of a vase into one of two faces in profile) that turns four truths into four tasks is the same perceptual switch that turns Buddhism 1.0 into Buddhism 2.0. It is a matter of reconfiguring the "nucleobases" of *dukkha,* arising, ceasing, and path. Instead of treating them as key elements of a metaphysical belief, one treats them as key elements of one's practice of living in this world.

For Buddhism 2.0 it is quite irrelevant whether the propositions "existence is suffering," "craving is the origin of suffering," "nirvana is the end of suffering," or "the noble eightfold path leads to the end of suffering" are true or not. The aim of one's practice is not to confirm or refute such time-honored dogmas but to respond in a radically different way to what presents itself at any given moment. Whenever suffering occurs in your life— whether that of coming down with flu or not getting the job you wanted—you seek to know it fully rather than resent or deny it. Instead of distracting yourself with fantasies or worries, you focus your attention calmly upon the felt sense of what is happening. As you perform this task you become acutely conscious of your reactive "arisings" and the potency of their force. They too are to be included within that same wide, still embrace. You do not free yourself from narcissistic or self-disgusted longings by suppressing them but by accepting them as the uprising of habitual inclinations, which may be psychologically, culturally, religiously, or instinctively conditioned.

Fully knowing suffering is not an end in itself but a precondition for being able to let go of the craving that habitually arises in reaction to suffering. In Buddhism 2.0 the problem with craving is not that it causes suffering (although obviously sometimes it does) but that it prevents one from entering the eightfold path. In this sense, craving is a hindrance (*nīvarana*), something that blocks unimpeded movement along a trajectory. As long as one consciously or unconsciously assents to the imperatives of the desires triggered by *dukkha* ("I want this!" "I don't want that!"), one will remain trapped in the powerful cycles of repetitive thoughts and actions that undermine any attempt to embark on a way of life that is no longer determined by them. Paradoxically, the letting go of craving is achieved not by willfully renouncing it but by deepening and extending one's embrace of the "great matter of birth and death"—as the Chinese call *dukkha*—that constitutes one's life.

In *fully* knowing birth, sickness, aging, and death one comes to understand the inevitably transient, tragic, and impersonal nature of human existence. Over time this erodes the underlying rationale of craving: namely, that this world exists for my personal gratification, and if I play my cards right by getting everything I want and getting rid of everything I hate, then I will find the lasting happiness I long for. Such a world is not the one we inhabit. Once this realization begins to dawn, the absurdity and futility of craving's ambitions are exposed. The longings, fears, and animosities that habitually arise begin to fall away of their own accord (or if they don't actually fall away, they lose their hold over us, which comes to much the same thing), culminating in moments when they stop altogether, thereby opening up the possibility of a way of life that is no longer driven by their demands and freeing us to think, speak, act, and work otherwise.

This process can be conveniently summarized under the acronym ELSA:

Embrace,
Let go,
Stop,
Act.

One embraces *dukkha,* that is, whatever situation life presents, lets go of the grasping that arises in reaction to it, and stops reacting so that one can act unconditioned by reactivity. This procedure is a template that can be applied across the entire spectrum of human experience, from one's ethical vision of what constitutes a "good life" to one's day-to-day interactions with colleagues at work. Buddhism 2.0 has no interest in whether or not such a way of life leads to a final goal called nirvana. What matters is an ever-deepening, ever-broadening engagement with a process of practice in which each element of ELSA is a necessary and intrinsic part. "Ceasing" is no longer seen as the *goal* of the path but as those moments when reactivity stops (or is suspended) in order that the possibility of a path can reveal itself and be "brought into being." Just as *dukkha* gives rise to craving (rather than the other way round), so the ceasing of craving gives rise to the eightfold path (rather than the other way round). Thus Buddhism 2.0 turns Buddhism 1.0 on its head.

( 13 )

"*Suppose, bhikkhus,*" said the Buddha, "*a man wandering through a forest would see an ancient path travelled upon by people in the past.*

*He would follow it and would come to an ancient city that had been inhabited by people in the past, with parks, groves, ponds and ramparts, a delightful place. Then the man would inform the king or a royal minister: 'Sir, know that while wandering through the forest I saw an ancient path. I followed it and saw an ancient city. Renovate that city, Sir!' Then the king or royal minister would renovate the city, and some time later that city would become successful and prosperous, well populated, attained to growth and expansion."*[14]

In explaining this story, the Buddha says that the "ancient path" refers to the "eightfold path" and the "ancient city" refers to the Four and conditioned arising. He compares himself to the man who went wandering in the forest and discovered these things, then returned to the world and, with the help of kings and ministers, established the dharma and sangha, which now flourish throughout the land.[15]

The narrative structure of this strikingly secular parable closely mirrors the narrative structure of *The First Discourse*. It too has four principal stages that correspond to those of *The First Discourse* outlined above in section 11.

1. The discovery of the forest path (= the declaration of a middle way).
2. The discovery of the ancient city (= the declaration of the Four).
3. Engaging in the task of restoring the city (= showing the Four as tasks to be recognized, performed, and accomplished).
4. Completing the task of restoring the city (= achieving peerless awakening as the result of accomplishing the tasks).

Whereas *The First Discourse* presents these four stages in terms of an individual's awakening, *The City* presents them in terms of a social project to be realized concretely in the world. As well as providing a template for leading one's own life, the Four are now shown to provide a template for the communal endeavor to realize another kind of society. The practice of the dharma, therefore, is not reducible to attaining awakening for oneself. It is a practice that necessarily involves cooperative activity with others to achieve goals that may not be realized until long after one's death.

Both texts suggest that the eightfold path is to be seen not as a linear sequence of stages that results in a final goal but as a positive feedback loop that is itself the goal. In *The City*, the eightfold path leads to the discovery of the Four, but the fourth of the Four is the eightfold path itself, which, according to the text, leads to the Four ad infinitum. To spell this out: fully knowing *dukkha* leads to the letting go of what arises, which leads to moments in which what arises ceases, which opens up a "complete view," the first step of the eightfold path. Such a view then informs how we think and make choices (step 2), which lead to how we speak (step 3), act (step 4), and work (step 5), which provide an ethical framework for applying oneself (step 6) to cultivate mindfulness (step 7) and concentration (step 8). But what is one mindful of? What does one concentrate on? One is mindful of and concentrates on life as it presents itself in each moment, which is how one fully knows *dukkha*. Thus one returns, at a deeper pitch of understanding and empathetic awareness, to the first task of the Four, which leads to the second task, and so on.

This loop I am describing, however, is not cyclical. If it were, one would keep finding oneself back where one started, which would be analogous to *saṃsāra*, the cycle of repeated birth and death from which Buddhists traditionally seek liberation. I compare the process of ELSA to a positive feedback loop, similar to that of contractions in childbirth that release the hormone oxytocin, which in turn stimulates further contractions, finally resulting in the birth of a child.[16]

( 14 )

And this is the path: the path with eight branches: complete
view, complete thought, complete speech, complete action,
complete livelihood, complete effort, complete mindfulness,
complete concentration.

— *THE FIRST DISCOURSE*

"When, bhikkhus, a noble disciple has abandoned perplexity
about the Four," declares the Buddha, "he is then called a stream
enterer (*sotāpanna*)."[17] Elsewhere, Sāriputta explicitly defines the
"stream" as the eightfold path, and a "stream enterer" as one who
has made such a path his or her own.[18] The unfolding process of
ELSA is comparable to the flowing water of a stream. Such imagery implies that once one embarks on fully knowing *dukkha,*
thereby triggering the positive feedback loop that is the path, one's
life no longer feels as if it were somehow "stuck" or "blocked"
or "arrested." It begins to flow. You realize that the frustration of
being hindered in realizing your deepest aspirations is due to the
instinctive cravings that arise unbidden, fixating you on the exclusive task of satisfying a desire or repelling a threat that has seized
your attention. At times, of course, it pays to heed such instinctive
reactions—after all, they are there because they have provided and
still provide "survival advantages." But these instincts are so in-
grained that they now override and subvert other concerns, which
one has committed oneself to realize.

The fullest account of stream entry (*sotāpatti*) in the canon is
found in the *Sotāpattisaṃyutta*—the penultimate chapter of the
*Saṃyutta Nikāya*. A stream enterer, says this text, is one who possesses "lucid confidence" (*aveccappasāda*) in the Buddha, dharma,
and sangha and embodies "the virtues cherished by the noble
ones."[19] The first part of this refers to what are commonly called

the "Three Jewels." Yet rather than presenting them as the objects of a ritual in which one affirms one's identity as a follower of the Buddhist religion, here they are understood as the parameters of a conscious reorientation of one's core ethical values. One who embraces *dukkha,* lets go of craving, experiences the ceasing of craving, and thereby enters the stream of the eightfold path is one who gains increasing lucidity and trust in a way of life that is founded on a set of values that are not driven by the imperatives of craving. "Buddha" refers to the awakening to which one aspires; "dharma" to the body of instructions and practices that guide one's realization of awakening; and "sangha" to those men and women who share such goals and through their friendship support your own realization of them.

At the same time, three "fetters" are said to fall away on entering the stream of this path: narcissism (*sakkāya diṭṭhi*), rule-bound morality and observances (*sīlabbata*), and doubt (*vichikicchā*).[20] A careful examination of one's human condition leaves one with very little to be narcissistic about. The closer one peers into the transient, tragic, and impersonal conditions of one's existence, the more the reflection of one's beloved, fascinating self-image breaks up and dissolves. Puṇṇa Mantāniputta, the nephew of Koṇḍañña and preceptor of Ānanda, compares the clinging (*upādāna*) that arises from craving to the way "a young woman or man, fond of ornaments, would examine her own facial image in a mirror or in a bowl filled with pure, clean water."[21] By clinging to their form in this way, he explains, the conceit "I am" (*asmi*) arises. *Sakkāya diṭṭhi,* which I have translated here as "narcissism," literally means "the view of one's existing body."

Moreover, to the extent that one understands the complexity and uniqueness of the peculiar *dukkha* of every moral dilemma, to that extent one recognizes how the strict moral rules of religion can be no more than broad guidelines for action. Empathetic awareness of another's suffering calls for a response that is driven not by the conceit of knowing what is the right thing to do in general, but by the courage to risk what may be the most wise and loving thing to do in that particular case. And since the process of ELSA is grounded in firsthand experience rather than belief, once this path has become "your own," it becomes difficult if not impossible to entertain doubts about its authenticity.

As a religious institution governed by a professional elite, Buddhism has tended over time to elevate stream entry to such a rarified spiritual height that it becomes all but inaccessible to any but the most dedicated practitioners of the dharma. Yet the *suttas* insist that numerous stream enterers at the Buddha's time were "men and women lay followers, clothed in white, enjoying sensual pleasures," who had "gone beyond doubt" and "become independent of others in the teaching."[22] Perhaps the most striking example of this is that of a drunkard called Sarakāni the Sakiyan, whom the Buddha affirmed to be a stream enterer in spite of the objections of the local people.[23]

## ( 15 )

Just as Christianity has struggled to explain how an essentially good and loving God could have created a world with so much suffering, injustice, and horror, so Buddhism has struggled to account for the presence of joy, delight, and enchantment in a world that is supposedly nothing but a vale of tears. Both cases illustrate the limitations of belief-based systems of thought. Once you commit yourself to upholding the truth of metaphysical propositions, such as "existence is *dukkha*" or "God is good," you will be drawn into the interminable task of trying to justify them. In Christianity this is known as "theodicy," whereas the Buddhist equivalent might be termed "dukkhodicy." Praxis-based systems avoid the dead end of such justification by founding themselves on injunctions to do something instead of on propositions to believe something. Thus rather than trying to justify your belief that "existence is *dukkha*," you seek to "fully know *dukkha*." And rather than struggling to understand how "craving is the origin of *dukkha*," you seek to "let go of craving."

The *suttas* contain a number of passages that suggest this more pragmatic and nuanced approach. "I do not say that the breakthrough to the Four is accompanied by suffering," declares the Buddha in the final chapter of the *Saṃyutta Nikāya*. "It is accompanied only by happiness and joy."[24] To fully embrace suffering does not increase suffering but paradoxically enhances your sense of astonishment at being alive. By saying "yes" to birth, sickness, aging, and death, you open your heart and mind to the sheer mystery of being here at all: that in this moment you breathe, you hear the wind rustling the leaves in the trees, you look up at the night sky and are lost in wonder. In another passage, the Buddha corrects his friend the Licchavi nobleman Mahāli, who holds the mistaken belief that life is nothing but suffering: "If this life, Mahāli, were exclusively steeped in suffering," he explains, "and if it were not also steeped in pleasure, then beings would not become enamored of it."[25]

And in another text, also from the *Saṃyutta Nikāya*, we find the Buddha reflecting on his own motives for embarking on his quest. "When I was still a bodhisatta," he recalls, "it occurred to me: 'What is the delight (*assādo*) of life? What is the tragedy (*ādhinavo*) of life? What is the emancipation (*nissaraṇaṃ*) of life?' Then, bhikkhus, it occurred to me: 'the happiness and joy that arise conditioned by life, that is the delight of life; that life is impermanent, *dukkha* and changing, that is the tragedy of life; the removal and abandonment of grasping (*chandarāga*) for life, that is the emancipation of life.'"[26] Only when he had understood all

three of these things, he concludes, did he consider himself to
have attained a peerless awakening in this world.

( 16 )

Let us imagine a child who was born in the year of the Buddha's death. Like the Buddha, that child also lived for eighty years,
and in the year of his death another child was born. If we continue this sequence up to the present day, two and a half thousand
years later, we will find that only thirty such human lives separate us from the time of the Buddha. From this perspective, we
are not in fact so distant in time from a period we habitually, and
sometimes reverentially, regard as antiquity. Buddhism's "antiquity" serves as another trope to burnish its teachings with greater
authority (which is further reinforced by the Indian belief in the
"degeneration of time," which maintains that, across the board,
things have been getting steadily worse since the fifth century
BCE). Yet what is remarkable about some of the *suttas* that originated in that "ancient" time is how directly and lucidly they speak
to the condition of our life here and now in the twenty-first century. In a primary, existential sense, human experience today is no
different from what it was at the Buddha's time.

This adjustment in temporal perspective throws into question the idea that we live in a "dharma-ending age," when it is
no longer possible to realize the fruits of the path as was done by
the great adepts of the past. One could just as well explain such
thinking in Feuerbachian or Marxist terms as an instance of the
progressive alienation that occurs when an established religious
system, often serving as the moral arm of an authoritarian political power, claims to be the sole true possessor of those human
values, such as wisdom and compassion, that the tradition up-
holds.[27] By elevating "stream entry," for example, into a rarified

spiritual attainment, one places it out of reach of the ordinary practitioner, thereby confirming both the higher authority of the religious institution and its representatives and the powerlessness of the unenlightened laity.

But couldn't we also imagine that instead of coming to an end, Buddhism might only just be beginning? The secularization of the dharma that seems to be currently underway might not, as its critics bemoan, be a further indication of the terminal watering down and banalization of the Buddha's teaching but rather a sign of the waning power of the orthodoxies that have held sway for the past two thousand or so years. Secularization might indeed mark the collapse of Buddhism 1.0, but it might also herald the birth of Buddhism 2.0.

For those, like Jane and others, who stumble across Buddhism through their practice of mindfulness in medical treatment (or, for that matter, through their appreciation of the philosophy of Nāgārjuna, their love of Zen haiku and brush painting, their admiration of the personality of the Dalai Lama, or their longing for social justice as former untouchables in India), Buddhism 2.0 offers a secularized dharma that dispenses with the soteriology of ancient India yet is founded on a critical reading of key canonical texts such as *The First Discourse*. By reconfiguring the operating code of the Four, Buddhism 2.0 offers a different perspective on understanding and practicing the dharma, one that is grounded in the positive feedback loop of ELSA. It remains to be seen whether this re-formation is capable of generating a consistent and coherent interpretation of Buddhist practice, philosophy, and ethics that could serve as the basis for a flourishing human existence in the kind of world in which we live today.

In the parable of the raft, the Buddha describes "a man in the course of a journey" who arrives at a body of water that he has to cross. Since there are no boats or bridges available, his only option is to assemble a raft out of the "grass, twigs, branches, leaves" and whatever other materials are to hand. Having bound them together, and "making an effort with his hands and feet," he manages to get across to the opposite shore. Despite its evident usefulness, he realizes that there is no point in carrying the raft any further once it has accomplished its purpose. So he leaves it by the shore and continues on his way. Likewise, the Buddha concludes, "I have shown you how the dharma is similar to a raft, being for the purpose of crossing over, not for the purpose of grasping."[28] This story shows how the dharma is an expedient, a means to achieve an urgent task at hand, not an end in itself that is to be preserved at all cost. It emphasizes how one needs to draw upon whatever resources are available at a given time in order to accomplish what you have to do. It doesn't matter whether these resources are "what the Buddha truly taught" or not. The only thing that matters is whether such a configuration of disparate elements is of any help in getting you across the river. So it is with Buddhism 2.0. In the light of this parable, it makes little sense to ask "Is this really Buddhism?" The only relevant question is "Does it float?"

# 3

## THINKING OUT LOUD

# REBIRTH:
## A CASE FOR BUDDHIST AGNOSTICISM

In 1254 the Franciscan friar William of Rubruck, a missionary in Mongolia, became the first Westerner to describe a reincarnate Buddhist teacher. In the report of his mission to King Louis IX of France he recounted the following episode:

> A boy was brought from Cataia [China], who to judge by his physical size was not three years old, yet was fully capable of rational thought: he said of himself that he was in his third incarnation, and he knew how to read and write.[1]

Seven hundred and thirty years later, the same phenomenon was reported in the heartland of Christian Europe:

> On February 12th, 1985, in the State Hospital of Granada, Spain, Osel Hita Torres was born. He came into the world without causing his mother any pain, his eyes wide open. He didn't cry. The atmosphere in the delivery room was charged—very quiet and yet momentous. The hospital staff was unusually touched. They sensed that this was a special child.[2]

This passage from Vicki Mackenzie's book *Reincarnation* describes the birth of a young boy who was shortly to be recognized by the Dalai Lama as the reincarnation of Lama Thubten Yeshe, a charismatic teacher and founder of numerous Tibetan Buddhist centers throughout Europe, Australia, and America, who had died in Los Angeles eleven months earlier of heart failure at the age of forty-nine.

Following the traditional ways of determining a future rebirth, Lama Thubten Zopa, Lama Yeshe's principal disciple, began examining his dreams and consulting oracles for signs that might indicate the whereabouts of his teacher. In one dream he beheld "a small child with bright, penetrating eyes, crawling on the floor of a meditation room. He was male and a Westerner."[3] Shortly afterward, he visited Osel Ling, a meditation center that Lama Yeshe had founded in Spain, and there, crawling on the monastery floor, was the very same child. According to Mackenzie, the fourteen-month-old boy was then subjected to a number of traditional tests to determine whether he was in fact Lama Yeshe.

> Lama Zopa sought out some of Lama Yeshe's possessions, mixed them with others of similar type, and asked Osel to pick out those that were rightfully his. He started with a rosary, a fairly ordinary wooden beaded one, a favorite of Lama [Yeshe]'s, which he placed on a low table along with four others almost identical in style and one made of bright crystal beads which he thought would act as a natural red herring. Then, with Maria [the mother] and a few Western disciples as witnesses, he commanded Osel, "Give me your mala [rosary] from your past life." Osel turned his head away as if bored. Then he whipped it back again and without hesitation went straight for the correct mala, which he grabbed with both hands, raising it above his head, grinning in a triumphant victory smile.[4]

In December 1990, I had the opportunity to meet the five-year-old Lama Osel, as he is now known, in a Buddhist center in Finsbury Park, London. He was a fair, attractive child, dressed in miniature Tibetan robes. For our meeting he sat cross-legged on a bed, looking down at myself and Roger Ash Wheeler, a former student of Lama Yeshe's (we were seated on the floor). After introducing ourselves, Roger said, "I studied with Lama Yeshe and Lama Zopa at Kopan [in Nepal]."

Lama Osel eagerly replied: "Before, I was Lama Yeshe."

"You remember that well, do you?" I asked.

"Not all," said Lama Osel.

"What do you remember?"

"When I was very sick they put me in the fire. . . ."

"What was it like being put in the fire?"

"Very hot. I couldn't see I was Lama Yeshe when they put me in the fire. I didn't see because I was in a stupa. In a photo, they put me into a fire like this—I saw. In one little hole, like this, then zzp!, they put here fire. All burn. I saw in photo that it was like a monster. Eyes like this all red."

Although we tried, he did not respond to our further questions about his past life; instead, he talked about what he had been doing in the previous weeks and months.

What impressed me most about the young boy was the calm and dignified way in which he carried himself. Although sometimes he would behave just like any other child of his age, as soon as he had to function as Lama Osel he displayed a maturity that seemed far in advance of his physical age—an impression similar to that of the boy described by William of Rubruck. That afternoon an hour-long ritual was offered by the center for Lama Osel's long life. He was placed on a throne about six feet high, wearing a pointed Tibetan hat and saffron robes. His high child's voice led the chanting in Tibetan, and he stayed completely composed to the very end without looking bored, neither fidgeting nor looking around distractedly—certainly not the kind of behavior I would have expected from a five-year-old.

Yet being around Lama Osel raised far more questions than it answered. The basic enigma that preoccupied me as I came away was quite simply: What on earth is going on here? The most straightforward answer would have been that what was going on was precisely what was claimed to be going on: that this five-year-old Spanish boy called Osel was the reincarnation of a Tibetan lama called Thubten Yeshe.

In support of this possibility is the fact that most religions assert the continuity of life after death in one form or another. In some, such as Hinduism or Buddhism, it is very specific: one is reborn in a form that corresponds to the kind of ethical or unethical actions (karma) that have been committed either in this or a previous life. In the monotheistic religions of the Middle East and Europe, the range of options is usually limited to either heaven or hell. The indigenous Chinese religion of Taoism does not have such a strong sense of individual identity; nevertheless some form of afterlife is suggested. A longstanding popular belief in Europe and America, moreover, posits an "other side" from which the intact personality of this existence is able, through the agency of mediums, to communicate with friends and relatives on "this side." Religious and spiritual traditions throughout history have explained that death is not the end of life but that some part of us, perhaps all of us, somehow carries on.

Buddhism is no exception to this. It is undeniable that the historical Buddha accepted the idea of rebirth. He spoke of rebirth and frequently described, sometimes in considerable detail, how actions committed in this life determine the form of existence in a future world. He also spoke of enlightenment in terms of how many times one must be reborn before one will be freed from the cycle of birth and death. Although there are instances in his discourses (the *Kālāma Sutta*, for example) where he says that the practice of dharma is meaningful, whether you believe in a hereafter or not, the overwhelming mass of evidence does not suggest that he held an agnostic position himself.[5]

On the basis of such authoritative statements, Buddhists of all traditions have used the concept of rebirth to make sense of the process of spiritual liberation and to provide an explanation of what carries the all-important imprints of karma that drive the cycle of birth and death itself. An action is judged to be right or wrong in terms of the kind of karmic consequences it will reap in the future—both in this life and after death. "After you die," declares the Tibetan lama Pabongka Rinpoche, "your consciousness does not end: it must definitely take rebirth, in the upper or the lower realms."[6]

In addition to these views about karma and rebirth, Tibetan Buddhists adhere to the Mahayana doctrine of bodhisattvas (beings who dedicate their lives to the enlightenment not only of themselves but of all others). Bodhisattvas strive to replace the force of karma with that of *bodhicitta,* the altruistic resolve to continue taking birth as long as there are living beings in the world that need to be saved from suffering. According to Mahayana Buddhism, at any one time numerous bodhisattvas are taking birth to help other beings in whatever ways are required.

Tibetans also accept the theory and practice of tantric Buddhism, which gives detailed instruction on how to control those psychic energies and subtle levels of consciousness that are attained through yogic disciplines. By utilizing energies and consciousness, it is believed that one can direct one's future rebirth to a specific place. In Tibet, this form of Buddhism became the prevailing ideology of the land.

The lamas of Tibet were political as well as spiritual leaders. Those lamas who were celibate monks had no natural heirs to assume their mantles after death, but as tantric Buddhists they could, for the benefit of others, direct their own consciousness to a suitable womb and ensure continuity of authority both within their monastery and over their political domains for many successive lifetimes. The best-known examples are such figures as the Dalai Lama, the Panchen Lama, and the Karmapa, all of whom wielded considerable political power across the whole country. For the method to work, it presupposes that their disciples have the skills to rediscover them in their new incarnation. This involves divination, oracular consultation, dream analysis, and so on. Only after having thoroughly tested the child and satisfied themselves that the boy (in one case, the girl) is in fact the lama, will the child be officially enthroned. He will then be brought up under the finest tutorial care his disciples can offer until he reaches the age of about twenty, at which time he will be reinvested with his full temporal and spiritual power. When he dies the process is repeated. Some of these lines are now in their twentieth or thirtieth incarnations.

While all religions believe that life continues in some form after death, it does not prove that the claim is true. Until quite recently most religions believed that the earth was flat, but such widespread belief had little effect on the shape of the planet. Even though the Buddha accepted the idea of rebirth, one could argue that he simply reflected the generally held beliefs of his time. By the time of the Buddha, India had already developed a cosmology which included the ideas of karma, rebirth, and liberation. (A curious twist here is that Westerners often find the idea of rebirth attractive, whereas in Buddhist terms, liberation or nirvana means freedom from the endless round of birth and death.) These ideas were taken for granted, just as we take for granted many scientific views, which, if pressed, we would find hard to prove.

Whether he really believed in it or not, the Buddha found the prevailing worldview of his time sufficient as a basis for his ethical system. It also provided an adequate set of metaphors for his doctrine of transcendence. His main concern, however, was not whether there is or is not life after death, but whether it is possible to live in such a way that one could transcend the dilemma of suffering.

Many contemporary forms of Buddhism in the West—especially Zen and Vipassana—seem to pay little attention to the doctrine of rebirth, emphasizing instead the importance of living more fully and authentically in the present. Teachers in these traditions often use the idea of rebirth metaphorically to describe the moment-to-moment process of "dying" and being "reborn." However appealing, psychologically astute, and didactically skillful such interpretations may be, they can give rise to the misleading impression that in traditional Zen or Theravāda Buddhist cultures the doctrine of rebirth is likewise not taken literally. Not only is belief in rebirth firmly adhered to in all Buddhist countries, from Japan to Sri Lanka, but—especially in East Asia—it has become the very basis for the livelihood of the majority of monks and nuns. A typical Zen temple in Korea or Japan spends far more time offering services to assist departed parishioners on their way to a better rebirth than on instructing the living in zazen (sitting meditation).

Institutionalized Buddhism throughout Asia not only has a doctrinal commitment to rebirth but also has an economic and political one. In contrast to most Tibetan lamas, for whom the belief in the doctrine of rebirth is essential to the continuing authority of their institutions in exile, other Asian Buddhists in the West have felt freer to adapt their teachings to suit the needs of a secular and skeptical audience whose interest in the dharma is as a way of finding meaning here and now rather than after death. One will search in vain for any discussion of rebirth in the numerous writings of Thich Nhat Hanh, for example. Although he comes from a country (Vietnam) in which the belief is deeply rooted, he now seems to be moving toward a view that equates karma with some form of genetic inheritance and transmission.

A concern often voiced by traditional Buddhist teachers is that denial of rebirth undermines the basis of karmic continuity and hence the need for morality. Similar fears were expressed at the time of the European Enlightenment in the seventeenth century by the Christian churches, who believed that loss of faith in the doctrines of heavenly reward and hellish punishment would likewise lead to rampant immorality. One of the most lasting and powerful realizations of the Enlightenment was that an atheistic materialist could be just as moral a person as a believer, and maybe even more so. This insight in the West led to a tremendous liberation from ecclesiastical dogma and was crucial in forming that vital sense of individual liberty, which today we take for granted. It also might explain why for so many Western Buddhists the notion of karma as a nontheistic version of punishments and rewards is felt at a gut level to be an inadequate and unconvincing basis for ethical conduct.

I do not believe, as is sometimes claimed, that the teaching of the Buddha stands or falls on the doctrine of rebirth and that one cannot really be a Buddhist if one does not accept it. Theologically, or "Buddhologically," it is indeed problematic to do away with the doctrine of rebirth, for numerous other basic ideas would then have to be rethought. But if liberation is the "taste" of the dharma, as the Buddha said,[7] then for its sake one should at least be prepared to put up with the unappetizing flavor of doctrinal inconsistency. Another problem, which has also beset traditional Buddhists, is the question of what it is that is reborn. Religions that posit an eternal soul that is essentially distinct from the body/mind complex escape this dilemma—the body may die but the soul continues to exist. One of the central Buddhist doctrines, however, is that of non-self (anātman): the denial of any intrinsic identity or soul or self that can either be found through analysis or mystically realized in meditation. The doctrine teaches that the notion of such a deep-seated, independently existing personal identity is a fiction, a tragic habit into which we have become locked since "beginningless time." In order to free oneself from suffering, one needs first and foremost to free oneself from clinging to such a notion of self-identity. But how does one square this with the idea of rebirth, of something distinct from that which dies but which is somehow reborn and so passes from life to life?

To answer this question, more or less every Buddhist school has come up with a different explanation—a fact that in itself suggests that their answers are based on speculation. Most schools claim that what is reborn is some kind of consciousness. Some say that this is simply the sixth sense (*manovijñāna*); others speak of a special existence-generating mind (*bhavangacitta*); still others propose the presence of an underlying foundation consciousness (*ālayavijñāna*); while the tantric traditions talk of a combination of extremely subtle energy and mind. But as soon as one hypothesizes the presence of some kind of subtle stuff, no matter how sophisticated the technical term one invents to denote it, one has already reintroduced the notion of some kind of esoteric self-substance.

For the Prāsaṅgika-Mādhyamika school of Buddhist philosophy, whose seventh- and eighth-century Indian proponents are often regarded as having taken the deconstructive logic of Nāgārjuna as far as it can go, adherence to any kind of reified self or substance, no matter how subtle, is essentially in contradiction to enlightenment and liberation. Having rejected all concepts of some esoteric stuff that sneaks across from one birth to the next, the most one can legitimately say about what gets reborn is "I do." Any further elaboration of this "I" will inevitably lead into reification. In his *Guide to the Bodhisattva's Way of Life*, the eighth-century Mādhyamika poet Śāntideva pushes the idea even further:

> It is a misconception to think
> That I shall experience (suffering in a future life),

For it is another who will die
And another who will be born.[8]

The sheer momentum of the actions I conventionally consider as "mine" will generate forms of life as different from myself now as you are different from me now. Thus, for Śāntideva, it is not only of lesser ethical value but actually meaningless to act out of concern for one's own welfare after death. The ethics of karma are thus turned on their head: the only meaningful motive for action can be compassion for others.

Several centuries after the historical Buddha, Buddhist philosophers became involved in all manner of controversies with other schools of Indian thought, some of which had a materialist outlook and denied the idea of rebirth. At this point "proofs" were devised to convince nonbelievers of the truth of rebirth. These are examined with great clarity in Martin Willson's book *Rebirth and the Western Buddhist,* in which the author shows that none of the arguments hold (while still insisting that the doctrine of rebirth is essential to Buddhism). The "proofs" rest on the assumption that any moment of consciousness must be preceded by a previous moment of consciousness and that it is impossible for something material (like a brain) to produce something immaterial (like a thought). Thus one classical argument runs: "The mind of a child that has just been conceived must have existed previously, because it is a mind." This may convince a hypothetical Buddhist meditator who has directly experienced how consciousness in its nature arises from consciousness, but it carries little weight with a modern Westerner who is unclear as to whether or not consciousness is an epiphenomenon of the brain.

But even if such "scientific proof" should appear, it would only lead to further problems. Many Buddhists would doubtless rejoice at this vindication of their beliefs, but the fact of rebirth in itself does not lead to any moral linkage between one existence and the next. Just to prove that death will be followed by another life in no way indicates that a murderer will be reborn in hell, whereas a saint will go to heaven. The doctrine of rebirth is meaningful in Buddhism only insofar as it provides a basis for the continuity of ethical consequences. Although rebirth and karma are often linked together, it is karma that is of primary importance; rebirth is secondary.

Even if research into the cases of young children who claim to remember their previous lives, or of people who recall them through hypnotic regression, should lead to certainty about these people having been reborn, this in itself would not furnish any proof whatsoever either that they themselves would experience rebirth again or that anyone else was reborn in the past or will be in the future. The most such research can do is suggest the possibility of rebirth. A plausible theory of two or three lifetime cycles could be posited (as it was in fact by some materialist Indian schools), after which the rebirth process would cease. Research into individual cases may be consoling to rebirth advocates, but to draw the inductive conclusion that rebirth is therefore a fact of life is unwarranted.

Another kind of evidence that is often cited to "prove" that there is life after death is that of people's reports of near-death experiences (NDEs). The difficulty here is that a near-death experience is, by definition, not a death experience. One does not return from death to talk about it; rather, it is the end of life. The very term "near-death" itself makes this crucial distinction. Although NDEs might give some indications of what will happen at death, they are not reports from beyond the grave.

Westerners who have had such experiences tend to draw extremely optimistic conclusions from them, claiming that they have now lost any fear of dying. Their whole attitude toward life is sometimes completely transformed. But I wonder how much these experiences feed a basic yearning for consolation in a post-Christian culture: a longing for a heaven that has been repudiated. Tibetan Buddhists, for example, would have no difficulty accepting the existence of such experiences but, given their different worldview, would be unlikely to interpret them in an optimistic way. The accounts of NDEs are similar to the descriptions of the initial stages of death in such writings as the *Tibetan Book of the Dead*. The difference is that, according to the Tibetans, the initial beatific visions of radiant light and so on are, for most unenlightened people, the calm before the storm. The so-called Clear Light is the point at which one touches the very ground of one's being. But once the patterns of karma begin to reassert themselves, one is expelled from this peaceful repose into a nightmarish series of visions that serve as the conduit to the next suffering-laced womb. Many of the tantric teachings of Tibetan Buddhism are concerned with preparing oneself to utilize the experience of death to transform fundamentally one's way of being in the world. If a Tibetan Buddhist were to have a near-death experience, he or she would have no difficulty in fitting it into their worldview, but it is unimaginable that they would interpret it as an indication that death is no longer something to fear but the gateway to eternal life. At best it would reinforce their resolve to prepare themselves through tantric practice for the Clear Light experience.

Now let us go back to the case of young Lama Osel and his predecessor. Although one hypothesis to explain his appearance in Lama Zopa's dream, and his choice of the right rosary, is that he is the reincarnation of Lama Thubten Yeshe, could we not conceive of an alternative hypothesis that would be no less problematic than the theory of rebirth? One has to remember the environment in which Lama Osel has been brought up. From a very early age he has been immersed in images of Lama Yeshe and the world of Tibetan Buddhism (like the photo he referred to in the interview), subjected to high-profile media attention because of his having been identified as a *tulku,* and surrounded by people with a high investment in believing that he is the reincarnation of their teacher. Let us imagine that the child is simply responding to the expectations of the adults around him. He already knows that when he makes certain gestures or speaks in a certain tone of voice, those who care for him will exclaim with joy, "Oh, that's just like Lama Yeshe!" So when this sensitive child is confronted with a range of rosaries, could he not simply be responding to the hopes and expectations of his audience—none of whom are indifferent to the outcome? One wonders if the same tests were run under laboratory conditions in the presence of neutral observers whether the results would be the same. Whether or not one accepts such a possibility—that a young child can "read" the expectations of those around him—is such a theory any more or less credible than that of rebirth? As for his "remembering" his former incarnation, it would seem quite possible to explain this in a similar way, namely that he is simply telling the adults around him what he thinks they want to hear. This is not to deny the possibility of rebirth in this case but to show that the same phenomena can be explained by other hypotheses every bit as plausible.

Where does this leave us? Are we any clearer as to what is going on? Having looked at the traditional Buddhist account of rebirth and having reflected on some of the difficulties it presents, where does one stand? It is often felt that there are two options: one can either believe in rebirth or not believe in it. But there is a third alternative: that of agnosticism—to acknowledge in all honesty that one does not know. One does not have either to assert it or to deny it; one neither has to adopt the literal versions presented by tradition nor fall into the other extreme of believing that death is a final annihilation. This, I feel, could provide a good Buddhist middle way for approaching the issue today.

How can one know about something that presupposes the absence of the very apparatus that does such knowing (the psychophysical complex of body and mind)? Whatever I say about what happens to me after death is inevitably said from the standpoint of that which will cease at death. No matter how philosophically cogent, Buddhologically sound, aesthetically appealing, or psychologically astute it may be, whatever theory I propose will be limited by the senses, language, brain activity, and consciousness of a finite being (myself) who cannot conceive of anything outside the aforementioned senses, language, brain activity, and consciousness.

The traditional Buddhist doctrine of the "Six Realms of Existence" (those of gods, titans, humans, animals, ghosts, and hell-denizens), which are considered the only possible options for rebirth, betrays the necessary anthropomorphism of such a belief. All these realms (except that of the animals) are imaginative extensions of aspects of the human situation. It is impossible to imagine, for example, a seventh-sense faculty, let alone the kinds of consciousness more complex brains would make possible. Yet death, as the disintegration of the senses and the brain we now possess, surely must open up the possibility of a potentially infinite variety of forms of existence (and even the possibility of something beyond the very ideas of existence and nonexistence).

In many cases we find ourselves drawn to doctrines such as rebirth not out of a genuine existential insight or concern, but rather out of a need for consolation. At the level of popular religion, Buddhism, as much as any other tradition, has provided such consolation. Yet if we take an agnostic position, we will find ourselves facing death as a moment of our existential encounter with life. Any examined human life involves the realization that we have been thrown into this world, without any choice, only to look forward to the prospect of being expelled at death. The sheer sense of bafflement and perplexity at this situation is crucial to spiritual awareness. To opt for a comforting, even a discomforting, explanation of what brought us here or what awaits us after death severely limits that very rare sense of mystery with which religion is essentially concerned. We thereby obscure with consoling man-made concepts that which most deeply terrifies and fascinates us.

Nonetheless, among otherwise critical and discerning practitioners of the dharma, the subject of rebirth is often treated as out of bounds for honest and penetrating inquiry. While Tibetan Buddhists tend dogmatically to assert it, practitioners of Zen and Vipassana tend either to overlook it or explain it away as a metaphor. Both these attitudes can equally serve to sidestep the encounter with the "Great Matter of Birth and Death." Failure to summon forth the courage to risk a nondogmatic and nonevasive stance on this central issue is also liable to blur one's ethical vision. For if my actions in the world are to stem from an authentic encounter with what is most vital and mysterious in life, then they surely need to be unclouded by either dogma or prevarication. A truly agnostic position is not an excuse for indecision. If anything, it is a powerful catalyst for action, since in shifting concern away from a hypothetical future life to the dilemmas of the present, it demands precisely the kind of compassion-centered ethic advocated by Śāntideva.

The practice of dharma requires the courage to confront what it means to be fully human. All the pictures I entertain of heaven and hell, or cycles of rebirth, merely serve to replace the overwhelming reality of the unknown with what is known and acceptable. In this sense, to cling to the idea of rebirth, rather than treating it as a useful symbol or hypothesis, can be spiritually suffocating. If we are to take Buddhism as an ongoing existential encounter with our life here and now, then we will only gain by releasing our grip on such notions.

# CREATING SANGHA

A Buddhist community—a sangha—is not something one is merely born into or chooses to join but something one is challenged to create. A sangha provides a matrix of communal support for people to realize their commitment to a common vision or concern. Yet it is always in danger of deteriorating into an institution intent on preserving the power of a minority of professionals. A sangha requires some kind of organized structure to serve an effective purpose within a given society and persist over generations. The sangha structures in Buddhism over the past 2,500 years have for the most part been monastic communities.

Few would disagree that monasticism, with its vows and disciplines, provides the time and freedom to reflect on the dharma and a conducive framework for cultivation of concentration and insight. For this reason, since the time of the Buddha, the survival of the dharma has been seen as dependent upon the survival of a monastic community. In most Asian countries, the very term "community" (sangha) has come to refer to the monastic community alone. While a sympathetic laity is required to support the monks and nuns, the lay people's limited opportunity for realizing the scholarly and contemplative goals of Buddhist practice has led to their assuming an inferior status to monastics.

We find ourselves in a very different kind of society from those that prevailed in Buddhist Asia. What kind of role might a monk or nun play in this world? A monk or nun acts as a visible challenge to the shallow, distracted lives in which many people find themselves trapped. By their very presence monastics assert values that are either ignored, denied, or simply forgotten. Monastics are a reminder of that part of our lives that may be dimly recalled but is usually neglected. Irrespective of one's opinions about monasticism, to encounter a monk or nun in the flesh can have a powerful impact: for the faithful they act as a concrete affirmation of their values; for skeptics, a challenge to preoccupations with what is fleeting and self-centered. Monastics are living symbols who point beyond their own personality to something that is always present, even though awareness of it may be suppressed.

According to the legend, Prince Siddhartha himself was motivated in his quest for awakening by encountering four sights, one of them a wandering monk. The encounter with the monk is put on the same level as those with the sick person, the old person, and the corpse. Just as the meeting with the concrete realities of sickness, aging, and death opened his eyes to his own existential dilemma, so the sight of the monk opened his eyes to the possibility of a response to this dilemma. It was not necessary for the monk to say anything: his mere presence as a homeless renunciate was sufficient to force upon the prince the awareness of the values he had neglected in his life of sensory indulgence. Here lies the meaning of monasticism as a form of life standing in a polar relation to secular society.

The issue of monasticism today does not concern its validity as an exemplary way of life in which to practice the dharma. It concerns its relationship to the sangha, the Buddhist community, as a whole. Should communities of monks and nuns still be considered as the core of the Buddhist sangha? Or does the present situation call for a definition of sangha in which the role of monastics is less central?

As Buddhism developed over centuries in different cultures, its form was determined by the economic and social conditions of former times. All traditional forms of Buddhism share in common the stamp of a medieval social structure. They emerged in societies with fixed class distinctions in which the course of a person's life was determined at the time of his or her birth. The division between monastics and laity was as sharply defined as the division between classes. The life of the majority of the laity consisted of agricultural labor and the raising of families. A formal education was very limited if not absent. Monastics, in contrast, were largely free from having to engage in manual labor and had no family responsibilities. They were able to devote themselves entirely to the dharma—through the study of philosophy, the practice of meditation, and by serving a pastoral role in the community.

As a consequence of this split, the practice of Buddhism assumed two distinct forms. The laity, with neither time nor education, engaged primarily in prayer and devotional practices aimed at improvements in a future life. In addition, they provided material support to the monastic communities as a means of accruing merit and maintaining the institutions that concretized their religious beliefs. The monastics' practice was entirely different. As a result, they developed sophisticated philosophies as well as a precise and detailed understanding of spiritual practice. Of course, occasional lay people sometimes attained comparable heights. But the very fact that so much attention is given to the lay status of such figures as Vimalakīrti and Marpa only illustrates how they were clearly the exceptions rather than the rule.

Quite understandably, the Buddhist community—the sangha —was identified with the monastic community. For given the nature of Buddhism, with its emphasis on prolonged practice aimed at awakening, together with the economic and social constraints on the laity, it could not easily have been otherwise. In former times, the vast majority of the laity lacked the possibility to actualize within their own lives the experience of awakening that is vital to the continuity of the Buddhist tradition. The question today is this: is the modern world sufficiently different to require such a radical departure from tradition that monasticism would no longer be considered central to the Buddhist sangha?

Nowadays, the condition of the laity, even in traditional Asian Buddhist countries, is being transformed. No longer is the intellectual or moral superiority of monastics taken for granted. The nature of both interpersonal and social relationships has undergone vast changes too. Education is no longer the privilege of aristocrats and monks. Intellectual inquiry and philosophical thinking are possible for whoever is inspired to undertake them. State education and the development of telecommunications provide the basis for an active and critical spiritual life for a growing number of people. Leisure time in which to pursue such matters is also no longer the privilege of minority groups. Moreover, these pursuits can no longer be considered primarily the affair of men.

In accordance with the central Buddhist doctrine of "conditionality," the concept of sangha and the role of the monastic in Buddhist societies were both conditioned by the socioeconomic conditions of their times. And in accordance with the equally central notion of "impermanence," they too are subject to change. There is, nonetheless, a trend to overlook the implications of these doctrines on Buddhism itself and its institutions. This may in part be due to the one-sided interpretation of impermanence as "subject to destruction." This negative connotation obscures how impermanence is equally a precondition for creation, transformation, and renewal. Change is neither good nor bad: it is simply what happens.

It would not be unreasonable to conclude that the traditional concept of sangha may no longer be relevant today. It would seem self-evident that for the Buddhist community to survive, it must

adapt itself to the changing world. To insist upon preserving traditional institutions irrespective of circumstances would be to indulge
in a dinosaur mentality. The question of survival depends essentially on the structure of the sangha, for the sangha is the communal expression of the Buddhist experience that needs to be rooted in
the soil of society as a whole. As such it draws its sustenance from
beyond its own immediate boundaries; but if its root structure demands a soil that no longer exists, it will inevitably wither and die.

Many traditional Buddhists would insist that communities of
monastics are necessary if the dharma is to survive. While it is
true that the sangha is essential to the survival of Buddhism, is
it justified to assume such an identity between the sangha and
the monastic community? For it may well be an identity formed
by socioeconomic rather than existential needs. While it is true
that most of what we know of Buddhism today was preserved and
handed down by monastics, it may also be that Buddhism's often
moribund condition in Asia is due to having embodied its communal center in monastic institutions. While tradition claims that
monastics are the greatest strength of the Buddhist community,
history suggests they are one of its greatest weaknesses.

Why was Buddhism unable to survive the Muslim invasion of
India during the twelfth century, whereas Hinduism, which suffered equal persecution, was? One major factor was that Buddhism
relied for its continuity and identity upon isolated monastic groups.
To destroy Buddhism it was only necessary for the Muslim armies
to destroy the monasteries. With the monasteries gone, the lay community swiftly disintegrated because of the lack of a cohesive center.
Hinduism, on the other hand, was far more integrated into the fabric of Indian society—and therefore much more difficult to destroy.

In Tibet, too, the rapid destruction of Buddhism can likewise
be blamed partially on the monasteries. Here Buddhism was more
socially integrated and had assumed political as well as spiritual

authority. But it was the monks' insistence upon preserving the rigid forms of their institutions and their pursuing an isolationist policy that left Tibet defenseless against outside interference. The transcendental aims of the monks were translated into a political apparatus, making not only the monasteries but the entire structure of society vulnerable to secular ambitions.

Likewise in China, Mongolia, Vietnam, Laos, and Cambodia, Buddhism was undermined through destroying the monastic framework upon which the community depended. Indeed, it is remarkable to compare the extent of the Buddhist world fifty years ago with what remains today. Never in human history has such a major world religion diminished in size and influence so rapidly. Three or four revolutions in the right places would more or less eliminate traditional Buddhism from the face of the earth.[1]

This is not to suggest that monastics are redundant or unimportant, but rather that their role in the Buddhist community should be reevaluated. If Buddhism is to survive, it needs to find a firm communal footing within the framework of secular culture. Insistence on monasticism as central to the survival of Buddhism could hasten its downfall rather than ensure its preservation. While the dharma certainly needs to be embodied in a distinctive sangha, it may no longer be necessary for this sangha to be identified primarily with monastic institutions. The emergence of those outside the monastic fold who are pursuing an intelligent and serious practice of the dharma is creating the communal matrix for a new conception of sangha. It is in such a setting that Buddhists are being challenged to maintain the rigor and depth of their traditions while at the same time to function both caringly and critically in a modern society.

Today one finds oneself adopting a practice of Buddhism that exceeds in depth and diversity the traditional lay practice of prayer and devotion. One's knowledge and experience of Buddhism may not always equal the depth of insight made possible through a monastic life of a single-pointed contemplation, but this lack needs to be seen in the light of an enhanced ability to apply the Buddhist teachings under a wider and more complex range of conditions. We find ourselves in a situation with an increased freedom to practice yet without being constrained in our social interactions by monastic vows. Here, it seems, we discover the seeds of a new conception of sangha.

Yet rather than theorizing about the nature of such a sangha, we need to act. The challenge is to imagine and then create a communal structure that works *in practice*. As with all good experimentation, we need to proceed with an open mind free from attachment to the outcome. We must be ready to learn from whatever historical alternative models already exist: from the noncelibate yogic tradition of the Tibetan Nyingma school to the Japanese system of hereditary priests. We also need to learn from history's mistakes and work to create a sangha that is no longer ridden with the sectarianism, dogmatism, authoritarianism, and sexism endemic to many Asian traditions.

For the creation of a viable sangha is the single most important challenge facing Buddhists throughout the world today. Without it, the dharma is liable to become either the preserve of benign eccentrics on the margins of the world or gradually absorbed into other disciplines and lose its identity altogether. Despite its failings, the monastic sangha has successfully weathered more than two and a half millenia of upheaval and change. Will the alternative we put in its place prove so effective and enduring? That will be the test. We need to be on guard against the giddy hubris of modern secularism that dismisses such a resilient institution as atavistic and irrelevant. Ultimately, whatever kind of sangha emerges in the West, it will do so out of a continuum of practice sustained over generations. In a way that no one can predict.

# THE AGNOSTIC BUDDHIST

Something I've noticed over the years is how, although we may start out at a young age rebelling against Christianity or Judaism and then finding in Buddhism a vindication for our rebelliousness, as we grow older, we begin in a strange way to recover our past. I was not brought up a Christian. In fact, my grandparents on my mother's side formally broke with the church, even though my great-grandfather was a Wesleyan minister. Under my mother's influence I grew up in an anti-church environment, one that might loosely be termed "humanistic." Now I find that, more and more, I am coming back to the culture in which I grew up. Although I admire many of Christianity's ethical values, I have no natural sympathy with the Christian tradition. But I do find myself increasingly sympathetic to my childhood experience as a humanist, a secularist, an agnostic. I'm even beginning to reconsider positively what it means to be a materialist—a term that has a rather bad press in Buddhism.

The term "agnostic" is the one I identify with most closely. It was coined only in the late 1880s, by the biologist Thomas Huxley —and as a joke. Huxley belonged to a small philosophical circle in London in which he increasingly felt out of place. Everyone else in the group could readily identify as a Christian, or a Rationalist, or a Schopenhaurian, or whatever, but no such term seemed applicable to him. So he decided to call himself an "agnostic" in order that he too could "have a tail like all the other foxes."[1]

Huxley began to develop the idea. He saw agnosticism as being as demanding as any moral, philosophical, or religious creed. Yet for him it was more of a method than a creed. The method he had in mind is broadly that which underpins scientific inquiry. It means, on one hand, taking one's reason as far as it will go and, on the other, not accepting anything as true unless it is somehow demonstrable. Here there are very clear parallels with the Buddhist tradition. Although we may not find it so much in Zen, in the Indo-Tibetan tradition there is a strong emphasis on rational inquiry. I spent many years as a young monk not working on kōans but studying formal logic and epistemology with Tibetan lamas. Buddhism is a very strong, rational tradition, and I'm immensely grateful to have had that training. All schools of Buddhism agree that one should not believe something simply for the sake of believing it but only if it can somehow be demonstrated as true, if it can be realized in some practical way.

Huxley even described his view as "the agnostic faith," thus giving it the kind of seriousness that one might otherwise expect only among religious people. And within fifteen years of Huxley coining the term, "agnosticism" was already being linked with Buddhism. It was first applied by a man called Allan Bennett who became a *bhikkhu* in Burma in 1901 with the name Ananda Metteyya. Bennett was the first Englishman to be ordained as a Buddhist and the first European who tried to articulate his understanding of the dharma as a practicing Buddhist rather than merely a scholar of Buddhism.[2] In a magazine he issued in Rangoon in 1905, he spoke of Buddhism as "exactly coincidental in its fundamental ideas with the modern agnostic philosophy of the West."[3]

At the beginning of the twentieth century, when Westerners were only just starting to embrace the teachings of the Buddha, why would this young English monk have regarded Buddhism as agnostic? I suspect that one of the key sources may have been this famous passage from the *Cūḷa Mālunkya Sutta* in the *Majjhima Nikāya* of the Pali Canon. The Buddha says:

> Suppose Mālunkyāputta, a man were wounded by an arrow thickly smeared with poison, and his friends and companions brought a surgeon to treat him. The man would say, "I will not let the surgeon pull out the arrow until I know the name and clan of the man who wounded me; whether the bow that wounded me was a long bow or a cross bow; whether the arrow that wounded me was hoof-tipped or curved or barbed." All this would still not be known to that man, and meanwhile he would die. So too, Mālunkyāputta, if anyone should say, "I will not lead the noble life under the Buddha until the Buddha declares to me whether the world is eternal or not eternal; finite or infinite; whether the soul is the same as or different from the body; whether or not an awakened one continues or ceases to exist after death," that would still remain undeclared by the Buddha, and meanwhile that person would die.[4]

This passage shows quite clearly both the pragmatic nature of the Buddha's teaching and its agnostic bent.

It is important to distinguish between those questions that are addressed by the core teachings of the Buddha and those which are not really of central concern. I was listening on the radio not long ago in England to a discussion about religious belief. All of the participants were engaged in a heated discussion about the possibility of miracles. It is generally assumed that being a religious person entails believing certain things about the nature of oneself and reality in general that are beyond the reach of reason and empirical verification. What happened before birth, what will happen after death, the nature of the soul and its relation to the

body: these are first and foremost religious questions. And the
Buddha was not interested in them. But if we look at Buddhism
historically, we'll see that it has continuously tended to lose this agnostic dimension through becoming institutionalized as a religion,
with all of the usual dogmatic belief systems that religions tend to
have. So, ironically, if you were to go to many Asian countries today,
you would find that the monks and priests who control the in-
stitutional bodies of Buddhism would have quite clear views on
whether the world is eternal or not, what happens to the Buddha
after death, the status of the mind in relation to the body, and so on.

This has led to Buddhism as it comes into the West being
automatically regarded as a religion. The very term "Buddhism," a
word for which there is no exact equivalent in an Asian language,
is largely an invention of Western scholars. It suggests a creed to
be lined up alongside other creeds, another set of beliefs about the
nature of reality that we cannot know by other means than through
faith. This assumption, though, tends to distort or obscure the encounter of the dharma with secular agnostic culture. Another problem is that today the very force of the term "agnosticism" has been
lost. If somebody says they're an agnostic, although they know it
means that one claims not to know certain things, it usually goes
hand in hand with an attitude that seems not to care much about
such things. "I don't know what happens after death" becomes
equivalent to "I don't care; I don't really want to know; I don't even
want to think about it." Modern agnosticism has lost the confidence that it may have had at the time of Huxley and has lapsed
into a superficial skepticism. Buddhism too has lost that critical
edge that we find in the early Pali discourses and, of course, in the
Zen kōans. Very often Buddhism as an institution has tended to
lapse into religiosity.

So, what would an agnostic Buddhist be like today? How would
we even start to think about such a stance? Firstly, an agnostic

Buddhist would not regard the dharma or the teachings of the Buddha as a source which would provide answers to questions of where we are going, where we are coming from, what is the nature of the universe, and so on. In this sense, an agnostic Buddhist would not be a believer with claims to revealed information about supernatural or paranormal phenomena and in this sense would not be religious. I've recently started saying to myself "I'm not a religious person" and finding that to be strangely liberating. You don't have to self-identify as a religious person in order to practice the dharma.

Secondly, an agnostic Buddhist would not look to the dharma for metaphors of consolation. This is another great trait of religions: they provide consolation in the face of birth and death, they offer images of a better afterlife, they offer the kind of security that can be achieved through an act of faith. I'm not interested in that. The Buddha's teachings are confrontative; they're about truth-telling, not about painting some pretty picture of life elsewhere. They're saying: "Look, existence is painful." This is what is distinctive about the Buddhist attitude: it starts not from the promise of salvation but from valuing that sense of existential anguish we tend either to ignore, deny, or avoid through distractions.

Buddhism is often misrepresented as something nihilistic or life-denying. This view fails to recognize that the project of the four noble truths is about resolving the dilemma of anguish, not about indulging human suffering. Again it's a praxis; it's something we can do. It starts with understanding the reality of anguish and uncertainty, and then applying a set of practices that work toward a resolution. But this kind of agnosticism is not based on disinterest; it's not saying, "I just don't care about these great matters of birth and death." It is a passionate recognition that I do not know. I really do not know where I came from; I do not know where I'm going. And that "don't know" is a very different order of "don't know" from that of a superficial agnosticism.

This process of stripping away consolatory illusions by holding true to this agnostic not-knowing leads to what we might call "deep agnosticism." I like to think of the dharma as the practice of deep agnosticism. This both leads away from the superficiality of contemporary Western agnosticism and begins to tap a dimension that seems essential to the heart of dharma practice. To illustrate this, here is a kōan, case 41 from *The Gateless Gate:*

> Bodhidharma sat facing the wall. The Second Patriarch, standing in the snow, cut off his arm and said, "Your disciple's mind is not yet at peace. I beg you, master, give it rest." Bodhidharma said, "Bring me your mind and I will put it to rest for you." The Second Patriarch replied, "I have searched for the mind but have never been able to find it." Bodhidharma said, "I've finished putting it to rest for you."[5]

This deep not-knowing, in this case the Second Patriarch's inability to find his anguished mind, takes the notion of agnosticism down to another depth. One might call it a contemplative depth. Such deep agnostic metaphors are likewise found in such terms as *wu hsin* (no mind), and *wu nien* (no thought), as well as in the more popular "don't know mind" of the Korean Zen master Seung Sahn.

Another striking feature of this kōan is its similarity with the process of understanding emptiness as found in the Mādhyamaka philosophy of India and Tibet. "Emptiness" is a singularly unappetizing term. I don't think it was ever meant to be attractive. The Tibetan Buddhist scholar Herbert V. Guenther once translated it as "the open dimension of being," which sounds a lot more appealing than "emptiness." "Transparency" was a term I played with for a while, which also makes emptiness sound more palatable. Yet we have to remember that even two thousand years ago Nāgārjuna was having to defend himself against the nihilistic implications of emptiness. Some of the chapters in his philosophical works start with someone objecting: "This emptiness is a terrible idea. It undermines all grounds for morality. It undermines everything the Buddha was speaking about." Clearly the word did not have a positive ring back then either. I suspect that it might have been used quite consciously as an unappealing term, which cuts through the whole fantasy of consolation that one might expect a religion to provide. Perhaps we need to recover this cutting edge of emptiness, its unappealing aspect.

Let's go back to Bodhidharma and his disciple, the Second Patriarch. It seems as though the pain of the disciple's dilemma was so extreme that he was prepared to cut off his arm to resolve it. This pain was centered around some kind of nugget of anguish within his own mind, his most intimate sense of who he was. Yet by inquiring deeply into this painful, isolated self-identity, he could find nothing he could ultimately grasp hold of and say, "That's my mind. There it is. I've got it. I've defined it. I've realized it." Instead, he discovered the ultimate unfindability of the mind and, by implication, the ultimate unfindability of self and things. And this gives us an important clue to understanding the notions of emptiness and "no mind." They do not mean that there is literally no mind; they're saying that if you try to understand the nature of anything in the deepest sense, you will not be able to arrive at any fixed view that defines it as this or that. The Dalai Lama uses a quaint expression in colloquial Tibetan—*dzugu dzug-sa mindoo*— which means "There's nothing you can put your finger on." Again, this does not imply that the thing in question does not exist at all. It simply exposes the fallacy of the deeply felt, almost instinctive assumption that our self, the mind, or anything else must be secured on a permanent, transcendental basis. Yet the uniqueness of a person's mind or identity, the uniqueness of a flower that's growing in the garden, does not require any kind of transcendent basis that's peculiar to that thing. Emptiness indicates how everything that comes about does so through an unrepeatable matrix of contingencies, conditions, and causes as well as through conceptual, linguistic, and cultural frameworks. Everything arises out of an extraordinarily complex combination of transient events that culminate, in this particular instance, in my saying these words to you.

Now, whether we follow the Indo-Tibetan analytical approach or the Zen approach of asking a kōan like "What is this?" such meditative inquiry leads to a mind that becomes more still and clear. But paradoxically this does not mean that things then become more clear-cut, that you reach some final understanding of who you are or of what makes the universe tick. Because at the same time as such things become more vivid and clear, they also become more baffling. One encounters, as it were, the sheer mystery of things. A deep agnosticism would be one founded on this kind of unknowing: the acknowledgment that, in terms of what life really is, I really do not know. And in that unknowing there is already a quality of questioning, of perplexity. And as that perplexity becomes stabilized through meditation, one enters increasingly into a world that is mysterious, magical in a sense, and not containable by narrow ideas and concepts.

But this is not where the practice ends. This is only half the project. What we also discover in this open space, in this mysterious experience of non-self, are the wellsprings of creativity and imagination. In Mahayana Buddhism particularly the Buddha is not just someone who had a wonderful mystical experience, whose mind is freed, but he is also this being who spontaneously and compassionately manifests and is embodied in the world through the *nirmāṇakāya* (emanation body).

I like to think of the Buddha's awakening under the Bodhi tree not as some kind of transcendental absorption, but as a moment of total shock. Niels Bohr supposedly once said about quantum mechanics, "Anyone who is not shocked by quantum theory has not understood it." I think we could say the same about emptiness: If you're not shocked by emptiness, then you haven't understood it.

The Buddha's awakening is followed by this strange period where, according to tradition, he hesitates for about six weeks before being prompted, by a god in this case, to go out into the world and do something. This process is similar in many respects to the process of artistic creation. When faced with the task of articulating a deep intuitive vision in words, clay, or paint, one might experience that same intense trepidation that one finds in meditation when the mind is very still but at the same time tremendously resistant about pursuing the inquiry any further. At this point the meditator usually lapses into fantasy and daydreams and drowsiness. The writer (one of my other personae) usually has an urgent compulsion to tidy up his desk. But it's the same kind of evasion; it's the same kind of hesitation in the face of what is deeply weird and mysterious.

For here we stand on the threshold of the imagination. We are challenged to imagine something that has never quite been thought of in that way before. The Buddha's genius lies precisely in his imagination. I don't believe that when he experienced awakening, suddenly the four noble truths appeared—1, 2, 3, 4—in words of fire in the sky or anything like that. Rather, his awakening did not become real until he had to stammer it out to his first disciples, the five ascetics, in the Deer Park in Sarnath. The model of awakening in Mahayana Buddhism is that of a process which is perhaps never completed. The process of articulating the dharma goes on and on according to the needs of the different historical situations that it encounters. We could read the whole history of Buddhism, from the moment of the Buddha's awakening until now, as a process of seeking to imagine a way to respond both wisely and compassionately to the situation at hand.

Awakening is only complete—in the same way that a work of art is only complete—when it finds an expression, a form, that translates that experience in a way that makes it accessible to others. That again is the balance between wisdom and compassion. The creative process of expressing the dharma is not just a question of duplicating in words something etched somewhere in the privacy of my soul. The living process of understanding is formed through the encounter with another person, with the world. You've probably had the experience of someone coming to you in a state of distress and blurting out their problems, and you suddenly find yourself saying things that you were quite unaware you knew. The process of awakening is one of valuing and connecting with that capacity to respond in authentic ways to the suffering of others. The imagination is the bridge between contemplative experience and the anguish of the world. By valuing imagination, we value the capacity of each person, each community, to imagine and create themselves anew.

Dharma practice is like creating a work of art. Our five *skandhas*—body, feelings, perceptions, inclinations, consciousness— they're the clay that we mold and form through our practice into a bodhisattva, or whatever we aspire to. Our very lives become the raw material of our imagination.

In the contemporary world Buddhism encounters a culture that places a positive value on the power of each individual's creativity and imagination. It's interesting that in most Buddhist traditions these things are not strongly encouraged, or, if they are, it's usually only within highly formalized settings. I like to think of dharma practice today as venturing into a world of imagination, one in which each individual seeks to articulate a vision in terms of the particular needs of his or her own situation. Buddhism would then become less and less the preserve of an institution, and more and more an experience that is owned by ordinary people in ordinary communities.

Of course, there are dangers here. But these are hardly new. Historically, Buddhism has always had to find ways of responding effectively to the danger of becoming too acculturated, of becoming too absorbed into the assumptions of the host culture. Certainly such a danger exists here in the West: Buddhism might, for example, tend to become a kind of souped-up psychotherapy. But there's the equal danger of Buddhism holding on too fiercely to its Asian identity and remaining a marginal interest. Somehow we have to find a middle way between these two poles, and this challenge is not going to be worked out by academics or Buddhist scholars; it's a challenge that each of us is asked to meet in our own practice from day to day.

Buddhism is not some ethereal thing that is being magically transferred from Asia to the West. Titles of books like *The Awakening of the West* might suggest that Buddhism is a thing that has this almost mystical capacity. But what is it that is transmitted? The only thing that is transmitted is the understanding and the way of life of those people who practice it, people like you and me. No one else is going to do it for us. The responsibility is ultimately our own.

We need to be particularly wary today of the modern conceit which assumes that our broad education, our easy access to information, and the sudden emergence of a readily available literature on Buddhism are somehow going to speed up the process, that we'll arrive at an American Buddhism or a Western Buddhism or a whatever Buddhism much more quickly than in the past. I think this is a serious misreading of cultural transition and change. A culture like Buddhism is something organic.

For example, we may have a great deal of scientific understanding about oak trees, but that knowledge in itself, and our access to that information, is not going to speed up the growth of oak trees. Historically, we can see that Buddhism has never managed to root itself in any culture until several generations have passed. This is a sobering reminder for individualistic Westerners who are proud of their capacity to solve problems quickly. We prefer to think that some bright spark will sooner or later figure out what needs to be done to create a Western Buddhism rather than emphasizing our own doing of it, our own cultivation of the wisdom and compassion that are at the core of Buddhism. Perhaps we have really to trust in the practice and find the humility to accept that we will probably not live to see a Western Buddhism. Maybe our children will, or our children's children. We need to acknowledge that we live in a time of transition, a time in which the dharma might be in crisis in Asia and yet has not really found its feet here. It's an exciting time to be in: one in which something is being created, and we are the participants in that creation.

# THE OTHER ENLIGHTENMENT PROJECT

A postmodern world that takes for granted the plurality and ambiguity of perception, the fragmented and contingent nature of reality, the elusive, indeterminate nature of self, the arbitrariness, inauthenticity, and anguish of human existence would seem to fit Buddhism like a glove. Yet this is nothing new. Western advocates of Buddhism, from Schopenhauer onward, have all tended to be impressed by the compatibility of its doctrines with their own way of seeing the world.[1] Kantians saw the views of Kant in Buddhism, logical positivists those of Bertrand Russell, just as today deconstructionists behold the unravelings of Jacques Derrida. Within the last hundred years the teachings of the Buddha have confirmed the views of theosophists, fascists, environmentalists, and quantum physicists alike. Then is Buddhism just an exotic morass of incompatible ideas, a "Babylon of doctrines," as the sixteenth-century missionary Matteo Ricci suspected? Or is this another illustration of the Buddha's parable of the blind men who variously interpret an elephant as a pillar, a wall, a rope, or a tube depending on which bit of the animal's anatomy they clutch? There may well be as many kinds of Buddhism as there are ways the Western mind has to apprehend it. In each case "Buddhism" denotes something else. But what is it really? The answer: nothing you can put your finger on. To fix the elephant in either time or space is to kill her. The elephant is both empty and perplexing. She breathes and moves—in ways no one can foresee.

This fluidity has enabled Buddhism throughout its history to cross cultural frontiers and adapt itself creatively to situations quite different from those in the lands of its origin on the Indian subcontinent. (The most striking example being that of its movement nearly two thousand years ago to China.) This creative process requires Buddhism to imagine itself as something different. It entails adopting compatible elements from the new host culture while at the same time critiquing elements of that culture that are at odds with its own Buddhist values. So it is hardly surprising that Buddhists today instinctively home in on elements of postmodernity that resonate with their own understanding of the dharma. The danger is that, for the sake of appearing "relevant," they sacrifice the equally vital need to retain a lucid, critical perspective.

The element of postmodernity that potentially promises Buddhist voices access to contemporary culture is implicit in Jean-François Lyotard's simplified but seminal definition of "postmodern" as "incredulity toward grand narratives."[2] The grandest of all these grand narratives for Lyotard and others is the European Enlightenment, the certainty of human progress through reason and science, which began in the eighteenth century. As soon as conviction in this myth wavers, a host of other assumptions are thrown into question. Through focusing on change and uncertainty rather than on assured continuity, through emphasizing contingency, ambivalence, and plurality, postmodern thinkers have come to hear voices of the Other: those the Enlightenment Project has either suppressed, ignored, or disdained—women, citizens of the Third World, non-European systems of thought such as Buddhism.

As a Buddhist I find myself reading erudite texts on themes such as the nature of the self, which explore ideas quite familiar to me as a Buddhist yet fail to make even a passing reference to the fact that this kind of analysis and discourse has been pursued in Asia for more than two thousand years. I sense at these times what women must feel about texts that blithely assume a male perspective as normative. The habit of treating the East as Other is a deeply engrained European trait that goes back at least as far as Euripides and is ironically perpetuated even by postmodern writers. Yet there are signs of change. After the usual Eurocentric analysis, Galen Strawson concludes in a recent article titled "The Sense of the Self": "Perhaps the best account of the existence of the self is one that may be given by certain Buddhists."[3] Note the hesitation: "perhaps," "may be," "certain Buddhists" (not all of them of course).

Whatever features of postmodernity may be apparent in Buddhism, it would be foolish to describe Buddhist thought as "postmodern"—for the simple reason that Buddhism has undergone no phase of modernity to be "post" of. Buddhist cultures have evolved according to the grand narrative of their own Enlightenment Project. Consequently, two broad but opposing trends can be seen in the way Buddhism encounters contemporary Western culture.

In recognizing, on one hand, the breakdown of the grand narratives of the West, Buddhists might seek to replace them with their own grand narrative of enlightenment. This is explicit in the stated goals of at least two of the most successful Buddhist movements in Britain today: the Friends of the Western Buddhist Order (FWBO),[4] which aims to create a "New Society" founded on Buddhist principles, and Soka Gakkai International (SGI), which seeks to realize "Kosen Rufu"—the worldwide spread of Nichiren Daishonin's Buddhism.[5] Although both organizations are contemporary reformed Buddhist movements, from a postmodern perspective they remain entranced by the legitimating myth of a grand narrative that promises universal emancipation. If a defining trait of our times is indeed widespread loss of credibility in such narratives and their inability any longer to compel consensus, then such ambitions may be doomed to frustration.

Yet if, on the other hand, Buddhists find themselves in sympathy with postmodern incredulity toward grand narratives, then they might be compelled to imagine another kind of Buddhism altogether. They will try to rearticulate the guiding metaphors of Buddhist tradition in the light of postmodernity. An attitude of incredulity would itself tend to resonate more with the metaphor of wilderness than with that of path, with the possibilities of unbounded landscape as opposed to the secure confinement of a highway.

The key notion in such an endeavor would be "emptiness." For here we have a notion that shares with postmodernism a deep suspicion of a single, nonfragmentary self, as well as of any "transcendental signified," such as God or Mind. It too celebrates the disappearance of the subject, the endlessly deferred play of language, the ironically ambiguous and contingent nature of things. Yet in other respects it parts company with the prevailing discourses of postmodernity. Meditation on emptiness is not a mere intellectual exercise but a contemplative discipline rooted in an ethical commitment to nonviolence. It is not just a description in unsentimental language of the way reality unfolds; it offers a therapeutic approach to the dilemma of human anguish.

Proponents of the doctrine of emptiness, at least from the time of Nāgārjuna, have been subjected to the same kind of criticism as postmodernists receive today. They too have stood accused of nihilism, relativism, and undermining the basis for morality and religious belief. And not only from non-Buddhists; the concept of emptiness is still criticized within the Buddhist tradition itself.[6] The history of the idea of emptiness has been the history of the struggle to demonstrate that far from undermining an ethical way of life, such a life is actually realized through embracing the implications of emptiness.

The emptiness of self, for instance, is not the denial of individual uniqueness but the denial of any permanent, partless, and transcendent basis for individuality. The anguish and uncertainty of human existence are only exacerbated by the preconceptual, spasm-like grip in which such assumptions of transcendence hold us. While seeming to offer security in the midst of an unpredictable and transient world, paradoxically this grip generates an anxious alienation from the processes of life itself. The aim of Buddhist meditations on change, uncertainty, and emptiness are to help one understand and accept these dimensions of existence and thus gently lead to releasing the grip.

By paying mindful attention to the sensory immediacy of experience, we realize how we are created, molded, formed by a bewildering matrix of contingencies that continually arise and vanish. On reflection, we see how we are formed from the patterning of the DNA derived from our parents, the firing of a hundred billion neurons in our brains, the cultural and historical conditioning of our times, the education and upbringing given us, all the experiences we have ever had and choices we have ever made. These processes conspire to configure the unrepeatable trajectory that culminates in this present moment. What is here now is the unique but shifting impression left by all of this, which I call "me."

Moreover, this gradual dissolution of a transcendental basis for self nurtures an empathetic relationship with others. The grip of self not only leads to alienation but numbs one to the anguish of others. Heartfelt appreciation of our own contingency enables us to recognize our interrelatedness with other equally contingent forms of life. We find that we are not isolated units but participants in the creation of an ongoing, shared reality.

A postmodern perspective would question the mythic status of Buddhism and Agnosticism. In letting go of "Buddhism" as a grand, totalizing narrative that explains everything, we are freed to embark on the unfolding of our own individuation in the context of specific local and global communities. We may find in this process that we too are narratives. Having let go of the notion of a transcendental self, we realize we are nothing but the stories we keep telling ourselves in our own minds and relating to others. We find ourselves participating in a complex web of narratives: each telling its own unique story while inextricably interwoven with the tales of others. Instead of erecting totalizing, hierarchic institutions to set our grand narratives in brick and stone, we look to imaginative, democratic communities in which to realize our own *petits récits:* small narratives.

Such a view is inevitably pluralistic. Instead of seeing itself in opposition to other grand narratives that seem to contradict or threaten it, Buddhism remembers how in its vital periods it has emerged out of its interactions with religions, philosophies, and cultures other than its own. It reminds one of the traditional Huayen Buddhist image of the Jeweled Net of Indra, that vast cosmic web at the interstices of which is a jewel that reflects every other jewel. Today this image suggests the biosphere itself: that vast interdependent web of living systems that sustain each other in a miraculous whole. Which brings us back to the metaphor of wilderness as an image of a postmodern, postpath practice of Buddhism.

# What's Wrong with Conversion?

On his recent visit to Britain, the Dalai Lama was widely quoted as saying that he did not wish to encourage people to convert to Buddhism. Instead, he emphasized the importance of staying with the religion in which one was raised.

On the surface this sounds like a reasonable and responsible piece of advice. It may well have allayed the fears of church leaders that the decline in their congregations would not be further accelerated by calls from this charismatic and charming Buddhist pope. The disquieting fact nonetheless remains that there are few others at the head of a major religious denomination who could fill the Albert Hall—let alone one who would then tell his audience not to look to the tradition he represents for answers to their questions. It seems that it is not so much what the Dalai Lama says that attracts people to his gatherings as the authority with which he says it.

This advice of the Dalai Lama's appears to grant broadly equal value to the world's established religions, to the point where it does not really seem to matter into which one you happened to be born. While he encourages mutual tolerance and ongoing dialogue between these faiths, the Dalai Lama seems unwilling to challenge the status quo. Yet one of the reasons why a small but steadily growing number of Europeans and Americans are drawn to Buddhism and other non-Judeo-Christian traditions is precisely because they do question the status quo.

The Dalai Lama has come to represent far more than just Tibetan Buddhism. Whether he likes it or not, he has become a postmodern icon, an uncannily successful performer on the stage of a pluralistic and individualistic world; religious belief and spiritual practice are here no longer regarded as elements of an inherited faith to be uncritically accepted but rather as choices to be made freely and responsibly. It is all too easy for traditional religious figures (including the Dalai Lama himself) to speak dismissively of a "supermarket spirituality." In so doing, they risk further alienating themselves from those who question the authority of their ancestral religion and seek instead commitment to and engagement with a practice that responds to the specific demands of their personal and social experience.

If the Dalai Lama's injunction is valid now, then presumably it would have been valid in the past too—in which case is one to assume that he disapproves of Tibetans having converted to Buddhism from their indigenous animist faith in the eighth century CE? But if, as one might reasonably expect, he regards the transmission of Buddhist teachings from India to Tibet as the glorious beginning of the religious culture he now struggles to preserve in exile, then on what grounds does he discourage his Western admirers from adopting Buddhism now?

In the past, whether in Lhasa or Rome, conversion was forced on subject peoples by a rhetoric of superiority and uniqueness, the repression of alternatives, threats of hell, or simply imperial decree. But today, when freedom of choice is celebrated as one of the great achievements of liberal democracies, why is the exercise of this freedom not more actively encouraged in addressing the most important and profound questions of our existence? Such encouragement might inspire each of us to face these questions honestly and directly rather than simply acquiescing in the established beliefs of our traditional religious and secular institutions.

Addressing people who were similarly confused as to what path in life to follow, the Buddha once suggested to the Kālāma people: "Do not be satisfied with hearsay or with tradition or with legendary lore or with what has come down in scriptures or with conjecture or with logical inference or with weighing evidence or with liking for a view after pondering over it or with someone else's ability or with the thought: 'the monk is our guru.' When you know in yourselves: 'these things are wholesome, blameless, commended by the wise, and being adopted and put into effect they lead to welfare and happiness,' then you should practice and abide in them."[1]

Although delivered to an audience in north India more than two and a half thousand years ago, the Buddha's skeptical and pragmatic advice has a curiously contemporary ring. Rather than suggest to his listeners that they either stay with the tradition in which they were born or convert to another because they are impressed by the credibility of its doctrines or a teacher's authority, he advises them to find out for themselves what actual benefits the practice of such a teaching can bring.

Those who adopt Buddhist ideas, values, and practices today in the West are not necessarily interested in joining another religious institution. They find the Buddha's "test it and see" approach to be perfectly compatible with a healthy skepticism. If one interprets the Dalai Lama's advice as an encouragement for Westerners to remain within their own secular traditions, then atheists and agnostics may be reassured to find the nontheistic and self-reliant approach of Buddhism to be broadly in keeping with their own outlook. At the same time, Buddhism may also be enabled to recover its own critical and pragmatic perspective, which, historically, has often been overshadowed by its having assumed the identity of a religious creed.

# LIMITS OF AGNOSTICISM

Many years ago I realized I could not accept the Buddhist doctrines of karma and rebirth. These two ideas provide the indispensable mythic foundation for traditional Buddhism. By questioning them one threatens to undermine not only the entire edifice of Buddhist ethics, doctrine, and practice but the authority of the Buddha himself. For without believing in some kind of consciousness that survives physical death, to be propelled by the force of its acts through a vicious cycle of rebirths, the raison d'être for embarking on the liberating path taught by Gotama and generations of his enlightened followers is lost. For orthodox Buddhists, this multi-life perspective is what endows the dharma with its redemptive grandeur.

To resolve this dilemma, I opted for an agnostic position, which was outlined in my book *Buddhism without Beliefs*. It seemed to provide an appropriately middle way solution to the problem. As an agnostic, I did not have to accept *or* reject the doctrines of karma and rebirth. In affirming that I did not know (*a-gnosis*) whether or not they were true, I was able to leave them open as questions to be pondered rather than dogmas to be believed or disbelieved. That I was not alone in finding this position attractive was attested to by the considerable popularity of the book. But (naively in retrospect) I was unprepared for the ensuing backlash from various quarters of the Buddhist establishment. I was accused of severely weakening the thrust of the Buddha's teaching, of subordinating the dharma to nihilistic Western views, of rendering a revered and ancient tradition banal.

I have now come to see more clearly the limitations of this agnostic approach. While agnosticism can offer a refreshingly open-minded contrast to the closed certainties of dogmatism, as a consistent position of principle it is both too broad and too noncommittal. All believers, by definition, must be agnostics. The moment you declare that you *believe* in God or the law of karma, you are acknowledging that you *do not know* whether they exist or not. For if you did know, you would have no need to believe. Only fools, fanatics, and omniscient beings would claim to know such things. To not know, to be agnostic, is nothing more than an honest acceptance of the limited human condition.

The strengths of agnosticism—tolerance and openness, ongoing inquiry, acceptance of uncertainty—turn out to be its weaknesses. For human beings cannot afford the luxury of remaining forever ambivalent. We are repeatedly confronted by challenges, which force us to take a stand, make commitments, defend what we value. We have to cast aside lingering doubts and decide to act in one way or another. We must be willing to take any number of leaps in the dark.

Self-conscious life has somehow come to flourish in the biosphere enveloping this planet. That is all I know about it with certainty. Human beings like us may never have evolved before and may never evolve again in this or any other universe. As far as anyone knows, we are alone in an inconceivably vast cosmos that has no interest at all in our fate. I do not believe that I existed in any meaningful sense before my birth or will exist again after my death either here on earth or in a heaven, a hell, or any other realm. All that will survive from my brief spell here as a rational animal will be the traces I leave behind in this world and the impact I have through my words and deeds on the lives of others.

This might strike you as a depressingly bleak picture that excludes any possibility of hope or redemption. I disagree. Such spiritual shudders of distaste are a reflex of that primal human longing for there to be more to life than just this. But *this,* I would argue, is where the religious quest not only begins but ends. God, the devil, heaven, hell, rebirth, karma are human inventions that we have projected beyond ourselves and invested with a separate reality of their own. The view of reality disclosed through the natural sciences evokes for me feelings of awe incomparably greater than anything religious or mystical writings of any tradition can inspire. Far from being just dumb, inert stuff, matter is wondrously, abundantly, profusely alive. The more we understand it, the less there appears any need for a divine spark or immaterial consciousness to animate it.

Let me repeat. I do not know if this is true; I just believe it is. Among all the accounts of the origin and nature of life currently on offer, that of modern science is by far the most convincing and compelling. Therein also lies its danger. One can be as inflexibly dogmatic about a scientific worldview as a religious one. Today's understanding will probably turn out to be partial and provisional. We can no more anticipate what Copernican revolutions future millennia hold in store than our forebears could imagine the ground beneath their feet to be the surface of a globe rotating in space around the sun. How we picture the universe now may represent only a few scattered pieces of a jigsaw puzzle that we cannot possibly conceive.

By abandoning religious cosmologies and metaphysics, one is able to see more clearly the transformative role spiritual practices can play in this life. Long before embracing agnosticism, my doubts around karma and rebirth were resolved when it dawned on me that even were they not true, it would not affect my commitment to a Buddhist *practice.* To live according to Buddhism's ethical precepts, to apply its instructions on meditation, and to engage with its philosophical ideas seemed sufficiently self-validating and worthwhile in themselves. None of these activities needed to be justified or motivated by arcane theories of multiple lives and karmic causation.

Practices such as generosity, tolerance, compassion, nonviolence, detachment, mindfulness, concentration, and inquiry into the nature of emptiness and contingency were not only compatible with my post-Christian, secular humanism and its scientific worldview but appeared to enrich and enhance them. In its unique configuration of these values Buddhism introduced an entirely new perspective on life and the world. It suggested the possibility of a culture of awakening. And, crucially, it provided a systematic body of practices whereby that perspective and culture could be embodied and realized. In the unfamiliar soil of a Western value system and cultural outlook, however, these practices began to yield unorthodox results. Meditation on impermanence, suffering, and no-self, for example, did not—as the Buddha insisted it would—lead me to disenchantment, dispassion, and a resolve not to be born again but to an ever-deepening awareness of life's infinitely poignant beauty.

# A Secular Buddhist

I am a secular Buddhist. It has taken me years to fully "come out," and I still feel a nagging tug of insecurity, a faint aura of betrayal, in declaring myself in these terms. As a secular Buddhist my practice is concerned with responding as sincerely and urgently as possible to the suffering of life in this world, in this century (our *saeculum*), where we find ourselves now and future generations will find themselves later. Rather than attaining nirvana, I see the aim of Buddhist practice to be the moment-to-moment flourishing of human life within the ethical framework of the eightfold path here on earth. Given what is known about the biological evolution of human beings, the emergence of self-awareness and language, the sublime complexity of the brain, and the embeddedness of such creatures in the fragile biosphere that envelops this planet, I cannot understand how after physical death there can be continuity of any personal consciousness or self, propelled by the unrelenting force of acts (karma) committed in this or previous lives. For many—perhaps most—of my coreligionists, this admission might lead them to ask, "Why, then, if you don't believe such things, do you still call yourself a 'Buddhist'?"

I was neither born a Buddhist nor raised in a Buddhist culture. I grew up in a broadly humanist environment, did not attend church, and was exempted from "scripture" classes, as they were then called, at grammar school in Watford. At the age of eighteen

I left England and traveled to India, where I settled in the Tibetan community around the Dalai Lama in Dharamsala. I became a Buddhist monk at the age of twenty-one and for ten years underwent a formal monastic education in Buddhist doctrine, philosophy, and meditation. Even in the wake of the 1960s this was considered a highly unconventional career path. Buddhism, when it was mentioned at all in those days, was dismissed by mainstream Western media as a marginal though benign spiritual preoccupation of ex- (or not-so-ex-) hippies and the occasional avant-garde psychiatrist. I would have dismissed as a fantasist anyone who told me that in forty years' time Buddhist meditation would be available on the British national health service and that a U.S. congressman (Tim Ryan, Dem.) would publish a book called *A Mindful Nation: How a Simple Practice Can Help Us Reduce Stress, Improve Performance, and Recapture the American Spirit.*

Buddhism has its origins in fifth century BCE India and eventually spread throughout the whole of Asia, but it was not until the middle of the nineteenth century that Westerners had any inkling at all of what it taught and stood for. The abrupt discovery that Gotama Buddha was a historical figure every bit as real as Jesus Christ, whose influence had spread just as far and wide, came as a shock to the imperial conceits of Victorian England. While a tiny handful of Europeans converted to Buddhism from the late nineteenth century onward, it was only in the late 1960s that the dharma started to spread rapidly in the West. In contrast to Christianity, which slowly and painfully struggled to come to terms with the consequences of the Renaissance, the European Enlightenment, natural science, democracy, and secularization, Buddhism was catapulted into modernity from deeply conservative, agrarian societies in Asia, which had been either geographically remote or cut off from the rest of the world through political isolation. When Buddhist communities collided with modernity in the course of the twentieth century, they were unprepared for the new kinds of questions and challenges their religion would face in a rapidly changing global and secular world.

I suspect that a considerable part of the Western enthusiasm for things Buddhist may still be a romantic projection of our yearnings for truth and holiness onto those distant places and peoples about which we know the least. I am sometimes alarmed at the uncritical willingness of Westerners to accept at face value whatever is uttered by a Tibetan lama or Burmese *sayadaw*, while they would be generally skeptical were something comparable said by a Christian bishop or Cambridge don. I do believe that Buddhist philosophy, ethics, and meditation have something to offer in helping us come to terms with many of the personal and social dilemmas of our world. But there are real challenges in translating Buddhist practices, values, and ideas into comprehensive forms of life that are more than just a set of skills acquired in courses on mindfulness-based stress reduction and that can flourish just as well outside meditation retreat centers as within them. Buddhism might require some radical surgery if it is to get to grips with modernity and find a voice that can speak to the conditions of this *saeculum*.

So what sort of Buddhism does a self-declared "secular Buddhist" like myself advocate? For me, secular Buddhism is not just another modernist reconfiguration of a traditional form of Asian Buddhism. It is more radical than that: it seeks to return to the roots of the Buddhist tradition and rethink Buddhism from the ground up.

In exploring such roots, the secular Buddhist finds herself excavating two fields that have been opened up in the past century by modern translators and scholars. The first of these fields consists of the earliest discourses attributed to Gotama, which are primarily found in the Pali Canon of the Theravāda school. We are exceptionally fortunate as English speakers to have not only a complete translation of the Pali Canon, but one that is continually being improved—something that speakers of other European languages can still only dream of. The second of these fields is that of our increasingly detailed (though still disputed and incomplete) understanding of the historical, social, political, religious, and philosophical conditions that prevailed during the Buddha's lifetime in fifth century BCE India. Thanks to the work of many scholars, we are beginning to see more clearly the kind of world *in which* the Buddha taught. Together, these two fields provide a fertile soil for the project of rethinking, perhaps reimagining, the dharma from the ground up.

Yet this very wealth of material also raises serious difficulties in interpretation. The Pali Canon is a complex tapestry of linguistic and rhetorical styles, shot through with conflicting ideas, doctrines, and images, all assembled and elaborated over about four centuries. The canon does not speak with a single voice. How then to distinguish between what is likely to have been the word of the Buddha as opposed to a well-intended "clarification" added by a later commentator? We are not yet—and may never be—at a point where such questions can be answered with certainty. Be that as it may, as a Buddhist practitioner, I look to the Buddha's discourses not just for scholarly knowledge but in order to help me come to terms with what the Chinese call the "great matter of birth and death." It is in this sense that my secular Buddhism still has a *religious* quality to it—because it is the conscious expression of my "ultimate concern," as the theologian Paul Tillich once defined "faith." As one who feels an urgency about such concerns, I am bound, therefore, to risk choices of interpretation now that may or may not turn out to be viable later.

My starting point is to bracket off anything attributed to the Buddha in the canon that could just as well have been said by a brahmin priest or Jain monk of the same period. So when the Buddha says that a certain action will produce a good or bad result in a future heaven or hell, or when he speaks of bringing to an end the repetitive cycle of rebirth and death in order to attain nirvana, I take such utterances to be determined by the common metaphysical outlook of that time rather than reflecting an intrinsic component of the dharma. I thus give central importance to those teachings in the Buddha's dharma that *cannot* be derived from the worldview of fifth century BCE India.

Tentatively, I would suggest that this "bracketing" of metaphysical views leaves us with four distinctive key ideas that do not appear to have direct precedents in Indian tradition. I call them the four *P*'s:

1. The principle of conditionality
2. The practice of four noble tasks (truths)
3. The perspective of mindful awareness
4. The power of self-reliance

Some time ago I realized that what I found most difficult to accept in Buddhism were those beliefs that it shared with its sister Indian religions Hinduism and Jainism. Yet when you bracket off those beliefs, you are left not with a fragmentary and emasculated teaching, but with an entirely adequate ethical, philosophical, and practical framework for living your life in *this* world. Thus what is truly original in the Buddha's teaching, I discovered, was his *secular* outlook.

And when you bracket off the quasi-divine attributes that the figure of the Buddha is believed to possess—a fleshy head protuberance, golden skin, and so on—and focus on the episodes in the canon that recount his often fraught dealings with his contemporaries, then the humanity of Gotama begins to emerge with more clarity too. All this supports what the British scholar Trevor

Ling surmised nearly fifty years ago: that what we now know as "Buddhism" started life as an embryonic civilization or culture that then mutated into another organized Indian religion.[1] Secular Buddhism, which seeks to articulate a way of practicing the dharma in this world and time, thus finds vindication through its critical return to canonical sources and its attempts to recover a vision of Gotama's own *saeculum.*

Above all, secular Buddhism is something to do, not something to believe in. This pragmatism is evident in many of the classic parables: the poisoned arrow, the city, the raft—as well as in the Buddha's presentation of the four noble truths as a range of tasks to be performed rather than a set of propositions to be affirmed. Instead of trying to justify the belief that "life is suffering" (the first noble truth), one seeks to embrace and deal wisely with suffering when it occurs. Instead of trying to convince oneself that "craving is the origin of suffering" (the second noble truth), one seeks to let go of and not get tangled up in craving whenever it rises up in one's body or mind. From this perspective it is irrelevant whether the statements "life is suffering" or "craving is the origin of suffering" are either true or false. Why? Because these four so-called truths are not propositions that one accepts as a believer or rejects as a nonbeliever. They are suggestions to do something that might make a difference in the world in which you coexist with others now.

Therefore "enlightenment"—though I prefer the term "awakening"—is not a mystical insight into the true nature of mind or reality (that always weirdly accords with the established views of one's particular brand of Buddhism) but rather the opening up of a way of being-in-this-world that is no longer determined by one's greed, hatred, fear, and selfishness. Thus awakening is not a state but a process: an ethical way of life and commitment that enables human flourishing. As such it is no longer the exclusive preserve of enlightened teachers or accomplished yogins. Likewise, nirvana—that is, the stopping of craving—is not the goal of the path but its very source. For human flourishing first stirs in that clear, bright, empty space where neurotic self-centeredness realizes that it has no ground to stand on at all. One is then freed to pour forth like sunlight.

Such a view of the dharma fits well with the theologian Don Cupitt's vision of a "solar ethics."[2] In Room 33 of the British Museum you will find a small clay, second century CE Gandhāran bas-relief, which represents the Buddha as a stylized image of the sun placed on a seat beneath the Bodhi tree. In the Pali Canon, Gotama describes himself as belonging to the "solar lineage" (*ādiccagotta*), and others call him by the epithet "solar friend" (*ādiccamitta*). A true friend (*kalyāṇamitta*), he remarks, is one who casts light on the path ahead just as the rising sun illuminates the earth.[3] Yet as Buddhism grew into an organized Indian religion, it seemed to lose sight of its solar origins and turned lunar. Nirvana is often compared to the moon: cool, impassive, remote, and also—as they didn't know then but we know now—a pale reflection of an extraordinary source of heat and light. Perhaps we have reached a time when we need to recover and practice again a solar dharma, one concerned with shedding its light (wisdom) and heat (compassion) onto and into this world, which, as far as we know, might be the only one that ever has been or ever will be.

# A MINDFUL NATION?

As one immersed in the practice of Buddhism for the past forty years—as a student, translator, writer, interpreter, and teacher—I may not be best placed to appreciate the impact of this tradition on the wider society of which I am a part. I may be unable to see the forest, as we say, precisely because of my professional concern with some of its trees. Nonetheless, I sense that seismic changes are afoot in the ways Buddhism is currently evolving in its adaptation to modernity.

In a recent article, "Facing the Great Divide," the eminent American scholar-monk Bhikkhu Bodhi suggests that Buddhism "has arrived at a major watershed from which two distinct streams have emerged, which for convenience we may call 'Classical Buddhism' and 'Secular Buddhism.'" Bodhi explains how the former largely perpetuates the heritage of Asian Buddhism, be that of the Theravāda, Tibetan, Zen, Nichiren, or Pure Land schools, while the latter "marks a rupture with Buddhist tradition, a re-visioning of the ancient teachings intended to fit the secular culture of the West."[1]

That Buddhism may indeed have arrived at such a watershed is further suggested by a recent book by the Dalai Lama entitled *Beyond Religion: Ethics for a Whole World*. "What we need today," he argues, "is an approach to ethics which makes no recourse to religion and can be equally acceptable to those with faith and those without: a secular ethics." Without for a moment rejecting his own Buddhist faith, he acknowledges how "the reality of the world today is that grounding ethics in religion is no longer adequate. This is why I believe the time has come to find a way of thinking about spirituality and ethics that is beyond religion."[2]

Without addressing concrete issues people face in their day-to-day lives, such stirring remarks remain vague and abstract. The deeper challenge confronting both these Buddhist authors is not merely one of "re-visioning ancient teachings" or finding "a new way of thinking about spirituality and ethics" but of advocating practices that can make a palpable difference to the way we live in this world now. And it is here, I believe, that the seismic change in Buddhism's relation to modernity is actually taking place: through the widespread practice of mindfulness.

"Mindfulness," writes its foremost proponent, the American emeritus professor of medicine Jon Kabat-Zinn, "is a way of being in wise and purposeful relationship with one's experience, both inwardly and outwardly. It is cultivated by systematically exercising one's capacity for paying attention, on purpose, in the present moment, and non-judgmentally, and by learning to inhabit and make use of the clarity, discernment, ethical understanding, and awareness that arise." What Kabat-Zinn presents here as mindfulness is more than just a short-term therapeutic intervention to treat a transient health problem. It is a practice that demands not only considerable mental discipline but also a revaluation of the purpose of one's life and the ethical values needed to realize that purpose.

The above definition of mindfulness is found not in a book on psychotherapy or meditation but in Kabat-Zinn's foreword to *Mindful Nation UK: Report by the Mindfulness All-Party Parliamentary Group (MAPPG)*, published in October 2015 in London.[3] This group was set up to review the scientific evidence on the effectiveness of mindfulness, develop policy recommendations for government, and provide a forum in Parliament to explore the role of mindfulness in public life. The report recommends four areas in which mindfulness could be implemented: healthcare, education, the workplace, and the criminal justice system. This was not just a theoretical exercise. One hundred and fifty parliamentarians and eighty of their staff have taken part in mindfulness courses offered in Parliament.

It is, of course, entirely appropriate that mindfulness be presented in such contexts as a practice that is effective irrespective of whether or not one regards oneself as a Buddhist. The report acknowledges the Buddhist origins of mindfulness as a historical fact but insists that the practice has been "freed from any religious or dogmatic content." This does not imply, however, that mindfulness is a therapeutic technique that is entirely value-free. By using such terms as "wise," "non-judgmental," "ethical understanding," and "awareness," Kabat-Zinn's definition of mindfulness endorses certain values. Such a set of values may be pointing to the kind of secular ethics envisioned by the Dalai Lama, but, at the same time, it has a distinctly Buddhistic ring.

Mindfulness is not a marginal practice among Buddhists. Mindfulness is the seventh element of the noble eightfold path, the doctrine the Buddha declared to constitute the very heart of his teaching. Together with appropriate vision, intention, speech, action, livelihood, effort, and concentration, it is a core value to be developed on the way to awakening. The Buddha even declared mindfulness to be the "sole path" to nirvana itself.[4] So when someone uses mindfulness-based cognitive therapy (MBCT) to counter relapse into depression, for example, she is employing a practice that potentially leads to the still, nonreactive freedom of nirvana.

I am as concerned as anyone else that the practice of mindfulness in secular contexts be entirely disassociated from the dogmas of the Buddhist religion. Beliefs in reincarnation or the law of karma, for example, are irrelevant in terms of its therapeutic benefits. That it was originally taught by a person Buddhists believe to be "enlightened" likewise has no bearing at all on whether one should adopt or reject it. The only criterion for its use in healthcare or elsewhere must be whether it can be shown to work in alleviating suffering and improving the quality of human life.

I cannot think of a single meditative discipline from any other world religion that could be utilized outside a religious setting in the way mindfulness is being used today. This leads one to wonder whether, in its essence, what we call "Buddhism" is best described as a religion at all. While the secularization of mindfulness is deplored by some classical Buddhists as a dumbing down or commodification of a revered practice within their tradition, one could also argue that the discovery of the effectiveness of mindfulness in reducing suffering allows Buddhism to recover its secular soul that has long been obscured by the encrustation of religious beliefs.

What matters for secular Buddhists is to live life in such a way that it results in a better world for those who are alive now as well as those who will inhabit it after their death. They understand how both their personal actions and the deeds of a society or state that they endorse will have consequences long after their own death. In accepting degrees of responsibility for these acts, they affirm a belief in natural justice, but they can do so without needing to entertain the idea that they will survive in any form to experience the results of those acts themselves.

For traditional Buddhists, by contrast, it is incoherent to consider oneself a "Buddhist" without believing that this life is but a brief moment in a succession of lifetimes in different realms of existence, driven by the moral force of one's deeds (karma). For without this belief, the Buddhist goal of enlightenment would make no sense, since the "enlightened one" is regarded as the person who has achieved liberation from this repetitive cycle of death and rebirth. To remove such core beliefs would be comparable for them to what denying the existence of God would be for a devout Jew, Christian, or Muslim. In both cases, they would argue, it would deprive the tradition of its very raison d'être.

Without underestimating the doctrinal and philosophical difficulties involved, I attempt in my writings to imagine what the dharma would be like were it divested of the cosmology and metaphysical beliefs of ancient India. I maintain that such a rethinking of Buddhism reveals a foundation on which to build a secular dharma that is based on the earliest texts and provides an entirely adequate framework for human flourishing.

The emergence of secular Buddhism is seen by its advocates as an overdue reformation of the tradition: one that empowers the individual by returning him or her to the core principles, values, and practices taught by the historical Gotama before they mutated into an Indian religion. In this light, secular Buddhism may be far closer in spirit and style to the Hellenistic philosophies of Skepticism, Epicureanism, or Stoicism than to Judaism, Christianity, or Islam. A secular Buddhist celebrates the adoption of mindfulness in nonreligious settings, while recognizing that for its potential to be fully realized a meditative practice alone is insufficient. Just as Jon Kabat-Zinn and others have secularized Buddhist mindfulness, the challenge now is to secularize Buddhist ethics and philosophy in such a way that they can address the current conditions of our world by articulating a way a life in which humans and other beings can flourish together on this earth.

4

# CONVERSATIONS

# THE ECLECTIC CLERIC

## Stephen Batchelor talks to Don Cupitt

**In 1980 you published a book entitled *Taking Leave of God*. For some this must have seemed a shocking idea for a theologian and Anglican priest to propose. It would seem to threaten the very foundation of Christian religious life.**

Although I've been temperamentally religious all my life, my philosophy of religion turned critical with the publication of *Taking Leave of God*. I argued that we should regard God not as a metaphysical being, an infinite spirit, but rather as a guiding spiritual ideal by which to orient one's life. This idea of God was explicitly put forward by Kant and arguably has always been present in the Lutheran tradition.

The older realistic understanding of and language about God leads to impossible intellectual difficulties. How can a person be infinite, timeless, simple, and immutable? It seems to be essential to most Christians' idea of God that God should somehow be thought of as personal, as having dealings with us, but the philosophical attributes of God make that unthinkable. To me it makes more sense to see God as a spiritual ideal. And perhaps the best way to interpret Christianity is to say that Christians see in Christ that ideal embodied in a human life. So I demythologize the idea of an incarnation of God in Christ into the idea of embodiment of Christian values in Christ, in his teaching. I see Christianity as a spiritual path in which one pursues various values, tells certain

stories, follows examples that in the end go back chiefly to Jesus of
Nazareth.

**To what extent was your taking leave of God a movement to-
ward other faiths, in particular Buddhism?**

Yes, that was the time when my path and [author] Iris Mur-
doch's crossed. She was getting very interested in Buddhism and
was taking instruction in meditation. Both of us were beginning
to feel that the metaphysical side of Christian belief was coming to
an end. We were attracted to Buddhism because Buddhism has always known how to bracket the metaphysical questions and to put
the following of the path first. Christians have a maxim, *lex orandi
lex credendi:* the way you pray should give you the general shape of
what you believe; the way you practice your religion should come
before the ideological form you later cast it in.

I've always liked Buddhism. I like its phenomenalist side, its
desire for a unified conception of reality as something like a flux of
minute events. The self is indissolubly part of that, it is not a spirit
that peers into the world from the outside. The self is itself a cloud
of minute events and as such is part of the world.

In my religious thought I don't try to save our immortal soul
from a wicked world but rather to realize my complete immersion in this one world of ours. I want to get myself into harmony
and into step with the world we've actually got. I don't believe we
should look to any metaphysical order on the far side of experience
nor to any metaphysical subject on the near side of experience but
simply, as it were, to life. We are our lives. If we give ourselves
wholly to our own lives, we'll find the best happiness that we as
human beings are capable of. I strongly oppose religions that ask
us to distance ourselves a bit from life.

**Surely Buddhism has a long record of distancing itself from
life. At times it can appear almost life-denying.**

Buddhism arose at a time when in India, as in Greece, there

was a feeling that the development of a state society required a disciplining of the passions, some distancing of oneself from one's own passions. For me, though, the problem now is rather the other way 'round. Ever since the Romantic movement began, we in the West have been struggling for an integral life of the body, the emotions, and religion. We want to get our values, our feelings, our senses, our bodies all singing from the same hymn sheet.

I'm looking for a more unified selfhood. I like the more integrated, this-worldly humanism that Christianity has always wanted but has very seldom consistently pursued. Evangelicals like to say how horrible secular humanism is, but in Christianity you might say that God is a secular humanist. God becomes man in the world; the human being is the best miniature of what the world is. We shouldn't try to split ourselves into different bits or separate ourselves from the world.

Nowadays I'm a bit of an emotivist. I define religion as cosmic emotion, a feeling for it all, a desire to place oneself in relation to everything: to understand what we are, how we should live, what we can hope for, how we should orient our lives, where we belong in the whole scheme of things. I stress the priority of the passions and would say that our emotional health is the fundamental precondition for personal happiness. This, I know, is rather different from some traditional Buddhist teaching, but I've noticed how many younger Buddhists in the West are not too keen on Buddhist asceticism and don't think that sexual asceticism is necessary for personal happiness at all.

**What do you think precipitated this radical shift in your thinking? Was it the natural scientific understanding of reality that forced you to cast aside old metaphysical certainties?**

Yes, that's right. But I emphasize history nowadays. Our life is not controlled by a timeless order or standards. It is profoundly historical. I've always been historically minded. I've always thought

I could only be the person I am in the particular historical period in which I live. So I now see religious belief systems and practices and values all as historical. We ourselves evolve within the historical process and the standards by which we measure ourselves and our lives. We shouldn't see ourselves as hooked up to an extrahistorical order. For me, critical history is even more important than natural science in requiring us to go over to a thoroughly this-worldly, humanistic kind of religion.

**In *Emptiness and Brightness* you speak of the need for a totally fresh start in what you call "pure religious thinking." You argue that it is the responsibility of each person to take on the task of thinking for themselves in a new religious way.**

My correspondence indicates to me that almost all people of my generation and younger are aware that their whole lives are spent in a personal religious quest. People feel the need to begin all over again. I think we are becoming detraditionalized very quickly. I now feel that we need a religious version of the scientific method.

I'll put it this way: the only religious convictions that are of any value to you are ones you have formulated yourself and worked out and tested in your own life and in debate with other people. In 1993 I came very close to death, and my own convictions and beliefs were tested. Not only was I going through a very severe period of poor mental health, but I also had a burst cerebral aneurysm. Surgery left me with severe head pain, and for a time it seemed I would never write or work again. I managed to survive that period. But I asked myself afterward how I had got through such an extreme time and how it was I had known moments of great happiness in that period. Out of the self-questioning that began early in 1994, all my later thinking developed. It reflects a complete break with dogmatism and a desire to make a fresh start in the religious life.

**Isn't there a danger that this approach might lead one to become rather self-centered? Christians have always emphasized the importance of being part of the church while Buddhists speak of belonging to the sangha.**

They both stress that religious life must be grounded in a sense of community. I like community, but I'm always afraid of the extent to which religious communities bully and pressure their members into conformity and tend to fall under the control of dominant personalities for whom the religious community is a theater in which they enact their own power fantasies. The Sea of Faith has always tried to be a completely free religious society in which people can debate and argue with each other, develop their vocabulary but also find their own voice, develop their own views. Most religious communities emphasize obedience and deference to religious superiors and vows as if they're trying to stop individuals thinking freely for themselves.

I'd like there to be a much greater degree of religious freedom than we have yet known. I'd like people on the whole to hold fewer dogmatic beliefs. I'd like people to know a lot about the Christian tradition but be largely independent of orthodox Christian religious commitments, for they seem to inhibit thought and stop people from responding spontaneously to life. I'm looking for postdogmatic religion, led by the individual's personal quest, the search for values and practices that really do help us survive when life gets tough.

**What, then, does it mean nowadays to have a religious identity in the traditional sense, to think of oneself as a "Christian" or "Buddhist"?**

I'm keen on religious and political eclecticism. Traditional identities are a bit of a mistake. I don't want to go back to any supposedly pure, original, and exclusive religious identity. From the sixteenth to the nineteenth centuries, it was usually believed that at the beginning of the Christian tradition the faith was pure. So if you went back you'd find that everyone agreed, everyone held a pure and simple form of the faith. What modern historical critical scholarship has shown is that in the New Testament period there was the most appalling jumble of different ideas, out of which something which considered itself orthodoxy did not develop for about four hundred years. There never was an original, pure, primitive identity. Dreams of purity are almost always a complete mistake. I don't see why one shouldn't be highly eclectic. Notice how the most gifted revolutionaries, intellectual and artistic, always know their tradition very well and are quite happy to borrow from the most unexpected places. I approve of the modern religious supermarket and the huge artistic, religious, and cultural wealth that is available to us nowadays to choose from and explore. I want to encourage people to find their own way.

I suppose I am about half Christian and part Jewish. I've always liked Jewish humanism, conviviality, and the tradition of locating religion in the family rather than in a monastic order. I like Buddhism because of its independence and intellectual purity of mind. There is a simplicity and clarity in Buddhist thinking which I approve of. Buddhism is cool, and that coolness is a great relief from Christianity's often overheated personalism. Perhaps a quarter of me is Christian, a quarter Jewish, and a quarter Buddhist, and I don't see why we shouldn't be eclectic nowadays. Our societies are becoming multifaith, and our culture global.

**In your book *Emptiness and Brightness* you propose an "empty radical humanism." What do you mean by that exactly?**

By "humanism" I don't mean that the world is human-shaped and I certainly don't want to deify "man," although I recognize that consciousness develops because the world takes definite shape— and becomes beautiful and bright—only in our language and in our theory. There's a certain sense in which we can't avoid anthropocentrism, but I also want to demythologize our sense of ourselves. I don't want to say that man is the crown of creation. So it's an "empty humanism." Here I refer to the traditional no-self doctrine of the Buddhists, *anattā*—"empty," in the Buddhist philosophical sense of nonmetaphysical, noninflated. I rather like the humanism of respect and even veneration for elderly or weak people that you find among the Jews and the best Christian artists: a humanism of human weakness and compassion, but not heroic.

**You also say in your book that rather than meditating on emptiness, we should discover how to live emptiness as freedom. How does that work in practice?**

The studies I've done on the word "life" and the way it's used in English show that increasingly we want to live life to the full, to commit ourselves to life. That means accepting that we are passing away all the time. The more we pour ourselves out into life, the more we live by passing away. This requires us to be very nonmetaphysical, nondefensive, not holding onto the self but giving ourselves away all the time, taking risks.

What I call "solar living" is living as the sun does or living as a fire does. I like personal magnanimity and generosity rather than the traditional reserve and caution of the Christian who says "Don't touch me!" and shrinks back. In Christian art, the classic image here is that of the risen Christ recoiling from Mary Magdalene and saying, "Don't touch me!" It is that fearful, defensive attitude that I want to get away from. I would like a religion of personal recklessness and generosity.

**The phrase "emptiness and brightness" is reminiscent of the Tibetan Dzogchen teaching that the nature of mind is empty, radiant, and unimpededly responsive. Were you thinking of that?**

No. In my own history it comes from the fact that I'm a highly visual person. I get intense religious and artistic pleasure from the sense of sight every day of my life. I develop enthusiasms for birds, for butterflies, for trees, for geology. The great enrichment of the human apprehension of the world, because of the extent to which we've described what is around us, gives us a very vivid and brilliant sense of the world just through our eyes. That to me is brightness, the sense in which the glowing cosmos takes shape in our seeing of it, covered all over with human language, very finely described, appropriated by us. It is a hard thing to describe. It means for me that the sense of sight is very important in our cosmology and a great source of religious happiness.

I wish there were a better education of the senses in the Western tradition. In the West, education is almost always seen in terms of drilling people into conformity, of repression, of preventing kids from knowing too much about things that we do not want them to know about. I'd like education to be a formation of the senses and in particular of the sense of sight. Perhaps leading to an education of the body, of movement. We haven't yet developed the sort of education that human beings of the future will want.

**Given the sort of resistance you meet from evangelical and conservative Christians, and given the growing forces of fundamentalism in all religions, are you optimistic about the future? Can you see your ideas and those akin to them ever making much headway against a tide that seems to be moving in the opposite direction?**

It's a hard battle to encourage people to develop new religious ways of thinking as an alternative to fundamentalism. The deterioration of my own tradition during my lifetime has been very depressing. When I was young, the Church of England still had some weight and was closely linked with the national culture. Nowadays it's mediocre. The outlook for religion might seem to be poor, but I think there is great need for it.

Even though we are the most privileged and richest human beings there have been so far, in terms of the stability and length of our lives and the cultural resources available to us, we're not as happy as we should be. I'd like to see politics more oriented toward the question of happiness; certainly I'd like to see religion more concerned with making integral, happy people and raising the quality of personal life in our culture.

There is so much talk about power relations, and about economic relations, but there's not enough talk about the quality of personal life and personal happiness. My religious humanism is about trying to invest this life of ours with very high religious value. I think it can be done. I think our best thinkers, people like Nietzsche or D. H. Lawrence, knew that this is what religious thought nowadays should be concerned about. We must press on with that even in difficult times because it is what we need in the long run.

# STUDY AND PRACTICE

## Jeff Hardin talks to Stephen Batchelor

**The theme of the inaugural edition of the *Sati Journal* is the role of study in dharma practice. Do you have any general comments to make about this topic?**

I think that there is a tendency within the Buddhist world, particularly in the West, to see study as merely an inessential adjunct to "practice." This reflects how much of the Western Buddhist community is still carrying the legacy of the 1960s, which was an anti-intellectual, romantic movement that denigrated study and theory in favor of direct experience. It is understandable why that was the case at the time, but I think it is dangerous to unthinkingly perpetuate that view. It risks giving rise to a noncritical discourse which presents the Buddha's teaching in a way that doesn't give sufficient weight to the need for developing a reasoned, coherent account of what Buddhist practice is about. If there happen to be internal contradictions in what one says, that is not seen as being too big a problem—after all, one might shrug, these are "just ideas."

Buddhist tradition, however, has a strong rational and critical thread running through it. When you read the Pali texts, you don't have the impression that the Buddha is a paradox-loving romantic. He is a very skilled dialectician. He argues and reasons with rigor and clarity and has enormous skill in using metaphor. He has a great sensitivity to the power of language and words and how to use them in transformative and often provocative ways. That was

STUDY AND PRACTICE 183

the source of the tradition that gave rise to such figures as Nāgārjuna and other Indian Buddhist thinkers, who developed the critical and rational side of the Buddha's teachings and founded the
different schools of Buddhist philosophy.

Some of the most valuable parts of my own training as a monk
were not in meditation skills but in dialectics, debate, and the rational
analysis of texts. I found that extraordinarily helpful. As long as we
are creatures who use language, we are bound to the principles of
rationality and reason simply in order to make sense. If the Buddhist
community is going to be able to communicate its ideas and values with the wider public, it needs to have a coherent and rational
discourse. I think if we abandon that, we do so at our own peril.

Study is integral to Buddhist practice. I remember a Mongolian
lama called Geshe Ngawang Nyima with whom I studied once. He
was teaching a class on Buddhist logic. Then someone asked him,
"Geshe-la, why do we have to do all this study? Why can't we do
more practice?" And he said, "If you really knew how to study, you
would be practicing." To learn how to think clearly, to express oneself articulately: these are practices of the dharma in themselves.

Moreover, study enables us to enter into a closer relationship
with the tradition. It provides us with a much clearer sense of
where its ideas are coming from and how they are expressed. And
modern scholarship, with its emphasis on historical criticism,
helps us understand how the teachings attributed to the Buddha
are often only intelligible as a critical response to the issues, ideas,
and philosophical views of his time.

**During the Buddha's time study was conducted by oral trans-
mission and today it is conducted through multiple media chan-
nels. Do you think that this has any bearing on the quality or scope
of study?**

No. These are just different ways of storing and retrieving information. Whether a text is written on paper, stored on a com-

puter, or recorded in the neurological structure of your brain, it is always inscribed somewhere. Nonetheless, I am very glad that I memorized as much as I did. I have a considerable database of Buddhist doctrines and definitions of terms that were laid down in my twenties, and they are still accessible—though no doubt age and senility will wipe them out eventually. I find that memorized material is closer to hand. You are that much more intimate with it.

**Do you encourage students to memorize texts?**

No. It is not part of our culture and we are not trained to do it—besides which we have nearly instant access to a vast amount of material through the Internet. Nonetheless, I think it is important for any serious practitioner to memorize the key Buddhist lists, such as the four truths, the eightfold path, the five aggregates, the twelve links of dependent origination, the four foundations of mindfulness, and so on. This is useful both as a memory aid for reading the texts and as providing themes for ongoing reflection and contemplation. I am always rather shocked when I meet a Buddhist teacher who does not seem to have at least internalized these primary doctrines.

**How has study informed your practice historically versus how you use study now to inform your meditation practice?**

My involvement with Buddhism has always had a strong component of study. Much of my first years of training as a monk was taken up with in-depth study of classical Mahayana texts. One of the most intensive studies I did was of the *Bodhicaryāvatāra* by Śāntideva. I spent a year going methodically through that text and a thirteenth-century Tibetan commentary to it with my teacher Geshe Dhargyey. Then I spent the next four years translating it into English. That was a very valuable experience. It enabled me to internalize somebody else's refined understanding of the dharma and to work very closely with it. Since I left the Tibetan tradition, I've not studied quite as systematically as that. In Korea, when I wasn't doing formal Sŏn practice, I spent a lot of time reading the classical Chinese records. In the last twenty years I have devoted myself to reading the *suttas* and *vinaya* of the Pali Canon. I have also started learning Pali—though I am very much an amateur and neophyte. I regret not having learned it when I was in my twenties; once you are past fifty it becomes that much more difficult to master another language.

Study informs my meditation practice by providing it with a clearer framework of meaning and purpose. In order to have meaning, experiences we have in meditation need be translated into some form of concepts and words. If we are practicing Buddhists, then surely we need to be as clear as we can about the Buddhist frameworks of meaning. In its broadest sense, practice involves two parallel processes: those of direct experience and those of conceptual and verbal articulation. These interfuse and interweave, sometimes in ways that are difficult to describe.

In the *Sangīti Sutta,* Sāriputta mentions three kinds of intelligence *(paññā).*[1] It is also a model I learned in the Tibetan tradition. There is intelligence that arises from hearing (*sutamaya paññā*), intelligence that arises from thinking (*cintāmaya paññā*), and intelligence that arises from cultivation or training (*bhāvanāmaya paññā*). In other words, you start by hearing the teachings, thereby acquiring information. But information alone is inadequate. You then have to think about it. You need to reflect upon what you have heard in a way that allows you to internalize it, so that it becomes part of a coherent and consistent view of oneself and the world. But this rational, conceptual exercise is still not enough. Whatever insights and understanding you have gained through such reflection need to be translated into actual felt experience. That is done through *bhāvanā,* cultivating yourself through meditative training so that what began as an idea is brought into being as a lived experience. For example, you hear that all things are impermanent. That is just information. Then you think about the implications. "If I am impermanent, that means I am going to die." "Impermanence" then starts to become a key idea that informs how you make sense of who you are as a person and what kind of world you live in. But it only becomes an existential understanding if you begin to directly experience the impermanence of things for yourself. You realize through mindful awareness that impermanence is a feature of your existence rather than just an idea. By sensitizing yourself over time to this mark of being, it becomes integrated into your sense of who you are. I have always found this to be a useful way of presenting the process of *vipassanā* meditation.

**Do you have any recommendations for a beginner on where to start in using study to inform practice?**

I would suggest that one start straightaway with the *suttas* themselves, rather than later commentarial works. My first exposure to the Pali *suttas* was Bhikkhu Ñāṇamoli's *The Life of the Buddha*. I read this while I was a Tibetan Buddhist monk, and it opened up the world of the Pali Canon for me. It is a marvelous anthology of key canonical texts.

Bhikkhu Bodhi's *In the Buddha's Words* is also an anthology well worth studying.

The problem with any anthology, however, is that it will unavoidably reflect the preferences of the author or the orthodoxy to which he or she belongs, which may not correspond with your own interests and needs. Yet simply to plunge straight into the canon can be rather daunting and bewildering because there is so much material. In my own case, I found the *suttas* that concerned Māra to be particularly helpful, but neither of the anthologies I've mentioned give them much importance. At some point you are probably just going to have to follow your own nose. You need to find those texts that speak to your own condition rather than feel obliged to read those *suttas* that tradition has privileged.

At the beginning it is useful to find a teacher who can help you find your way through this morass of texts. Once you get a toehold into the body of material, you can more easily pursue your study yourself, by looking up related passages where the Buddha or one of his monks expands and elaborates on the theme that engages you. This will require a certain amount of legwork, some of which might lead you up blind alleys, but if you persist, you will find that after a while your study becomes a kind of adventure, which can lead you to remarkable discoveries and insights. If study is to become a practice, then it needs to become an open-ended quest of following your own intuitions. I think that is how it should be. But orthodoxies tend to say, "This is what the Buddha's teachings really mean," then selectively give readings that support the orthodox view. That can be a useful starting point, but if we are really going to get into this material, we have to make it our own.

**You mentioned earlier that you have studied Pali. Do you think that it is important to study the texts in their original languages?**

I'm afraid it is. English translations, no matter how competent the translator, will always leave you one step removed from the original. You will inevitably be subject to the biases of the translator. All translation, as the cliché goes, is interpretation. I realize that most *vipassanā* meditators will baulk at the idea of learning Pali. Particularly in the United States, where few people will have studied a classical language such as Latin or Greek at school and are unlikely to be familiar with any spoken language except English, you will lack the basic learning tools. If, in addition, you run a business and have a family to raise, to start learning Pali from scratch is not going to be easy. I was fortunate that from the age of eight, I studied French and Latin at school. When I was nineteen, I started learning Tibetan.

We are very fortunate in that we have so many different translations of the primary Pali texts available in English. If you are studying a *sutta,* read as many different versions as you can. Don't just rely on one translator. That will allow you to see the different shades of meaning a single word in Pali can possess. Each translator helps you get a sense of the nuances of a given Pali word. Any term in a classical language is unlikely to have an exact, one-to-one equivalent with an English term. Yet the translator is always obliged to select one English word among several possible options. In addition, the chosen English word is very likely to carry associations that the Pali word doesn't. It will have resonances for you as an English speaker that the Pali word may not have for a Pali reader.

**Do you see a movement among contemporary Western Vipassana teachers or other contemporary Buddhist teachers toward advocating study to their students?**

Well, some do, and some don't. But I wouldn't say that I see a movement. In some of the "dedicated practitioner" programs offered by Vipassana centers there is a recognition that to understand the dharma you need to do more than just become proficient in mindfulness, so a certain emphasis is given to gaining some knowledge of the traditional texts. But I still have the impression that study and thinking are seen as something optional, an adjunct to what really counts, that is, meditation. On the other hand, I don't see why meditators should be forced to study Pali texts if that doesn't suit their temperament or fit with their way of incorporating their practices into their lives.

There is still this common idea that texts only provide concepts and what really matters is your own experience. This may be true to a point. But "experience" is a vague and tricky term. Your experience might be nothing more than your own highly subjective and idiosyncratic take on something. My experience of meditation has always served as a conversation partner with my knowledge of the textual tradition. I see the two as having an interactive relationship. I would certainly not just trust my experience alone. I would always want to check it against the wisdom of the tradition. But I wouldn't want to be slavishly devoted to the authority of a textual tradition without it having a connection to my own life. In other words, dharma practice is an ongoing conversation, even an argument, with tradition. You meditate, you do retreats, then you go back to the texts and reflect further on their meaning. That helps inform, clarify, and integrate your experiences so that when you return to the cushion, you bring that knowledge of the tradition with you in a subliminal way.

**Do you encourage the study of the traditional commentaries? And what about more contemporary writings on Buddhism?**

I don't believe that any one commentarial tradition has the final word on the meaning of the primary canonical texts. I am not a Theravādin, and I do not hold Buddhaghosa's commentaries in any particular esteem. I have been influenced in this regard by the writings of the late Ñāṇavīra Thera. I think he is an important modern interpreter of the Pali *suttas*. But he is very critical of the traditional commentaries, which he says you should unlearn as fast as possible. That might be going a little too far, but I think he has a point.

There is also much to be learned from such scholars as Richard Gombrich, who are not necessarily practicing Buddhists but have made a lifelong study of the canonical texts using Western historical-critical methods. Gombrich and others seek to locate the Buddha's *suttas* in the context of fifth century BCE India, where they were taught. I feel this is crucial for our understanding of the dharma. The Buddha did not teach in a vacuum or from some transcendental perspective, but in the context of a culture, in response to particular beliefs held at the time, in dialogue with people from a specific kind of society. Modern scholarship is now able to tell us a great deal about the kind of world in which the Buddha worked.

**What are some pitfalls of combining study with meditation practice?**

Well, I suppose you could get carried away and put off your meditation because you are more fascinated with some technical problem in Pali grammar. But if your approach to the dharma involves a personal commitment, and you keep your broader goals in perspective, you will be fine. If you have a good teacher and a supportive community, that should be sufficient to prevent you from becoming either a blinkered meditator or a neurotic scholar.

**Can study lead to discursive thinking and *papañca* [mental proliferation]?**

You mean meditation can't? Scholar and meditator alike have to be alert to their own tendencies to an unnecessary proliferation of thoughts. I don't think that study is more or less prone to these things than meditation. You can sit in meditation while your mind wanders all over the place, generating all sorts of fantastical theories and stories. This kind of objection to study again reflects the anti-intellectual, romantic bias of many students of Buddhism. We really have to get over that and try to reach a more integrated notion of study-practice rather than constantly being suspicious that study is going to take us away from the path. Why don't we worry that meditation might take us away from the path? There are just as many pitfalls in practicing meditation; we can end up in all kinds of weird and self-deluding states. Study and careful reflection, however, can serve as a useful safeguard against such perils.

**In your recent book *Confession of a Buddhist Atheist* you give a secular interpretation of the life of the Buddha as represented in the Pali *suttas* that differs from the traditional, more religious or mythological approach that has been taught historically. How do you think that your pragmatic approach will affect how Western students study and practice the dharma?**

Well, it may have no effect at all. That depends on whether students are willing to take my writing seriously. For myself, I have found that the more human the Buddha becomes, the more his teachings connect to experience in the real world. The Buddha's life is in itself a teaching of the dharma. It shows us how the Buddha addressed the specific situations of his sociopolitical world. It demonstrates how he was not indifferent to the plight of that world. He was constantly involved with people—not just his monks but powerful rulers, wealthy merchants, religious opponents, simple farmers, his ambitious relatives. He had to do whatever was necessary to ensure the survival of his teachings and community. The *suttas* show us how the Buddha taught not just by words but by his actions. The Buddha struggled with the same sort of issues and conflicts much as we do. He was beset by all manner of crises, threats, scandals, and compromises.

By humanizing the Buddha, one humanizes the dharma. This does not mean, however, that one should reject the well-known mythic accounts of his life. The story of Prince Siddhattha growing up in his palace and seeing the four sights is a powerful universal myth that speaks to the core existential dilemma of humankind. But it says nothing about Gotama's life as the eldest son of a local oligarch in a failing republic in fifth century BCE Kosala. As long as we don't confuse myth with history, we can appreciate the value of both.

As a Westerner, I am formed both by a secular tradition that values historicity and a religious tradition where the narrative of Jesus's life plays a central role in his message. You cannot separate the teachings of Jesus in the Gospels from the drama of his life. The life is the teaching. The same is true of much the Old Testament as well. But that narrative dimension has never been given much attention in Buddhism. You have the legend of how Gotama became the Buddha, then you have the dharma. After the awakening, you hear about a number of disconnected episodes, whose main purpose is to set the scene for a teaching, and finally the Buddha dies in Kusinārā. I wonder if this is one of the reasons why Buddhism has often tended toward abstraction, transcendence, and an indifference to the affairs of the world. So in one way, what I am doing in this book is giving a historically conscious, Judeo-Christian reading of the Buddha's life. I am searching for a gospel-like narrative that can weave the threads of teaching together with those of the life. My quest for the historical Buddha has served to ground his teaching in the world. The model of the Buddha's life also challenges me to apply the dharma in the social, economic, political, and religious context in which we live. It is an unapologetically pragmatic and secular approach. If Buddhists choose to model their lives on the liberated *arahant*—or the idealized Mahayana bodhisattva, for that matter—rather than follow the example of Gotama, then I wonder how Buddhism will find a compelling voice to address the pressing issues of our world today. That is important. I don't want Buddhism to become ghettoized.

**What do you mean by "ghettoized"?**

I mean you get lots of Buddhist groups that are absorbed in what they are doing but have relatively little interaction with the wider world of which they are a part. To some extent this is inevitable with any new religious movement. We are still working toward a Western Buddhist language and identity, to a time when Buddhists will no longer be perceived as some sort of alien presence. We have some way to go before the average person walking down the street doesn't do a second take when a non-Asian like myself announces that he is a Buddhist.

**In our culture, in addition to Christianity we have the religion of psychology. What do you think of the impact of Western psychology on Buddhism in America?**

If you look at how Buddhism has entered into different cultures in the past, it has tended to do so by finding points of common interest within the new host culture. In the case of China, for example, Buddhism attracted Taoists, who had an interest in meditation. In the secular West, it is hardly surprising that Buddhism attracts those interested in psychology. The Buddhist analysis of the causes of suffering, for example, immediately strikes us as psychologically astute. But it is a two-way process. As Buddhist teachers recognize the interest among psychologists and therapists, they tend to highlight the psychological aspects of the dharma, more so than would be the case when teaching in traditional Asian societies. In contrast, it would be alarming if Buddhism in the West were to be overdetermined by psychological discourse and Buddhism evolved into a kind of spiritual psychotherapy. That would be far too reductive. The practice of the dharma embraces the totality of the eightfold path. It is an integral way of life that balances philosophical insight, ethical commitment, right livelihood, spiritual discipline, and the forming of community. To overemphasize its psychological dimension risks losing sight of its complex reality as a culture that addresses every aspect of human need.

**How can we know which parts of the Brahmanical tradition the Buddha accepted and which he rejected?**

It is very important that we understand the Buddha's teachings in the context of his times. And there is plenty of material in the canon where the Buddha seems to accept elements of traditional Indian belief. Yet I must confess that what I find least appealing and helpful in Buddhism are precisely those elements it shares with Hinduism—rebirth, karma as a scheme of moral bookkeeping, the goal of freeing oneself from the cycle of birth and death, the idea that there is a transcendent consciousness or absolute that underpins phenomenal experience. Not only do these ideas not speak to me, they often seem to obscure what was truly original and distinctive in what the Buddha taught: the principle of conditioned arising, the four noble truths, mindful awareness of phenomenal experience, and the emphasis on self-reliance. I admit that my approach is subjective. I am concerned with those teachings and texts that address my condition as a human being here and now and provide an inspiring and practical framework for living in this world.

I don't believe the Buddha had a detailed metaphysical theory that he sought to impose on the world irrespective of whom he was addressing. He was a situationalist. His teachings were given to specific people in specific situations at specific times in their lives. He considered himself a physician, and his dharma a medicine. He prescribed different treatments to different people in different situations. That is the great message of the Buddha's teaching. It is not dogmatic or doctrinaire but therapeutic and pragmatic. Of course, I am following my own intuitions as to what is universal in his vision of what human life could be. I am not interested in those teachings that are only intelligible to those who uphold an Indian worldview. I doubt Buddhism will get very far in the modern world if one insists that to really understand and practice it you have first to embrace the cosmology of ancient India. Such an insistence is likely to condemn Buddhism to marginality. Nor do I believe that science will one day finally vindicate these dogmas. That is clutching at straws. Perhaps the Buddha did believe in some of these things. I don't find that problematic—like all people he was a product of his time, and the teachings he gave were embedded to some degree in the context of his Indian culture. But I don't think those beliefs are what is really universal and liberating about the Buddha's dharma.

# AFTER BUDDHISM

Chris Talbott talks to Stephen Batchelor

**With proper caveats about speculation, in *After Buddhism* you go after a historical Buddha—a real, if extraordinary, flesh-and-blood person. You do this by careful research of the texts and commentaries, and also by creating, based on that research, historical sketches of several other people who were his contemporaries. Some we know, such as Ānanda; others we recall from reading texts, such as King Pasenadi; and others, such as Mahānāma, we might pass by without much thought in the texts; also wanderers or ascetics that the Buddha encounters, such as Vacchagotta. You've carefully figured out all the kinship, political, and other relationships these people have to the Buddha. What do you try to accomplish with that?**

I've been working on trying to reconstruct the Buddha's life and social-political-economic world for more than ten years now. This project actually started out as the foundation for a screenplay. I recall once when reading the *Discourse on the Monuments to the Dharma,*[1] which describes the final meeting between King Pasenadi and Gotama, I had this odd experience of suddenly seeing how the whole life held together, almost like your life passing before your eyes. That *sutta* provided me with the missing link, and suddenly I figured out how it all worked. Since then I've been trying to bolster that understanding by getting more and more data. The screenplay never came to anything. Then I worked on a

six-part TV miniseries with the same material; that didn't go anywhere. In between doing those two things, I wrote it as a novel: the
life of the Buddha from the point of view of Ānanda, as he recalls it
on the eve of the First Council. That took me a year or more; that
didn't go anywhere either. Nobody wanted to publish it.

The next attempt was in my book *Confession of a Buddhist Atheist,* where the second part of the book interweaves a travelogue
through modern-day India, a pilgrimage as it were, with a recon-
struction of the life. The attempt in this new book is by far the
most detailed and, I think, probably the most assured reading.

The great difference is that this version relies on the work of
W. W. Rockhill. Rockhill was an American diplomat who lived in
China in the nineteenth century, a linguistic genius—he must
have been the first American to know Tibetan; he also produced a
Chinese-English dictionary. And in 1884 he published a life of the
Buddha according to the Tibetan canon. It draws from material of
equivalent antiquity to that of the Pali Canon, from a source called
the *Mūlasarvāstivāda Vinaya.* He went through it in the 1870s and
pulled out of it a story that is almost identical to the story that I re-
constructed from the Pali materials. Somewhat embarrassingly, I
hadn't actually read Rockhill until quite recently. I didn't think the
Tibetan material would be relevant. But I was wrong. The Tibetan
*Vinaya,* from the *Mūlasarvāstivāda* school, gives us the same story,
with the same characters, and the same relationships. The two
versions don't agree in every detail, but they're remarkably similar.
So we actually have two independent sources, pretty much, that
seem to be referring to a common source, that must have predated
both, that would go back I think very close to the Buddha's time.
So all of that work, in a sense, has come to fruition in this book.

**Was Rockhill familiar with the Pali Canon?**

He was a polymath. He refers to Sanskrit sources, to Pali
sources; how well he knew those languages, I don't know. I don't

think he knew the Pali Canon in detail. Certainly none of that had been translated or published in his lifetime. If he had known about it, it would have been through his own reading of the Pali, but judging by his footnotes, he doesn't seem to have much sense of it. So he was working independently.

**It's remarkable that we have two seemingly independent sources that agree so well.**

Yes, very remarkable, and I'm amazed nobody else has spotted that. G. P. Malalasekera, whom I refer to in my book, quotes Rockhill quite a lot, actually, but he never really draws together all the threads in a way that allows a coherent narrative to unfold. So I'm very excited about the fact that at this distance in time we do seem to have far more material than anyone might have guessed. The trouble of course is that all of these stories are scattered through the discourses and the *Vinaya*. So when you find yourself reading through the *Majjhima Nikāya,* for example, you simply don't get a sense of who these people are. It takes a long time to pick out all the little fragments and reassemble them. What's amazing is that these characterizations are always consistent. Even if a person appears only half a dozen times in the canon, that person will appear in a consistent guise on each occasion. Which to me suggests that there must at one time have been a single, freestanding account, probably retained orally, that actually told the story of the Buddha's life. That then got lost in its entirety, leaving only disconnected fragments in the canon.

**The theme for your analysis of the teachings might be that the Buddha was not a metaphysician but more of a physician, a healer, that his method was pragmatic, ethical, and philosophical. He was helping us see what to *do* rather than what to *believe*. You say he wanted "a task-based ethics rather than a truth-based metaphysics." You say, "The point of the doctrine is not to provide a true account of reality but an effective framework for the performance of a task." Talk about that if you will.**

Well, one obvious value is that at a single stroke, we can dispense with having to worry about ancient Indian cosmology and metaphysics. It's no longer a question of being either pro or contra the doctrine of reincarnation, let's say. Such metaphysical claims no longer have significance. It's as simple as that. It also allows us to go back to that other quote that I used to open, I think, chapter 11, where the Buddha says, "I do not dispute with the world; the world disputes with me. What the wise in the world would agree upon as existing, I too say that exists. What the wise in the world agree upon as nonexisting, I too say that does not exist."[2] Now that's a powerful statement, and it supports my whole approach very well. (That's why I quote it!) But to me it shows quite explicitly that the Buddha's not actually interested in getting his view of reality correct. That's not what he's into. Whereas Buddhism, from the *Abhidhamma* on, has more or less committed itself to that sort of approach. In other words, enlightenment becomes a cognitive understanding of the true nature of reality. The person who's got that, who's arrived at it through meditation, that's the person we consider enlightened, and if somebody's account of the nature of reality doesn't agree with that, then they're not enlightened. So in other words, the whole discourse around enlightenment becomes about being cognitively correct or incorrect. The whole way in which Buddhist epistemology developed, certainly in India in the early centuries CE, was very much down that track. It didn't question that assumption.

By approaching the dharma as a task-based ethics, we don't have to deal with that anymore. It's no longer relevant to get into a battle with beliefs, because beliefs, one way or another, are not terribly significant, and we kind of miss the point. We get sidetracked, much as the Buddha said in the parable of the arrow, where the person just endlessly discusses what kind of arrow it was, what kind of bow it was, what kind of person shot it.[3] Other texts too seem to be clear that the approach of the dharma is entirely pragmatic and therapeutic and ethical. That's what it's all about. And somehow that idea got lost, as Buddhism mutated into a metaphysical religious system dominated by people who claimed to know "the truth."

**Your analysis of the texts of the Pali Canon uncovers what seem to be a lot of contradictions in how the teachings are portrayed. To uncover the historical Buddha, you have to peel away a lot of later additions. Your hypothesis is that these were added later to bolster Buddhism in its competition with other Indian traditions, such as Brahmanism and Jainism. You quote the scholar Johannes Bronkhorst as saying how "the brahmins colonized the past." You even note that the contradictions help us uncover what might have been there before those additions. Talk about this and what it means to us today.**

I doubt that a group of monks actually sat down around a table and said, "OK, how are we going to deal with all this material?" I've a feeling that what happened probably felt quite organic to the people who were doing it. Much in the same way as what we're doing here! People read this book that I've written, and many of those who are acculturated in the West and have a secular humanist background like me will say, "Oh, of course." But we're no different from those people who did the original shape-changing all that time ago. I think this is just how the dharma moves from one culture to another.

So I don't want to make a case that the earlier generations got it all wrong and now we clever Westerners have got it right. I don't think that's true. I can't rule out that in another two or three hundred years *we'll* be seen as just a bunch of guys in a smoke-filled room configuring Buddhism to our liking.

But I don't think that is how it works. If the texts speak to you—not in an intellectual way, but actually speak to your human condition—you enter into a dialogue with the texts. In the course of that dialogue, you start to argue with the text. You start to notice the conflicting voices. You start to prefer certain voices that seem to be speaking to you more truly, more honestly, more usefully, and they're the ones you privilege. And every Buddhist tradition, I think, has done something very similar. No Buddhist tradition gives equal weight to every word in the canon. It's impossible. Every tradition is based on a relatively small percentage of the overall canonical material, upon which it bases and it builds its own particular orthodoxy.

We do have certain advantages—easy access to materials through the Internet—that make us able to collate this data much more easily than in the past. But I still feel the basic process is a slow, organic adaptation that occurs through an ongoing dialogue and conversation with the texts themselves.

Some will say, "Batchelor is just cherry-picking the bits he likes." He just selects the passages that agree with his secular worldview and ignores everything else. That's a very common criticism, and I think it's a good criticism. That's why, at the beginning of the book I try to lay out a hermeneutic strategy.

It's clear that if my sole criterion for valuing a text is because I like it, because it doesn't conflict with my view of the world, that would be a very poor way of constructing a theological thesis, as it were. So I try to identify what are the distinctive elements in the Buddha's teaching that you can't derive from other sources. I also lay out that the *suttas* probably have the most authority, then the *Vinaya*, and then commentaries. Sometimes I have to deal with material that I might prefer to say, "Oh, this must be something that was added later." That's the easy way out of a problem, but if that doesn't agree with the criteria that I've established, then I have to keep it in.

**You trace a line of thought about the rejection of views in the *Book of Eights*, a very old text, through Nāgārjuna's teachings cen-**

turies later on emptiness, and finally to the Korean Sŏn teachings about "great doubt." Walk us through the connections and then how this understanding might help us to practice today.

I do feel that this is very much another aspect of the Buddha's suspicion of metaphysics. In other words, to adopt a position that in Western philosophy we would call skepticism. Now skepticism, in the early Greek Pyrrhonian sense, simply meant to always be inquiring, to not assume that there was a final end to your inquiry, and to valorize the quality of inquiry as a perspective, a sensibility that somehow underpins your whole practice. We see this in the *Book of Eights* (*Aṭṭhakavagga*):[4] it's very explicit. And, as you point out, it also resurfaces in Nāgārjuna, but it resurfaces in Nāgārjuna by way of the *Discourse to Kaccānagotta*,[5] which again I make into a rather important *sutta* in my own presentation. It's about finding a middle way that is not premised on the dualism of *being* or *non-being*, *it is* or *it is not*. Nāgārjuna then takes that starting point and develops his whole philosophy of emptiness. Likewise in Chan or Sŏn Buddhism, we have this very persistent emphasis on questioning, perplexity, or doubt.

In terms of its practice this kind of questioning unavoidably entails suspending whether something either is or is not the case. If you ask "Where is Boston?" and you don't have a clue where Boston is, you can't say that it's in Massachusetts or it's not in Massachusetts—you just don't know. So you're put into a quandary where you simply hold the quality of questioning as a value in its own right. That, I feel, is quite compatible with the suspension of metaphysical belief; it's also compatible with a kind of ongoing skepticism, inquiry, and examination of the condition you're in, without being prejudiced with any particular habits, views, or opinions that you might have formed. It's about keeping a very open mind concerning yourself, not with what is right or wrong, true or false, but with what is the most skillful, compassionate way to respond to this condition I find myself in here and now. It's not having a sort of a game plan that is already encoded in your belief system that you somehow just apply.

**So we don't have to wait until we feel like we have a perfectly coherent intellectual understanding of everything before we proceed to practice.**

Well, if it were, you'd never get round to practicing: that's the problem. Orthodoxies, of course, like to suggest that that's the case. That until you've understood the Buddha's teaching—and usually that's code for "until you've understood our school's particular interpretation of the Buddha's teaching"—you don't have any authority that qualifies you as someone who can make any claims on your own behalf. It's also political: claiming to have insight into an ultimate metaphysical truth is how representatives of a given orthodoxy maintain their authority over the unenlightened. So it also has a knock-on effect on the hierarchies and the political structures that Buddhism has evolved. You can't separate metaphysics from issues of control and power.

**To sum up about the value of this analysis for those of us practicing today, talk about the recasting of the four noble truths as the four great tasks. Why do you think that is closer to what the Buddha had in mind, and why is it helpful to us today? What would we be doing differently?**

Well, in some ways you may not be doing much different at all in terms of your actual day-to-day practice. But you will be operating from a different set of assumptions. I feel that in many ways each of the tasks is obviously a practice. But you'll find that the practice, for example, of comprehending *dukkha,* or embracing life, as you might put it more colloquially, is an umbrella term that covers most Buddhist practices, from just a simple practice of mindfulness, a practice of philosophical inquiry in Mādhyamaka

Buddhism, a practice of Sŏn. They're all ways of embracing *duk-kha,* of coming to terms with the condition that we are in.

What I find strange is that what is considered to be the first discourse, the *Dhammacakkappavattana Sutta,* does in fact conclude with this "fully knowing *dukkha,* letting go of craving," etcetera. But that language and that model somehow got lost. You find very, very few references in the canon, in the *suttas,* to that sort of terminology. So I've tried to restore that terminology and paradigm.

In my own practice, I find it makes a big difference. I find that mindfulness and, let's say, Sŏn practice no longer have to be thought of as being in any way in competition with one another. They're just different ways of getting a handle on life. It somehow opens up a much more pluralistic kind of practice.

Take *pariññā,* which I translate as "comprehend"; quite literally, *pari* means "around" or "about." It means a kind of awareness that tries to look at things from as many different angles as possible. It's a comprehensive kind of attention rather than one that focuses on a single point. That is something that one cultivates over the course of one's life. It leads into another rapport, another relationship with life as a whole, and that relationship in itself, I feel, begins to erode the habitual patterns of activity which commit you to a particular stance centered around "me": getting what I want and getting rid of what I don't like, a governing perspective that determines how most people, all people perhaps, lead their lives.

So we begin to see that there's a very intimate connection between embracing the condition we're in—which of course includes our reactivity, that's part of our *dukkha*—and having that embrace morph into a kind of release, which sounds paradoxical. But the more we embrace and open our hearts and minds in the deeper sense, the more that exposes the pettiness of our reactivity. We cease to be so much in thrall to it. It begins to fade away of its own accord, until we arrive at moments where we suddenly realize "Oh, well—that's stopped!" That reactivity's no longer such a dominant force, as it tends to be. We've opened up a kind of clearing, a space within, in which we're no longer determined or conditioned by reactivity. That is nirvana. It's from that nirvanic experience that new possibilities open up.

So what I've done is taken the four noble truths and torqued them into another shape. This reconfiguration enables us to revise the standard understanding of causality that underpins them. So instead of seeing craving as the cause of suffering, and the noble eightfold path as what leads to the end of suffering, I've turned that on its head. The experience of *dukkha* is actually what gives rise to reactivity. And the experience of nirvana is what allows the possibility of another way of life in this world.

Now there's plenty of material in the canon that supports that kind of reading, but orthodoxies, whether they're Theravāda, Zen, or Tibetan or whatever, have all more or less opted—in perfectly good faith—for the four noble truths model with its twofold causality built in.

So in offering a critique of the traditional view of the "operating system" of the four noble truths, I'm basically attempting to rewrite the operating system of the dharma itself, at least, as it's been widely taught up to now. This is not going to go down terribly well, I suspect. But it's very much the outcome or the fruition of all of the work and study I've been doing for the last forty-odd years. To me it's an entirely natural outcome from what I've been doing.

That's basically what *After Buddhism* is trying to do. It's trying to give that perspective the kind of canonical grounding that I feel would be necessary to be able to say, "This is another way in which we can practice the Buddhadharma." It has as much canonical

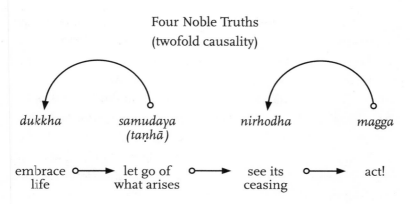

Four Noble Truths
(twofold causality)

dukkha          samudaya              nirhodha              magga
                (taṇhā)

embrace ○——▶ let go of ○——▶ see its ○——▶ act!
life             what arises            ceasing

Four Great Tasks

Four noble truths or four great tasks?

authority, I would argue, as that of the four noble truths in the standard kind of orthodox views that we're familiar with.

**Do we need a whole new language game, to borrow the idea from Wittgenstein, whom you quote a few times?**

I agree with you. I think Wittgenstein's idea of the language game is exactly what is evolving in the Western dharma world. And I think in these sorts of conversations, books, discussions, and debates—although people get very hot under the collar about maintaining their position or their point—what's actually going on, if we step back a bit, is the emergence of an idiom. We're struggling and groping to find a language that speaks English rather than what has been called "Bunglish" or "Buddhist Hybrid English," which is just jargon, really. This kind of speech might work perfectly well while you're doing a retreat at a Buddhist center, but it sounds like gobbledygook when you go back home and try to explain to your family. So we do need to find a language that is true to the tradition and the original discourses but is also current in our own lexicon, in our own way of speaking in the twenty-first century. That's not easy. How exactly it will play out, we don't know. But yes, we're trying to develop another language.

**Would you encourage more people to study the texts themselves? Your insights appear to make this seem more fruitful for more people; it provides a wonderful set of analytical tools, in a way. How would people go about this?**

Whatever practice you're doing, you cannot but be doing that in the framework of certain assumptions, ideas, preferences, and beliefs. You can't get round that. You're not a machine. You're a philosophical being. So to deepen one's practice I think you can benefit enormously from a study of the canonical texts. We owe an extraordinary debt of gratitude to people all the way from T. W. and Caroline Rhys Davids, right through to Bhikkhu Bodhi and Ajahn Thanissaro today, for the incredible work they've done. It makes available a body of material that otherwise would be inaccessible to anyone apart from specialists in Pali, Sanskrit, and Chinese.

**Why do you prefer "the sublime" to "the sacred"?**

The background here is to remember that I was not brought up in a Christian family. I never identified as a Christian. I was brought up in a humanist, nontheistic world. I was educated in that world. And I've never really been able to make much sense of words like "God" or "the sacred." The same goes for "the absolute" or "the non-dual," or other terms borrowed from Vedanta. That language doesn't speak to me. And I'm somewhat uncomfortable when Buddhists start employing these terms. It seems to be a last-ditch attempt to keep God in the picture somewhere, even though we don't call it God. I think we have to go beyond God language altogether. There is a dimension of our experience—certainly as soon as we start doing mindfulness practice—that opens up a kind of humility within ourselves with regard to the overwhelming experience of finding ourselves as this little brief human being in a vast universe, and that actually brings our minds to a stop. We're simply thrown into a condition of awe or wonder. My sense is that Buddhism is not concerned at all with trying to say what that overwhelming sense of awe or wonder is about. What it's interested in doing is cultivating certain forms of practice that actually make us more receptive to that kind of experience.

Again I would go back to the same sources, the *Book of Eights,* the suspicion of "is" and "is not," the middle way between eternalism and nihilism, and the kind of questioning you find in Sŏn, of simply being able to enter the world in an open-minded, questioning kind of way.

Some of the Romantic poets did something somewhat similar. Coleridge, for example, talked of "the sublime" as the suspension of the powers of comparison.[6] It's about learning to drop certain habits of mind that cause our experience of ourselves in the world to be very narrow, limited, self-interested, and driven by our wants and our dislikes. I think what Buddhist practice does is dismantle, or erode, that whole reactive strategy. One of the ways it does it is by encouraging us, as much as we can, to live in a state of questioning and inquiry. If that questioning and inquiry operate within the frame of a therapeutic practice, then that, I think, allows them to become more emotionally and bodily embedded in experiences that poets would call "the sublime."

Now if people are comfortable with words like "sacred" and so on, I don't have a big issue with that. It just doesn't work in my case. But I find the notion of the sublime a very helpful one. Admittedly in our culture it becomes somewhat misused. But if we go back to its sources, it is a conveniently nontheological term that doesn't have the whiff of God about it, even though some theologians have tried to turn it into a theology (in Rudolf Otto's *The Idea of the Holy,* for example). But it allows us to come to an understanding of our experience in which the narrowness of our self-perspective is gone. The openness to the wonder of experience, if anything, is greatly enhanced. We can locate that experience as a part of the experience of nirvana, the unconditioned, the deathless, which opens up to a way of life, the eightfold path. And if we use the language of the sublime, it also allows us, I think, to valorize imagination and creativity as part of the process. It's an experience that actually can become a turning point in how you express yourself in the world, of how you relate to other people, of how you write poetry or music or art. That, to me, is a bit that is often missing in Buddhism—how does Buddhism understand the interface between contemplative experience and the making of art, poetry, or music? By bringing in notions of the sublime, as opposed to the sacred, you keep the experience as an aspect of our own secular tradition that is very intimately involved with imagination and creativity.

So I guess I'm confessing at this point that my approach to the dharma is not that of a scientist or a technologist, but more that of a poet or an artist. I also start feeling uncomfortable when I hear claims such as "Buddhism is a science of the mind." I think that's going off in the wrong direction. I'm looking for a vision, a framework of how to live my life that will valorize creativity, imagination, poetry, and beauty. And the term that I currently use is "the everyday sublime." "Everyday," because I feel the sublime is not reducible to magnificent sunsets and vast views of the Himalayas. If you look carefully and mindfully at the tiniest detail of what's going on, that is just as awe inspiring as the stars in the night sky. When you look at a leaf or a blade of grass—very Sŏn, I suppose—that's the sublime. The sublime has to be here and now. Your American artist Barnett Newman wrote an essay in the 1960s titled "The Sublime Is Now." That is a phrase I found very helpful and it seems to me very central to the experience of mindfulness or Sŏn practice.

We first heard some of the ideas in this book at the conference on secular Buddhism at the Barre Center for Buddhist Studies in 2013. Have your feelings about the word "secular" changed?

To be honest, in the writing of this book I've become a little more cautious in my use of the word "secular." I don't really know whether it's so helpful to frame this argument in terms of whether it's secular or religious, to get into that debate. I think it is an important debate, but I don't want to sideline what I think is far more important: whether we think of ourselves in terms of being a secular or a religious Buddhist, we are involved in a much broader process than that of our own self-interest. We find ourselves as part of a growing community that is practicing similar values, with great sincerity—even though we may not agree with each other all the time—and the consequence of that will be the emergence of a culture. I think that such a "culture of awakening" has been evolving now for the last twenty or thirty years, at least. There are certain signal moments, such as the publication of *Tricycle* magazine, for example, which broke the mold of the parochial Buddhist newsletters that used to be all you could get. Suddenly you have a magazine that actually includes everybody, and is nondenominational.

But the reason I want to emphasize culture is to get outside this idea that what we have to do is to create another version of the Buddhist religion. Can we imagine a society and a practice that doesn't carry any of the conventional tropes of religion? I find it dispiriting that some teachers still claim that "you can't be a Buddhist unless you believe in reincarnation."

If we can get round that kind of thinking altogether, and bring people together into a framework of value, meaning, purpose, and practice, it starts generating other possibilities of human culture. That's something I'm very passionate about. And I'd far rather expend my energies working toward such a vision than setting up some sort of institution or defining things in a more narrow way.

# 5

# ART AND IMAGINATION

# A Convenient Fiction

Imagine returning to your desk to continue writing a letter in which you were interrupted in the middle of a word, having typed, say, *e-n-i*, leaving *g-m-a* still to be completed.

Any typist knows how one writes blocks of words or clusters of thoughts without being aware of the individual letters (unless uncertain of the spelling). Even when my wife calls me with some urgency in her voice, I finish at least the word—more likely the sentence (it usually only takes a few seconds) before getting up to do what she asks. But to be pulled away from a letter in the *middle of a word* suggests a sudden, unexpected, and shocking interruption: like a stranger abruptly appearing unannounced in the room, a scream, a gunshot from a bedroom upstairs.

I did not know Gert Bastian and Petra Kelly well. I met them only twice: once with Arnie Kotler, our common friend and publisher, over a dinner of intense, animated discussion at an outdoor café on the Kurfürstendamm in Berlin, then again, briefly, the following afternoon at a Buddhist conference we were attending in the city. Only the dates make the meetings significant: Saturday, September 26, and Sunday, September 27, 1992. Gert and Petra left Berlin the following Wednesday afternoon to arrive home in Bonn late that night. The next morning they were both lying dead from gunshot wounds.

According to official reports, in the early hours of the morn-

214 ART AND IMAGINATION

ing, halfway through typing the word *müssen* in a letter to his lawyer, Gert Bastian was abruptly wrenched away from his typewriter,
either by the compulsion to kill his lover and companion of the
past nine years and then shoot himself, or by the sudden urge
to go upstairs to her bedside to carry out a suicide pact. He took
his twin-barreled .38-caliber derringer pistol, shot her in the left
temple, and then shot himself in the crown of his head. The badly
decomposed bodies were discovered by police nearly three weeks
later on Monday, October 19. The electric typewriter was still hum-
ming. Powder burns were found on Gert's hand. "Murder by third
parties," declared the Bonn prosecutor's office the next day, "is
certainly excluded."

In the café on the Kurfürstendamm, Petra and I ordered tor-
tellini, Arnie a salad, and Gert a potato broth. Petra discoursed
incessantly on her current passions, with Gert injecting brief supportive comments in his softly caring voice. She told us of a film
they had seen that afternoon on the effects of radiation on the
children of Chernobyl; she predicted that the extreme Right would
win seats in the Bundestag at the next election; she admired the
sweet mournful voice of a Vietnamese nun we had heard sing that
morning; she bemoaned the fact that the principles of Green politics seemed incompatible with the holding of power. Her eyes
were like animated emeralds, glittering from the dark brown pools
that encircled them.

I need to be careful, for already I find my recollections of our
meeting blurred and tainted by the media's explanations for their
deaths. "A deeply exhausted and increasingly neurotic Petra Kelly
held on tightly in a suffocating symbiosis with the aged general,"
wrote *Der Spiegel*. Such snippets combine to form a perception in
the public eye that seems to make sense of what happened. As we
ate dinner I did not know that Gert was a former major general.
In fact, I knew nothing about him or their relationship. I was in-

terested only in meeting Petra. Later that night, I dictated my impressions of the day into a tape recorder. "She's a very intense, passionate, obsessed woman," I said. "Her husband/friend/partner is a very sweet, elderly man. They are both very committed and inspiring."

History is a selection of memories credibly arranged in chronological order. The episodes of which it is formed are, as Voltaire noted, convenient fictions. The evidence—powder burns, increasing neurosis, despair about Germany's future, political marginalization—is structured to assure both author and reader alike that things really did happen in the way they have been described. No matter how Gert and Petra died, their lives are now history. They have joined those mute, powerless faces about whom endless stories can be spun but who can never answer back.

As the evening grew late a chill breeze wafted up the Kurfürstendamm. I doubted whether Petra would ever pause long enough for me to ask the question that burned on my lips. As part of my research into a book on Buddhism in Europe (*The Awakening of the West*), I wanted to hear her account of the Dalai Lama's brief stopover in Berlin in December 1989 on his way to receive the Nobel Peace Prize in Oslo. I seized a rare gap in the rush of syllables.

She and Gert had arranged the visit, she said. At the time they were both members of the Bundestag and were pressing the German government to take a more pro-Tibetan stance. By chance, the Tibetan leader arrived on the very day when Egon Kranz was toppled from power and East Germany was plunged into a leaderless uncertainty.

As the Dalai Lama recalls in his autobiography *Freedom in Exile*, he was able—"thanks to the co-operation of the East German authorities"—to stand by the crumbling Berlin Wall in full view of a still-manned security tower. An old woman handed him a red candle, which he lit and held up. "For a moment the tiny dancing flame threatened to go out, but it held and, while a crowd pressed round me, touching my hands, I prayed that the light of compassion and awareness would fill the world and dispel the fear and oppression."[1]

Petra laughed as I recounted the episode. Not only was the "old woman" the young East German human rights activist Bär-bel Bohley, the "crowd" was a hand-holding circle of radicals from both Germanys, including Gert and herself, and the location was unambiguously the *East* Berlin side of the wall. Against all regula-tions, Petra had made an official government car available for the Dalai Lama and his staff to cross into the Soviet zone at Check-point Charlie. "I was very afraid," she remembers the Dalai Lama telling her. Having performed the ceremony, they were escorted by the East German secret police (Stasi) to a Jewish old people's home, where His Holiness laid a white Tibetan offering scarf on a gravestone that stood as a memorial outside. The party was then driven to a meeting of the Round Table of the Citizen's Action Movement.

By now I was scribbling Petra's words on to a paper napkin. It was the first time the Dalai Lama had encountered "a genu-inely revolutionary situation," she said. With the fall of Kranz, the Communist Party had lost its grip on power. In the chaotic but potent vacuum that now prevailed, the Citizen's Action Movement was confident that it would take over the government to create an independent, demilitarized, nuclear-free, and environmentally aware East German state, which would subscribe neither to the capitalist nor communist dogmas. The Dalai Lama was assured that he would be the first official guest of the new rulers, who also promised to recognize the independence of Tibet.

She recalled how both the Dalai Lama and the aspiring gov-ernment were deeply moved by the meeting. She also remem-bered the nervousness of his staff, some of whom wanted to cut the meeting short and hasten back to the safety of the West. The dreams of the Citizen's Action Movement were never to be realized. They had underestimated the power of the West German institutions to control the course of events. Within a matter of weeks the stage was set for the reunification as defined by the Federal Republic.

Petra's heartfelt respect for the Dalai Lama often clashed with her frustration with his political advisors, whom she considered largely reactionary and ill informed. She told us how she and Gert would insist on meeting His Holiness alone, so she could vent her passion freely and he could speak frankly with them. The autobiography's failure to mention the meeting with the Citizen's Action Movement could simply reflect a concern of the Dalai Lama's staff that His Holiness would be associated with a failed political movement. History is a process of selection, its convenient fictions as much a reflection of what one chooses to omit as what one decides to include.

It was nearly eleven o'clock. Arnie made some final arrangements about a manuscript of speeches and essays that Petra had just given him to publish. Gert stood up to take a photograph. Arnie, Petra, and I moved our chairs together to get into the picture. The flash didn't work. Petra jumped up and took the camera from Gert, who sat down in her place. We smiled. She pressed the shutter. The flash dazzled us. It was the last frame on the roll of film.

The second and last time we met was at two o'clock the following afternoon when I bumped into them in the foyer of the conference hall. Petra mentioned that she had caught a slight chill from sitting outside so late. As a result of her staying in bed that morning they had missed the conference's concluding panel discussion. They were in the same buoyant spirits as the night before. We shook hands and said good-bye.

They arrive at their small terraced house in Bonn late on Wednesday night and go straight to bed. As is his habit, Gert rises in the early hours of the morning, dresses in shirt and trousers and sits at his desk. He types a letter to his estranged wife Charlotte in a casual, chit-chat tone, and seals it in an envelope. He inserts another sheet of paper in the typewriter and begins writing to his lawyer. He stops after typing the letters *m-ü-s.*

October 20. I am staying with friends in Big Sur, California, idly gazing at the sun-speckled Pacific while breakfast is being prepared. Arnie Kotler and his wife, Therese, had driven down the day before. Now they are strolling in the garden on the clifftop. It's a holiday, a reunion. The phone rings. A friend from Berkeley announces in a shocked and urgent voice what he has just picked up on cable TV: Petra Kelly has been murdered, probably by Gert Bastian. No dates, no details. Arnie and Therese come in, relaxed and smiling. They sit down. I tell them.

Two days later Arnie and I issue a statement describing our meeting. "The relations between them seemed caring, relaxed, and intimate," we write. "Since the entire tenor of their presence was overwhelmingly forward-looking, courageous, and life affirming, we cannot believe that either Gert would murder Petra and then take his own life or they would both choose to die as part of a suicide pact."

Now, a week later, my certainty is being upset by a flood of counterevidence from the media. A court psychiatrist in Berlin explains that the tragedy obeyed the "specific laws" peculiar to their kind of relationship. Close friends of Gert Bastian suggest a tragic "accident" in his heart or brain that triggered the fatal deed. In the very course of writing this piece, I have typed *e-n-i-g-m-a* in the opening paragraph rather than *m-u-r-d-e-r.*

I cannot reconcile the memory of those two compassionate and vital people sitting across the café table with the image of their bullet-pierced, decomposing corpses. I cannot accept that I would not have noticed at least some indication of the fate that would befall them four days later. I cannot bear the awful possibility that people so committed to the exposure of injustice and the relief of suffering might be presenting a brave facade that conceals their own unbearable agony.

# A DEMOCRACY OF THE IMAGINATION

Ernest Hemingway spoke once of sitting at his desk each morning to face "the horror of a blank sheet of paper." He found himself (as any writer can confirm) having to produce by the end of the day a series of words arranged in a way that has never before been imagined. You sit there, alone, hovering on the cusp between nothing and something. This is not a blank, stale nothing; it is a nothing charged with unrealized potential. And the hovering is the kind that can fill you with dread. Rearrangement of the items on your desk assumes an irresistible attraction.

I was once reminded of Hemingway's phrase while poised to write an essay after the completion of a meditation retreat in a Korean Sŏn monastery. Hovering on the cusp between nothing and something at my desk was not at all dissimilar from sitting on a cushion in an empty room asking myself, "What is this?" Such meditation requires that you rest in a state of perplexity about "the great matter of birth and death," hovering, as it were, in an abyss of unknowing. You still the mind, ask the question, listen, and wait. Like Hemingway's blank sheet, this too can give rise to dread. But with no objects at hand, no books on any shelf, the mind flees its predicament by erupting into an orgy of distraction or by lapsing into sleep.

The artist's dilemma and the meditator's are, in a deep sense, equivalent. Both are repeatedly willing to confront an unknown and to risk a response that they cannot predict or control. Both are disciplined in skills that allow them to remain focused on their task and to express their response in a way that will illuminate the dilemma they share with others.

And both are liable to similar outcomes. The artist's work is prone to be derivative, a variation on the style of a great master or established school. The meditator's response might tend to be dogmatic, a variation on the words of a hallowed tradition or revered teacher. There is nothing wrong with such responses. But we recognize their secondary nature, their failure to reach the peaks of primary imaginative creation. Great art and great dharma both give rise to something that has never quite been imagined before. Artist and meditator alike aspire to an original creative act. The primary imaginative act in the Buddhist tradition occurred when Gotama addressed the five ascetics in the Deer Park at Sarnath and "set in motion the wheel of dharma." It was here, rather than at the moment of awakening itself, that the Buddha expressed an original response to the dilemma he shared with others. His originality lay with the conception of the four noble truths, which set the template for all subsequent Buddhist thought. Since that moment, for any human endeavor to be "Buddhist"—whether in psychology, philosophy, or aesthetics—it needs to fit that template.

According to early tradition, the awakening left the Buddha in a stunned silence. He saw the benighted world as incapable of understanding what he had experienced, and he sat there serenely poised on the edge of nirvana. But is this not just a way of saying that he was at that time incapable of imagining how to express his experience? If so, it would also confirm the doctrine of Mahayana Buddhism that buddhahood is fully realized not at the moment of awakening, but only when the awakened imagination begins to creatively emanate images.

While widely accepted, this "lost weekend" account of the gap between the Buddha's awakening and his subsequent teaching career is awkward. An alternative version portrays the awakening as triggering a veritable explosion of the imagination. The opening passage of the *Avatamsaka Sūtra,* a vast compendium much loved in East Asia, reads:

> At one time the Buddha was in the land of Magadha, in a state of purity, at the site of awakening, having just realized true awareness. The ground was solid and firm, made of diamond, adorned with exquisite jewel disks and myriad precious flowers, with pure clear crystals. The ocean of various colors appeared over an infinite extent. There were banners of precious stones, constantly emitting light and beautiful sounds. Nets of myriad gems and garlands of exquisitely scented flowers hung all around. The finest jewels appeared spontaneously, showering innumerable gems and flowers all over the earth. There were rows of jeweled trees, their branches and foliage lustrous and luxuriant. By the Buddha's spiritual power, he caused all the adornments of his awakening to be reflected therein.[1]

The sixth-century monk Zhiyi, founder of the syncretic Tiantai school of Chinese Buddhism, regarded the *Avatamsaka,* which he believed to have been delivered in the first three weeks after the Buddha's awakening, as a spontaneous poetic outpouring of enlightenment intelligible only to gods. Realizing that its imagery was inaccessible for the people of his time, the Buddha left the Bodhi tree for Isipatana (Sarnath), where he embarked on the next phase of his teaching. In so doing, he was moved to engage with the anguish of human beings and thereby enter into history.

"Few men," J. W. N. Sullivan wrote in 1927, "have the capacity fully to realize suffering as one of the great structural lines of human life." Interestingly enough, he was speaking not of the Buddha, but of Beethoven.

"Bach," continued Sullivan, "escaped the problem with his religious scheme. Wagner, on the basis of a sentimental philosophy, finds the reason and anodyne of suffering in the pity it awakens. Mozart, with his truer instinct, is bewildered. To Beethoven the character of life as suffering became a fundamental part of his outlook. . . . Suffering is accepted as a necessary condition of life, as an illuminating power."[2]

As with great dharma, great art begins with an unflinching acceptance of anguish as the primary truth of human experience. A self-portrait by Rembrandt or one by Zen master Hakuin, a fragmentary piano sonata by Schubert or an adagio from a late Beethoven quartet, a haiku by Bashō or a verse by Eliot: all are united by the terrible beauty of anguish. They are also held together by a vivid stillness of mind, what Sullivan calls "a serenity which contains within itself the deepest and most unforgettable sorrow, and yet a sorrow which is transformed by its inclusion in that serenity."[3] Thus does a work of art come to "fit the template" of the four noble truths.

There is no reason why a Buddhist should not profoundly value works of art that are not intentionally Buddhist. For if a work of any tradition heightens awareness of the three marks of existence (impermanence, suffering, not-self), it will serve the fundamental tasks of Buddhism: to fully know anguish, to let go of self-centered craving, to realize cessation, and to cultivate the path.

Like great dharma, great art begins in anguish. It is through knowing suffering, rather than evading or ignoring it, that the door to beauty is first opened. Bashō's aching words

> Departing spring!
> birds crying;
> tears in the eyes of fish.[4]

are illuminated by T. S. Eliot's

> . . . notion of some infinitely gentle
> Infinitely suffering thing.[5]

Contemplative experience is not merely cognitive and affective but aesthetic.

In a confined, opaque world given to the ephemeral gratification of desire, we merely skim the surface of things. We rarely stop long enough to pay attention to anything. "It takes an artist to make us attend to the message of reality,"[6] wrote E. H. Gombrich of Henri Cartier-Bresson, the photographer who once described his art as "holding one's breath when all faculties converge in the face of fleeing reality. . . . It is putting one's head, one's eye, and one's heart on the same axis." A meditator who articulates his vision of such moments also makes us "attend to the message of reality." And he does so most effectively when he finds his own voice. "It is a way of shouting," says Cartier-Bresson of photography, "of freeing oneself, not of proving or asserting one's originality."[7]

The pivotal moments in the history of Buddhism have been defined by comparable instances of great dharma. Each has been marked by an original creative act in which the dharma has been reimagined in a way appropriate to the prevailing circumstances. These moments have occurred each time political, social, or religious conditions have shifted and, above all, whenever Buddhism has crossed into another culture.

The historical visionaries of Buddhism have all arisen in response to such challenges. The greatness of Nāgārjuna, Huineng, Śāntideva, Padmasambhava, Milarepa, Dōgen, Tsongkhapa, and Hakuin (among others) lay in their capacity to imagine something that had never quite been imagined before. While the imagination found its raw materials in tradition, it transformed them through

wisdom and compassion, and was further enabled by literary, poetic, or rhetorical skills.

Yet, as far as I am aware, there is no term in any of the classical Buddhist languages that corresponds to the English "creative
imagination." I can think of no doctrine that actively celebrates it.
Moreover, such a notion is at odds with the conservatism of traditional Buddhist institutions. Like those of all religions, these institutions maintain their power by controlling the imagination. By
explicitly and implicitly decreeing what can and cannot be imagined, they not only dictate the moral framework of punishment
and reward but also constrain the free and creative urges of the
individual. Not surprisingly, the greater an institution's political
and social power, the more clerical and repressive it becomes.

Without exception, moments of great dharma have been followed by periods of dogmatic ossification, in which preservation
of the outer forms of a great teacher's legacy has suppressed the
creative impulse that inspired him. Given the generally inert, isolationist, and autocratic character of premodern Asian societies,
these periods of ossification have sometimes lasted centuries. To
offer a fresh, imaginative vision became seen as a threat to an established hierarchy of power.

Even when the imagination is used in traditional practice, as
in Tibetan Buddhist tantra, it rarely goes beyond the affirmation
of a symbolic or archetypal truth. Each practitioner is instructed to
identify with and visualize in painstaking detail exactly the same
god with precisely the same attributes. In some traditions, one
must promise to recite the form without variation every day until
one dies. Failure to do so, one is warned, will result in birth in the
excruciating Vajra hell. The imagination is dangerous and subver-
sive. If it is to be used at all, then it must be strictly controlled.

Historically, such ossification of religious structures has been periodically rejected by a resurgence of the creative dimension of Buddhist practice. In Buddhism, the two most striking instances of such movements are those of the *mahasiddhas*, the eccentric tantric adepts of India, and their almost exact contemporaries in China, the iconoclastic Tang dynasty Chan (Zen) masters. Both of these groups, celebrants of the free imagination, rebelled against the suffocating clericalism of the times and initiated ways of life provocatively at odds with the established religion. Yet the conservatism and autocratic nature of their respective cultures allowed them to flourish only for relatively short periods of history before they became either marginalized or normalized through reincorporation into a renewed clerical orthodoxy.

The technological paradigm that dominates modern culture easily leads to the assumption that Buddhist practice is a set of spiritual techniques aimed at successfully solving the problem of anguish. While there clearly is a technical dimension to Buddhist practice, it is no different from the technical skill of an artist or writer. What matters in the creation of a work of art is the capacity to place that skill in the service of the imagination. The same is true of dharma. No matter how accomplished one's technical proficiency in meditation (for example) may be, such skill in itself can lead to no more than becoming an expert, a master craftsman as opposed to an artist.

In fact, the practice of dharma is more truly akin to the practice of art. With the tools of ethics, meditation, and understanding, one works the clay of one's confined and tragic existence into a bodhisattva. Practice is a process of self-creation.

In a pluralistic and agnostic culture, might there not emerge a way of Buddhist practice founded on a democracy of the imagination? While it would be naive to assume that clerical institutions could vanish overnight (or even that this would be desirable), the conditions of life are such today that a more resilient alternative can certainly be imagined, whether it can be realized or not.

In sharp contrast to their medieval predecessors, modern societies are frenetic, pluralistic, and individualistic. As the dharma seeks ways to respond to their suffering, may they not in turn transform Buddhism in ways hitherto unimagined? Rather than remaining the discrete preserve of the rare spiritual genius, might creative imagination not be released into the hands of every practitioner? Could we not envisage a democracy of the imagination, in which each individual ceases to be a passive recipient of spiritual truths and becomes instead their active creator?

Buddhism is often criticized for regarding the world as an illusion. Such criticism, however, is founded on a misunderstanding. Buddhism says not that the world is an illusion but that it is *like* an illusion, thus highlighting the crucial distinction between a literal and a metaphoric truth.

And not just any old illusion. The term specifically refers to the kind of theatrical illusion a magician in ancient India would produce for an audience. The texts describe how such illusions are the product of a variety of conditions: occult substances, spells, and the magician's hypnotic power. The resultant illusion, say, of a dancing horse, only arises in dependence upon these conditions. Although a horse appears to be there, under closer scrutiny it would be exposed as a magical illusion rather than a flesh-and-blood animal. Only because of the audience's credulity does the illusion seem to be something other than it is.

We do not have to believe in magic spells for this to work. We only have to be able to enjoy a film. The same elements are at work: cinematic technology, suspension of disbelief, the director's skill in organizing a compelling narrative. The result is the same.

Life, too, is like this. What appears to us through the senses seems real and solid enough, but once we submit it to deeper scrutiny (whether through physics, postmodern philosophy, or Buddhist meditation), that out-thereness-in-its-own-right of the thing starts to dissolve. Once we notice its utter contingency, the gut feeling that there must be something solid and unchanging at its core weakens. The thing is seen not only to emerge from a complex set of causes and conditions but also to depend on a vast number of parts, attributes, and components. If we look closer still, we find that it is what it is because of the way we talk and think about it, because of the peculiar way in which our culture perceptually organizes it so that it makes sense. Nothing else, no extra metaphysical essence, is necessary. While language forces us to use the word "it," ultimately there is nothing to which it refers.

Life is like a movie. It is like an unfolding story that we read and interpret, while identifying with the stars (i.e., gods) and immersing ourselves in the drama. When we start to notice this, life becomes lighter. The monotony fades and the magic begins. For when we turn our attention to our bodies, feelings, perceptions, inclinations, and consciousness, we find that we are woven of the quixotic threads of ongoing stories. For only such a self can create and be created. A fixed, intractable one is as good as dead.

In the individuated culture of the West, spiritual inspiration and meaning are found less in static icons and religious archetypes and more in the unfolding dramas of theater, music, novels, and films. We find our heroes and heroines not in timeless icons but in flesh-and-blood characters forging themselves from the tensions of real and fictional dramas. A democracy of the imagination is one in which the stories of the gods (myths) are brought down to earth and incarnated through individuated narratives. Not only might it free the creative impulses of the individual but also of communities to envision afresh how they might tell the story of their own unfolding.

# SEEING THE LIGHT

Taking photographs and practicing meditation might seem at first glance to be unrelated activities. For while photography looks outward at the visual world through the medium of a camera, meditation focuses inward on unmediated experience. And whereas photography is concerned with producing images of reality, meditation is about seeing reality as it is. Yet in taking photographs and practicing meditation over the past three decades, I find the two activities have converged to the point where I no longer think of them as different.

As practices, both meditation and photography demand commitment, discipline, and technical skill. Possession of these qualities does not, however, guarantee that meditation will lead to great wisdom any more than that photography will culminate in great art. To go beyond mere expertise in either domain requires a capacity to see the world anew. Such seeing originates in a penetrating and insatiable curiosity about things. It entails recovering an innocent, childlike wonder at life while suspending the adult's conviction that the world is simply the way it appears.

The pursuit of meditation and photography leads away from fascination with the extraordinary and back to a rediscovery of the ordinary. Just as I once hoped for mystical transcendence through meditation, so I assumed exotic places and unusual objects to be the ideal subjects for photography. Instead I have found that meditative awareness is a heightened understanding and feeling for the concrete, sensuous events of daily existence. Likewise, the practice of photography has taught me just to pay closer attention to what I see around me every day. Some of the most satisfying pictures I have taken have been of things in the immediate vicinity of where I live and work.

Both photography and meditation require an ability to focus steadily on what is happening in order to see more clearly. To see in this way involves shifting to a frame of mind in which the habitual view of a familiar and self-evident world is replaced by a keen sense of the unprecedented and unrepeatable configuration of each moment. Whether you are paying mindful attention to the breath as you sit in meditation or whether you are composing an image in a viewfinder, you find yourself hovering before a fleeting, tantalizing reality.

At this point, the tasks of the meditator and the photographer appear to diverge. While the meditator cultivates uninterrupted, nonjudgmental awareness of the moment, the photographer captures the moment in releasing the shutter. But in practice the aesthetic decision to freeze an image on film crystallizes rather than interrupts the contemplative act of observation. Aligning one's body and senses in those final microseconds before taking a picture momentarily heightens the intensity and immediacy of the image. One is afforded a glimpse into the heart of the moment that meditative awareness might fail to provide.

"To take photographs," wrote Henri Cartier-Bresson, "is to hold one's breath when all faculties converge in the face of fleeing reality. . . . It is putting one's head, one's eyes and one's heart on the same axis. . . . It is a way of shouting, of freeing oneself, not of proving or asserting one's originality. It is a way of life." These words of the renowned French photographer define photography as an ongoing meditative relationship to the world. For

Cartier-Bresson, photography is not merely a profession but a liberating engagement with life itself, the camera not just a machine for recording images but "an instrument of intuition and spontaneity."[1]

To be moved to take photographs, like being inspired to practice meditation, is to embark on a path. In both cases you follow an intuitive hunch rather than a carefully considered decision. Something about "photography" or "meditation" draws you irresistibly. While you may initially justify your interest in these pursuits with clear and compelling reasons, the further you proceed along their respective paths, the less you need to explain yourself. The very act of taking a photograph or sitting in meditation is sufficient justification in itself. The notion of an end result to be attained at some point in the future is replaced by an understanding of how the goal of photography or meditation is right here, waiting to be realized each moment.

Both meditation and photography are concerned with light. Meditators speak of "enlightenment": an experience in which light metaphorically dispels the darkness of the mind. Similarly, by means of an odd angle, an unusual arrangement of light and shade, or an adjustment in the depth of field, a photographer illuminates something about an object that had previously been unnoticed. Such photography has nothing to do with preserving a pictorial record of things, places, and people that are already familiar. It opens up the world in a startling and unexpected way that can be both compelling and unsettling.

The photographer's concern with light is also a real one. For with insufficient light, one simply cannot take a photograph. Yet the closer you attend to what is seen in the viewfinder, the more you notice how the light which illuminates and the object being illuminated are not two separate things. An object is just as much the medium through which light becomes apparent as light is the medium through which an object becomes apparent. You cannot have one without the other. In taking a photograph of an object, you are taking a photograph of a condition of light.

When this separation between what illuminates and what is illuminated begins to dissolve, it becomes increasingly difficult to regard the object being photographed as a thing existing in its own right "out there." As soon as you make the perceptual shift to seeing the object as a condition of light, what you observe becomes as tentative, shimmering, and luminous as light itself. In paying more attention to the display of light rather than "something" illuminated by light, photography starts to move away from representation toward abstraction. The photographer becomes absorbed by the restless contrasts of line, color, shading, and what is in and out of focus to the point where the object as a recognizable "thing" disappears.

This is where the path of photography has led me at the time of writing. My photographs, taken over many years, reflect various stages in this journey. They also mirror my engagement with the process of Buddhist meditation. For both paths have served to deepen my understanding of the fleeting, poignant, and utterly contingent nature of things.

# A Cosmos of Found Objects

In the end, after much delay and misinformation, I retrieved my new passport from the Customer Service Center near Victoria Station in London. As an unexpected bonus it was given to me, together with its worn and now corner-clipped predecessor, inside a yellow envelope. What immediately caught my eye was that it was not a dull bureaucratic yellow—closer, really, to a brownish orange— but a shiny lemon yellow. Moreover, the paper of the envelope was agreeably smooth and uniform in texture and thin enough that the honeycomb patterning on its reverse side just showed through. This was a gift, a blessing perhaps, entirely unintended by the smiling young woman who handed the package to me across the counter. She probably thought my look of delighted surprise had something to do with a love of travel documents rather than a long-standing obsession with the detritus of the modern world.

Most eager recipients of a new passport would probably have had no interest at all in the envelope, only in what it contained. Once the passport was safely stowed in a wallet or bag, the envelope would doubtless be discarded: either crumpled into a ball and thrown into the nearest receptacle or, by the environmentally correct, recycled in an appropriate bin. In either case, its fleeting purpose fulfilled, it would become waste.

I had come to London that weekend for a public conversation with my brother David, an artist and writer whose book *The Lumi-*

*nous and the Grey* was being launched at the Whitechapel Gallery in the east end of the city. Inspired by Wittgenstein's gnomic remark "Whatever looks luminous does not look grey,"[1] David, in this book, continues the sustained meditation on color that began in his earlier work *Chromophobia*. A committed denizen of the city, my brother shuns the bucolic tints of ferns and buttercups in favor of bright, chemical, industrialized hues that assail us from billboards, plastic bottles, LCD screens, and fluorescent tubes.

David's latest reflections turn away from a direct contemplation of the vivid colors themselves to focus on the background conditions from which they appear. Rather than be dazzled/seduced by the glare of artificial lights, he notices how they also softly shimmer in the damp asphalt of the sidewalk beneath one's feet. Such moments of fugitive luminosity emerge most brilliantly from the grayscape that is the city at night. The two go hand in hand: "They cohabit and sustain one another," he remarks, "in an unacknowledged relationship of interdependence."[2]

The practice of such art is honed by learning to notice what is around us all the time but habitually overlooked. This discipline of attention is every bit as rigorous as that of the solitary contemplative who strives to turn her mind away from the prompts of compulsive and repetitive reactions in order to glimpse the world afresh and see it as though for the first time. By presenting experience as more or less constant and predictable, our perceptual habits can be consoling. Each morning the sight of the same undulating meadows from the train window, the same city streets on the way to work reassure and comfort us. But the meadows and streets are not the same. They have changed in unremarkable but discernible ways. The light that falls on them today is not the light that fell on them yesterday. Just take a photo of the same view every day at exactly the same time and you will see that no two pictures are ever alike. For, unlike the brain, the camera doesn't lie.

Mental habits do not just impose a veneer of sameness on the ever-shifting detail of the present. They also dull our senses, blinding us to the perplexing uniqueness of each moment. And they flatten our emotions, leaving us listless and bored, hankering after the intense bursts of stimulation promised in those brightly colored ads.

So just as a meditator mindfully attends to the passage of breath across the upper lip—cooler as it comes in, warmer as it goes out—the artist focuses attention on those details of the world that are likewise forgotten, taken for granted, or ignored. The aim of these practices is not to acquire esoteric knowledge about the subtleties of breathing or the peculiar qualities of neon light reflected in a puddle. One trains oneself to see the world anew, no longer wholly determined by the biological, social, and cultural habits we have acquired as human animals. "If the doors of perception were cleansed," noted another London artist, William Blake, "everything would appear to man as it is, Infinite." The poet is not advocating a proto-psychedelic mysticism here. Blake's vision is a tragic one. "For man has closed himself up," he concludes, "till he sees all things thro' narrow chinks of his cavern."[3]

Scraps of discarded paper, plastic, and cloth are as transient and contingent as the distended patch of sodium light on the hood of a parked car. Like reflected light, they bear the imprint of the world that produces and sustains them.

On my first (of three) visits to Her Majesty's Passport Office, I had spotted a piece of white paper lying on the road at the side of Bridge Place. I snatched it up. One corner was already torn off. Someone had scrawled on it a large letter *E* with a thick black marking pen (though had this been Guangzhou, I would have held it at another angle and seen the Chinese character for "mountain"). The rest of the paper was stippled, soiled, and, in a couple of places, perforated by tiny holes: the typical inscriptions of passing shoes and tires. Its world was written into this distressed sheet of paper, just as the prints of official fingers were invisibly traced on the surface of the yellow envelope in which the passport was finally delivered.

You have to be quick. If such found objects are not immediately retrieved, they will soon be swept away, gathered up, crushed, and destroyed. I keep them in a ziplock plastic folder in order to preserve them just as they were found. At this stage I strive to keep myself and my actions as much out of the process as possible. On returning home, these things become the raw material of my art. They will be glued to card, cut and recut with scalpels into squares and rectangles, then organized alongside other scraps in a formal mosaic generated by simple algorithms. This is an attempt to redeem the world by harvesting and transforming its rubbish into objects of contemplation that might even pass for beauty. "For even the fairest cosmos," wrote Heraclitus in the sixth century BCE, "is but a pile of sweepings heaped at random."[4]

# An Aesthetics of Emptiness

While preparing this essay, I found myself thinking about Immanuel Kant's understanding of aesthetics in his *Critique of Judgment* (*Kritik der Urteilskraft*, 1790). Kant considers three kinds of aesthetic experience: what he calls the "agreeable," the "beautiful," and the "sublime."

The "agreeable," however, is not for Kant a genuine aesthetic experience: it simply refers to what we feel to be pleasant, which triggers desires that serve our short-term self-interest. An example would be our liking for a particular food or drink. The experience of the beautiful is also based on feeling, but it differs from our experience of the agreeable in two ways: first, it is "disinterested," that is, not something that prompts a self-interested desire, and second, we regard it as something that everyone, in principle, ought to enjoy and appreciate in the same way we do. Examples would be a rose or a sunset. Kant says less about the sublime but recognizes, along with Edmund Burke and others, that it concerns experiences that are overwhelming and exceed our capacity for representation—whether it be the mathematical idea of infinity or the witnessing of a violent storm at sea.

I wonder whether Kant's distinctions might provide a clue as to how to formulate a Buddhist theory of aesthetics. The experience of something agreeable, which prompts self-interested desires, is what the Buddha described as the experience of a pleasant feeling (*vedanā*) that triggers a self-interested craving (*taṇhā*) to possess or enjoy the object or person with which the feeling is associated. This would suggest that those who cultivate mindful attention to pleasant (and unpleasant) feelings but do not get swept away by self-interested desires would therefore be opening themselves to the possibility of experiencing the beautiful. Indeed, it is frequently reported by meditators how when the mind becomes quiet, attentive, and still, the world—particularly the natural world—is revealed as radiant and beautiful. If, through *vipassanā* practice, we then deepen this further by contemplating the transient, tragic, impersonal, contingent, and empty characteristics of what we attend to, we might then reach what "exceeds our capacity for representation" and come to experience what I have called in *After Buddhism* the "everyday sublime."

Furthermore, Kant's tripartite view of aesthetic experience neatly maps onto the tripartite Buddhist distinction of the world into three realms: that of sensual desire, pure form, and formlessness. Thus, the experience of the agreeable would correspond to the realm of sensual desire, the experience of beauty to that of pure form, and the experience of the sublime to that of formlessness. In a more dynamic and experiential way, these distinctions might also reflect the Mahayana Buddhist account of awakening in terms of the three "bodies" of the Buddha: the *nirmāṇakāya,* the *sambhogakāya,* and the *dharmakāya.* I will say more about this as we proceed.

( 1 )

I began making collages from found materials on the afternoon of Sunday, July 2, 1995, while sitting in a train from London Paddington to Totnes, Devon. I was on my way home from a weekend with my mother, brother, and wife in London, attending a family wedding and visiting art galleries. For some reason, I found myself emptying out my pockets and shoulder bag and placing the accumulated detritus of our trip on the table in front of me: train and museum tickets, the wedding invitation and service, various flyers and pamphlets, an article on Camille Pissarro torn from a Sunday newspaper, a crumpled paper bag. Then and there, as a kind of epiphany, I knew that I would organize these things into a collage of identically sized squares.

I can trace my love of collage to a moment when I was in class 2C (C was not an academic grade but stood for the chemistry master "Killer" Collins) of Watford Grammar School for Boys. I was twelve years old. Seated at my wooden desk, I was admiring a maroon, plastic-covered ring binder, which I used at the time to keep homework and other hole-punched papers. Between the clear plastic cover and the surface of the folder itself I had inserted some scraps of paper that I had found here and there (the only one I remember now is that of a partial photograph of a clock). I was thrilled by the way these otherwise unrelated things were brought together: both in the way they contrasted with each other and in how they were pressed together to create a smooth, uniform plane. I can't imagine I thought in these terms at the time, but this is the best way I can put into words now the still vivid impression it left on me then.

Even further back in my childhood, I can recall the painstaking concentration it required to embroider an image of a yacht at sea onto a pre-traced and pre-colored fabric—a child's educational toy of the period. In particular, I remember my annoyance at having pulled the thread too tight on five successive stitches, thereby spoiling the uniform texture of the finished piece. My mother framed this work and it hangs today in my office. On the back she wrote: "STEPHEN about 1958." So I would have been five or six

years old when I did it. More than half a century later, I still feel a
pang of irritation on seeing those poorly executed stitches.

Before I was able to embark on collage work, however, one
other element needed to fall into place. It was provided by the late
British communist, trade unionist, poster designer, cartoonist,
artist, and therapist Ken Sprague (1927–2004). In 1988, when I
was thirty-five, Ken led a printmaking workshop at the Sharpham
community in Devon where I lived at the time. Each participant
was handed a sheet of cardboard and a surgical scalpel. Ken taught
us how to cut designs into the card with the scalpel, then carefully
peel away layers of the card in order to produce a printing block—
like the linocuts that I had made at school. The cardboard block
was then rolled with printers' ink. A sheet of paper was placed on
top of it, and the two were then fed together into an old wrought-
iron mangle of the kind used to squeeze water out of clothes in
the days before washing machines and tumble dryers. The result
was a printed image on the piece of paper. In the course of this
workshop, I produced a single print that likewise hangs today on
the wall of my office.

Ken's workshop did not inspire me to pursue printmaking,
but it introduced me to surgical scalpels and cardboard, which,
in addition to found materials, are the essential elements of my
collage work. More important than the tool and material, though,
was my rediscovery of the delight in making things with my
hands, which reverberated to the very tips of my fingers. Unlike
being seated at a desk tapping away at a keyboard as I wrote, here
my entire body was engaged in the task. By the end of the day, I
felt strangely invigorated and tired. I was deeply satisfied by what
I had produced with my labor. Yet it would still be another eight
years before these and other threads in my life coalesced into the
practice of making collages.

Two primary themes connect these three episodes from my past with my current collage work: *composition* and *texture*.

## ( 2 )

How do things go together? How does a composition "work"? These are aesthetic questions. Be it the notes of a piece of music, the words of a poem or novel, or the shapes and colors of a painting, in the end it comes down to how these things are put together to create a work of art. Out of the myriad different ways these things *could* be arranged, the musician, poet, or painter chooses to organize them in a highly specific way until, at a certain point, the work is deemed to be "finished." When I reflect on how, as a writer or artist, such judgments are made, I am unable to answer. My mind and senses are aligned in a wordless conviction that this is how the piece should be. It feels right. I know it in my bones. I am satisfied.

A successful work of art is transcendent. The haiku, sonata, or sculpture transcends the raw materials of which it is composed. The work is neither reducible to the sum of its parts nor could it possibly exist without them. It is something "more." Yet the exact nature of this "more" is difficult if not impossible to articulate. Carl Andre's sculpture *Equivalent VIII,* which was derided in the British press when it was bought by the Tate Gallery in 1972 as an egregious waste of public money, is more than a stack of 120 rectangular firebricks. But exactly how its transcendence is achieved is not easy to say. No matter how much erudite art theory I read about it, I am left with the funny feeling of being left shortchanged. All the words devoted to explaining it seem to talk around it rather than to it. I experience the same frustrated disjunction when reading the liner notes that accompany a recorded piece of music. When Henry Moore was once asked to explain what a particular sculpture meant, he reportedly said, "If I could tell you what it meant, I would not have had to make it."

Yet the longing for someone to tell me what a work or art is about persists. When I find myself in the presence of a "difficult" work, I am unsure how to respond. It makes me uneasy. Not only do I want to be told what it means, I want to be told how to feel about it as well. In both fascinating and repelling me, the encounter risks "a suspension of the power of comparison," which is how Coleridge spoke of the experience of the sublime.[1] In exceeding my capacity for representation, the work inclines my mind to stop, leaving me suspended in a Keatsian "*negative capability:* that is when a man is capable of being in uncertainties, mysteries, doubts, without any irritable reaching after fact or reason."[2]

This may remind us of the Madhyamaka (middle way) philosophy of Nāgārjuna and his followers, who conclude that a thing is neither identical to nor different from what constitutes it. In this sense, it is said to be "empty" of any intrinsic existence. Here is how Nāgārjuna understands the person:

> If mind and matter were me,
> I'd come and go like them.
> If I were something else,
> They'd say nothing about me at all.[3]

Nāgārjuna shows how the basic grammatical categories of identity and difference cannot account for the unique individuality of a person. For if you were identical to your body, feelings, perceptions, inclinations, and consciousness, then you would be as fleeting, contingent, and discontinuous as they are. But this is clearly not the case: for while you remain constant under different circumstances, all these things can be observed to "come and go." It is equally absurd to claim that you are something different from the physical and mental features that make you up. For the only way either I or you can know anything about me is through coming into contact with one or all of my features. If one were to delete physicality, feelings, perceptions, inclinations, and consciousness from one's experience, there would be nothing left over for me to be.

The self, like a work of art, is transcendent. It is not reducible to its parts, nor does it exist independently of them. Yet such transcendence is not in any way permanent or unconditioned. If the painting is destroyed or the person dies, they are gone forever. Over the years, my study of Madhyamaka philosophy has provided me with a language to align my childhood intuitions with what matters for me now as a Buddhist artist-practitioner. It has helped me formulate what might be called an "aesthetics of emptiness."

All the collages I have produced since 1995 are meditations on identity and difference. From 1998 to 2007 I made two large-scale triptychs of found materials entitled *Trikāya I* and *Trikāya II*. Both works are made up of three 72-cm-square mosaics, each of which is composed of 1,296 pieces.[4] Every mosaic contains 81 different scraps of found paper, plastic, or cloth. Each of these pieces is then cut by scalpel (in two stages) into a number of squares or rectangles. In the way they are finally arranged, however, none of the squares or rectangles is contiguous—either above, below, or diagonally—with a square or rectangle of the same original piece. So although they are repeated in the work, no piece ever touches another part of the paper, plastic, or cloth to which it was once joined. In this way, I seek to maximize differentiation out of a finite number of identical parts.

When reconfigured as a collage, each of the 1,296 pieces stands out as unique. This uniqueness is not due to any essential nature but to its being surrounded on all sides by colored squares and rectangles different from itself. The context in which it is now placed modifies how it appears. This became particularly clear in

*Trikāya I, 1,* a mosaic entirely composed of 2-cm-square pieces of found white materials. Each of the 81 discarded bits of paper, plastic, or cloth I came across appeared at first sight to be self-evidently "white." But when rearranged into a mosaic of 1,296 noncontiguous squares, it became evident that none of them were in fact the same "white" at all. There was no such thing as "white," only infinite shades of whiteness.

Composing a collage is a practice of transformation. Whatever lies discarded on roadsides and cast into bins is considered as rubbish. These are just bits and pieces of redundant matter with no further value or utility. Their fate is to be trampled on, shredded, burned, reduced to pulp by rain, buried, and forgotten. In training the eye to notice these overlooked or unsightly things, then picking them up, gluing them to card, cutting and recutting them, they are restored. I find myself caring for what the world rejects. The slow and laborious task of creating a collage transforms litter into art. Something you might have looked upon with mild disgust becomes an integral part of a work that you may find beautiful.

This practice of transforming rubbish has led me to understand why the traditional Buddhist meditation on the foulness of the body is ineffective. In order to combat sexual lust, the practitioner is often instructed to contemplate the unpleasant, ugly, and foul (*asubha*) aspects of the desired person's body. But this reductive exercise is based on a philosophical mistake. As a thought experiment, think of a beautiful painting. Then imagine you are told that it is painted with pigments formed entirely from urine, excrement, and other body parts. To learn that the work is composed of shit might discourage you from touching it, but it will have no effect at all on its beauty. Likewise, to visualize your lover's kidneys and intestines might momentarily revolt you, but these have nothing whatsoever to do with her physical or personal allure. As in

Gestalt psychology, Madhyamaka philosophers understand how the whole is not equivalent either to all or some of its parts.

Each collage is also a meditation on chance and order, chaos and cosmos. I do not select my materials and then purchase them. I only make use of what I find lying around, unowned and freely available. Of course, I may decide to pick up one scrap of litter and ignore another, but I have no control over what other people discard and where they discard it. Likewise, in organizing the cut pieces I follow formal rules laid out in advance from which I try not to deviate. Part of this reconfiguration includes "chance operations," where I select a piece at random before gluing it in an assigned place in the mosaic. I thereby override any personal preference I might have for what seems to fit well together in the composition. In both these regards, I seek to remove as far as possible the sense of "I" and "mine" from the work.

*Trikāya I* and *Trikāya II* are named after the Mahayana Buddhist doctrine of the three "bodies" of the Buddha: the *dharmakāya, sambhogakāya,* and *nirmāṇakāya.* This teaching maintains that awakening (*sambodhi*) cannot be adequately understood as a private, subjective experience alone. While awakening might originate in such an experience (*dharmakāya*), it becomes complete only upon achieving form (*rūpa*). The process of assuming form has two phases: first, the achieving of an archetypal or symbolic form (*sambhogakāya*), that is, through abstract images or concepts, and second, the manifesting in a concrete form (*nirmāṇakāya*) embodied in a specific flesh-and-blood existence in a public world.

In Vajrayana Buddhism, these three "bodies" are understood to be immanent within the dynamic structure of life itself. The *dharmakāya* is compared to deep sleep; the *sambhogakāya* to dreaming; and the *nirmāṇakāya* to the waking state.[5] The *Trikāya* collages seek to reflect this dynamic concept of a three-phase awakening. As triptychs, each mosaic represents a different phase in this process: the *dharmakāya* mosaic suggests the unformed contingency of emptiness, and the *sambhogakāya* and *nirmāṇakāya* mosaics express the unfolding of the *dharmakāya* into increasingly concrete patterns of form. At the same time, the construction of each individual mosaic also mirrors how the final image (*nirmāṇakāya*) comes into being through randomly distributed materials (*dharmakāya*) being organized through applying the principles of an abstract conceptual scheme (*sambhogakāya*).

An explicit theory of a three-part awakening is not found in the *suttas* of the Pali Canon. A similar pattern can nonetheless be detected in the structure of the eightfold path. The first step of this path, complete vision (*sammā diṭṭhi*), emerges out of the nirvanic emptiness of greed, hatred, and confusion. This vision is what then allows for the unfolding of forms of life no longer conditioned by the imperatives of greed, hatred, and confusion. As in the *trikāya* doctrine, these forms also come into being through progressive stages of increasing concreteness and embodiment in the public world: namely, intentions (*sankappa*), speech (*vācā*), physical acts (*kammanta*), and livelihood (*ājīva*). In this context, it is worth noting how the second step, *sankappa,* usually translated as "intention" or "thought," comes from the Pali *kappeti*, which, according to the dictionary, means "to cause to fit, to create, build, construct, arrange, prepare, order."[6]

# ( 3 )

To consider these collages in terms of their composition risks overlooking the equally crucial element of their texture. In my ongoing quest for materials, I am particularly drawn to discarded pieces of paper, cloth, and plastic that have been *distressed.* It might take the form of the indelible creases in a sheet of paper that someone has scrunched up into a ball and tossed aside. No matter how much I flatten the paper when gluing it to card, it will retain the distress marks of having once been crumpled. Or the distress might be visible in the object's having been repeatedly trodden on by passing feet, run over by cars, punctured by the gritty surface of a road, alternately soaked by rain and dried by sunlight, inadvertently or deliberately torn into pieces, snagged on a thorny bush then shredded by the wind, or degraded and discolored by immersion in seawater. In picking it up and gluing it on card, I arrest its decay and save it from further damage. Once preserved, each salvaged object bears witness to the history of its frictive and entropic relationship with the world.

There is something almost unbearably poignant for me about these distressed surfaces. In revealing the *dukkha* of the material world, they mirror the distress of vulnerable creatures of flesh and blood like ourselves. The stresses to which they have been subject reflect the stress of our own lives. We often talk of suffering in such terms. We complain about being "rejected," "ignored," "forgotten," "trodden on," "torn," "worn out," "scarred," "damaged." These are all metaphors drawn from the distressed things around us. And in opposition to our society's obsession with unblemished youth, these objects rendered fragile with wear echo the beauty of aging in the finely wrinkled skin of an old person's face.

On completion of the two *Trikāya* collages, in 2008 I embarked on another large-scale work entitled *Quadrants,* which at the time of writing is still unfinished. *Quadrants* consists of eight 48-cm-square mosaics. Each mosaic is divided into four quadrants, consisting of two squares and two rectangles. The eight mosaics in turn comprise four works, each of which is thus a dyad of two mosaics side by side. As a further meditation on identity and difference, the mosaics of each dyad are identical in terms of the alignment of their four quadrants and their being composed of 51 pieces of the same size, which are positioned in the same place in each mosaic. They differ in that the quadrants of one mosaic are composed of found materials in one of the four primary Buddhist colors (white, yellow, red, and blue),7 while the quadrants of its companion mosaic are made up of found materials of nonprimary colors and old photographs, letters, and postcards. Each dyad also differs from each other dyad because the square template, which determines the placing of the 51 pieces, is rotated 45 degrees, thus allowing for four different positionings.

Most of the old photographs, letters, and postcards are not, strictly speaking, found objects. Throughout the making of this work I have regularly visited *vide greniers* (attic emptyings), which are held during summer weekends in the villages near where I live in southwest France. There I rummage through shoe boxes filled with discarded photographs and postcards, images that have often been found in the attic or cupboards of a house bought by new owners after its former occupants have either moved or died. That they have survived at all is due to the sentimental value they had for a man, woman, or child. Over time, as the people they depict are forgotten by subsequent generations, they too are forgotten in dark, dusty corners. Their preservation hangs on an increasingly tenuous ancestral attachment, until the time comes when they are finally cast out and end up on a trestle table in a market square or farmer's field. For a small sum, often haggled over, I purchase them for my art.

Given this gradual forgetting, the photographs tend to be very old—some of them date to the nineteenth century. As a result, the images are often badly faded; sometimes one can barely make out the faces. Others suffer from chemical degradation, prolonged exposure to sunlight, or indeterminate spillages and accidents. The photographs are often cracked, torn, curled, or buckled. Yet here are found the very last traces of a human being, "drawn by light"—as the word "photograph" implies. They capture a moment—or with the older images several moments—in which light reflected off a face and body passed through a lens and was preserved in a chemical film on glass or plastic. A century later, people, frozen in time, still gaze out at us. Their shyness, awkwardness, or vanity is touchingly visible. It is quite possible that no one now alive remembers who they are. The sole vestige of their existence may be their fortuitous presence in my collage.

Each mosaic in this series is initially composed of 51 unequally sized pieces. These are then cut into 2-cm squares, making a total of 576 equally sized pieces. Moreover, this second scalpel cut is made into the back of the piece, which further distresses its surface by producing a slightly elevated ridge. The overall effect of these operations is to produce a texture that is simultaneously uniform and differentiated. The contrast between, say, a degraded photograph and a scrap of discarded plastic also stands in contrast to a flat plane interrupted by regular ridges that unites all the pieces. I love the variegated textures created by this process, so much so that I run my fingers over the surface with tactile delight.

Because of their textures, these collages do not lend themselves to photographic reproduction. Partly it is because in reality they are very thin sculptures, three-dimensional objects that cannot be replicated in a two-dimensional image. But what truly renders them incapable of being photographed is the way in which their textured surfaces reflect light depending on (1) the quality of the light source and (2) the position from which one views them.

In 2001, Martin Creed won the Turner Prize for a work called *Work No. 227: The lights going on and off.* The exhibition room was empty. The only thing to be seen was the lights turning on for five seconds, then off for five seconds, repeating the cycle endlessly. Predictably, *Work No. 227* elicited the same howls of outrage from the popular British press that had greeted Carl Andre's *Equivalent VIII* some thirty years earlier. I was moved by Creed's piece because it exposed something I had been puzzling over while contemplating my collages. I became aware of how their colors and textures varied according to both the way the light changed through the course of day and night and the angle from which I looked at them. While these facts should be self-evident and un-remarkable, I tended to picture the work in my mind as though it were always illuminated by a steady light source and observed from the point of view of someone standing directly in front of it—an illusion that is reinforced by the way work is habitually dis-played in art galleries. In contrast to my *actual* experience of the work as constantly changing under varying light conditions and viewing angles, I conceptualized it as something fixed and static.

This observation finds an echo in Buddhist thought. In re-sponse to Kaccānagotta's question "What is complete vision (*sammā diṭṭhi*)?" Gotama replies, "By and large, Kaccāna, this world relies on the duality of 'it is' and 'it is not.' But one who sees the arising of the world as it happens with complete understanding has no sense of 'it is not' about the world. And one who sees the ceasing of the world as it happens with complete understanding has no sense of 'it is' about the world."

The lights go on: "it is." The lights go off: "it is not." But the world is endlessly variable in its arising and ceasing. As light and viewpoint change, so does our experience of what is happening: it cannot be reduced to the crude polarities of "is/on" and "is not/off." Yet we are instinctively committed to such dualities. They are embedded in the grammar of our language. "But one with complete vision," explains the Buddha, "does not get caught up in the habits, fixations, prejudices or biases of the mind. He is not fixated on 'my self.' He does not doubt that when something is occurring, it is occurring, and when it has come to an end, it has come to an end. His knowledge is independent of others."[8]

The *Kaccānagotta Sutta,* as this Pali discourse is known, serves as a primary source for Nāgārjuna's philosophy of emptiness; it is the only discourse cited by name in his key work the *Mūlama-dhyamakakārikā*. As Nāgārjuna and his followers developed their middle way philosophy of Madhyamaka, other conceptual polarities were subject to the same scrutiny as that of "it is" and "it is not." Among these we find the examination of "identity" and "difference," which has been so central to my collage work. The same is equally true of the polarity between "self" and "other." In the end, all such dichotomies are exposed as inadequate for capturing the profoundly contingent, relational, and tragic character of lived experience. An aesthetics of emptiness, therefore, originates in suspending belief in the inviolability of these distinctions, while simultaneously highlighting the radiant contingency of life that is revealed once the grip of such dualistic thinking is loosened.

As a practice, the Buddha does not present emptiness as something to be understood or known. He describes it as a *vihāra*, a place to dwell or live (*viharati*). "I mainly live," he says to Ānanda in the *Shorter Discourse on Emptiness*, "by dwelling in emptiness." Such emptiness refers to the nonreactive space that opens up once the effluences (*āsava*) of cupidity, becoming, and ignorance are no longer conditioning one's mind. "This state of awareness," says Gotama, "is empty of those effluences. And that which is not empty is this: the six sense fields of a living body." Such a person regards this awareness as "empty of what is not there. And of what remains, he knows: 'this is what's here.' So is this entry into emptiness in accord with what happens, undistorted and pure."[9]

The challenge facing every Buddhist artist-practitioner is to learn how to dwell in such an empty, nonreactive space, which allows the kind of "complete" vision (*sammā diṭṭhi*) that enables appropriate intentions (*sammā sankappa*) to be formed. As we saw, the term *sankappa* has the root meaning of "to cause to fit, to create, build, construct, arrange, prepare, order." From here, one can then embark on a course of speech (*vācā*) and action (*kammanta*), which, in my own case, translates into writing books, teaching dharma and making art. Thus one's livelihood (*ājīva*) as a writer or artist or both becomes an integral part of cultivating (*bhāvanā*) the middle way.

# ( 4 )

Ever since I began making collages in 1995, I have come to regard this work as a silent counterpoint to what I write. I do not regard it as accidental that *Buddhism without Beliefs,* the book that established my reputation as a writer, was published two years after I completed my first collage. Since then, each book I compose in words for my public is paralleled by a composition in shapes and colors that is largely private. Yet there is no one-to-one correspondence between a specific book and a specific collage. What unites them are the ongoing acts of composition themselves: the putting of things together, regardless of whether they be words and sentences or scraps of paper, cloth, and plastic. Intuitively, I sense that these two processes are engaged in an unspoken dialogue, but I have no idea what they communicate to each other or what it might mean. All I know is that the writing and collage making are mutually illuminating activities that yield aesthetic delight.

During my first years of writing books and making collages I suffered from an underlying anxiety that once a work was completed, I would not know what to do next. For as long as I was absorbed in the task of making a work, it seemed inconceivable that I could ever embark on anything else. I worried that when a particular book or collage was finished, it would also mark the end of the creative process itself. I imagined coming to a dead end, bereft of any further ideas or inspiration. Over time this anxiety has evaporated. I now understand that it is only upon the completion of one work that you are able to see what work comes next. It is a bit like climbing a mountain. You ascend toward a ridge that looms above you, behind which is only sky. But once you arrive at the ridge, the view is abruptly transformed, revealing to you the next stage of the ascent. I have now (almost) complete trust in the unfolding of the imagination. The more I pursue my vocation as a writer-collagist, the greater my confidence that something other than my petty desires and fears will determine what comes next.

As this joint practice of writing and collage enters its third decade, I find myself toying with the idea of formally integrating these two dimensions into one. Instead of treating the book and collage as two distinct works, could I produce a single work in which both book and collage would be subsumed as constitutive elements? This would require subjecting both the book and the collage to the same formal constraints. It could be done, for example, by deciding that the book consist of a set number of chapters, with each chapter consisting of a set number of words, which would correspond to an equivalent numbering pattern of the found objects that make up the collage. Whether or not such a *Gesamtkunstwerk* will ever come to fruition, I cannot say.

# NOTES

## In Search of a Voice

1.  Śāntideva, *Bodhicaryāvatāra* 2:35.
2.  Śāntideva, *Bodhicaryāvatāra* 7:6.
3.  Śāntideva, *Bodhicaryāvatāra* 7:60.
4.  Śāntideva, *Bodhicaryāvatāra* 3:18–19.
5.  Śāntideva, *Bodhicaryāvatāra* 7:52.
6.  Śāntideva, *Bodhicaryāvatāra* 8:25.
7.  Śāntideva, *Bodhicaryāvatāra* 7:2.
8.  Śāntideva, *Bodhicaryāvatāra* 7:63.
9.  Śāntideva, *Bodhicaryāvatāra* 7:66.
10. Śāntideva, *Bodhicaryāvatāra* 7:67.
11. Augustine, *Confessions*, book 2, section 4, p. 47.
12. Augustine, *The Trinity*, 1.5. Quoted in an article by Garry Wills, *New York Review of Books*, January 14, 2016, pp. 71–72.
13. Hadot (1995), p. 3.
14. Ibid.
15. Ibid., p. 75.
16. A quote from Ritesh Batra's 2013 film *The Lunchbox*.
17. See, for example, Bronkhorst (2007, 2011), Gombrich (1996, 2009), Schopen (1997), and Schumann (1989).
18. See Stephen Batchelor (2010) and (2015).
19. *Majjhima Nikāya* 26. Cf. Ñāṇamoli and Bodhi (1995), p. 260.
20. Personal communication from Geoffrey Bamford.
21. To be technically precise, they "appear in the form of gods" (Tibetan: *hla'i rnam par shar ba*).
22. Feuerbach (1957), p. 3.

23. Ibid., p. 16.
24. Ibid., p. 65.
25. Marx wrote his eleven "Theses on Feuerbach" in 1845, the last of which is the famous "The philosophers have only interpreted the world, in various ways; the point is to change it." This passage cited here is from the fourth thesis. They were first published in 1888.
26. Śāntideva, *Bodhicaryāvatāra* 2:50.
27. Śāntideva, *Bodhicaryāvatāra* 5:31–32.
28. Feuerbach (1957), p. 10.
29. Feuerbach built on David Strauss's groundbreaking *Leben Jesu* that appeared in 1835, six years before *The Essence of Christianity*. Both books were first translated into English by George Eliot.
30. On the everyday sublime, see Batchelor (2015), ch. 9.

## EXISTENCE, ENLIGHTENMENT, AND SUICIDE

Epigraph: Ñāṇavīra (1987), p. 390.
1. *The People,* September 26, 1965, Ñāṇavīra (1987), p. 536.
2. Somerset Maugham (1990), p. 272.
3. Ibid., pp. 73–74.
4. Ibid., p. 298.
5. Ibid., p. 307.
6. Robin Maugham (1975), p. 186.
7. Ibid., p. 189.
8. Ibid.
9. Evola (1982), p. 12.
10. Ibid., p. 13.
11. Ibid.
12. Ibid. This is my translation of Evola's French text. "Extinction" is Evola's rendering of "nirvana." The passage is found in the *Mūlapari-yāya Sutta* (M.1). In Ñāṇamoli and Bodhi's translation of the *Majjhima Nikāya,* it reads: "He perceives Nibbāna as Nibbāna. Having perceived Nibbāna as Nibbāna, he conceives [himself as] Nibbāna, he conceives [himself] in Nibbāna, he conceives [himself apart] from Nibbāna, he conceives Nibbāna to be 'mine,' he delights in Nibbāna. Why is that? Because he has not fully understood Nibbāna." See Ñāṇamoli and Bodhi (1995), p. 87.
13. Evola (1982), p. 14.

14. Ibid., p. 86.
15. Ibid.
16. Ibid., p. 138.
17. Evola (1951), p. 95.
18. Ibid., p. 17.
19. Ibid., p. 43.
20. Ibid., p. 135.
21. Ibid., p. 129.
22. Ibid., p. 16.
23. Ibid., p. 14.
24. Ibid., p. 17.
25. Ibid., p. 20.
26. Ibid., p. ix.
27. Evola (1982), p. 142.
28. Robin Maugham (1975), p. 190.
29. Ibid., p. 189.
30. Ibid., p. 190.
31. Ñāṇavīra (1987), p. 368.
32. Ibid., p. 367.
33. Robin Maugham (1975), p. 198.
34. Ñāṇavīra (1987), p. 440.
35. Ibid., p. 485.
36. Ibid., p. 310.
37. Ibid., p. 305.
38. Ibid., p. 5.
39. Robin Maugham (1975), p. 194.
40. Ñāṇavīra (1987), p. 223.
41. Ibid., p. 495.
42. Ibid., pp. 396-97.
43. Ibid., p. 386.
44. Ibid., p. 529.
45. Ibid., p. 386.
46. Ibid., p. 216.
47. Ibid., p. 241.
48. Ibid., p. 276.
49. Ibid., p. 238.
50. Ibid., p. 376.

51. Ibid., p. 253.
52. Robin Maugham (1975), p. 198.
53. Ibid., pp. 197–98.
54. Ibid., p. 192.
55. Ibid., p. 200.
56. Ñāṇavīra (1987), p. 403.
57. Robin Maugham (1975), p. 202.
58. Evola (1982), p. 142.
59. Ibid., p. 143.
60. Ñāṇavīra (1987), p. vii.
61. Ibid., p. 5.
62. Ibid., pp. 321–23.
63. Ibid., p. 339.
64. Ibid., p. 254.
65. Ibid., p. 337.
66. Ibid., p. 240.
67. Ibid., p. 302.
68. Ñāṇavīra (1987), p. 261.
69. Ibid., p. 12.
70. Ibid., p. 259.
71. Ibid., p. 357
72. Evola (1951), p. ix.
73. Ñāṇavīra (1987), p. 397.
74. Ibid., p. 296.
75. Ibid., p. 270.
76. Ibid., p. 292.
77. Ibid., p. 444.
78. Ibid., p. 282.
79. Ibid., p. 452.
80. Ibid., p. 466.
81. Ibid., p. 255.
82. Ibid., p. 442.
83. Ibid., p. 307.
84. Ibid., p. 243.
85. Ibid., p. 256.
86. Ibid., p. 381.
87. Ibid., p. 279.

## "A Much Younger Man, but No Less Charming"

When I started my research into the life of Ñāṇavīra Thera, I tried without success to identify Maugham's companion. I did manage to trace William Lawrence, who had assisted Maugham on his 1975 book *Search for Nirvana*, which recounts the meeting with Ñāṇavīra, only to learn that he was not the person who accompanied Maugham to Ceylon in 1965. Lawrence suggested that Peter Maddock may have been the man I was looking for, but he did not know of his current whereabouts. At that point, in those pre-Google days, the trail went cold. In 2007, I read by chance an interview by the journalist Mick Brown, whom I knew, with Peter Maddock about the production of the latter's play *Charlie and Henry*. Since this Peter Maddock was about the right age and alluded in the interview to Somerset Maugham's *The Razor's Edge*, I wrote to Mick Brown, who kindly put me in touch with Peter, who confirmed that he was indeed the person who met Ñāṇavīra Thera with Maugham. Brown's interview with Maddock can be found at: http://www.telegraph.co.uk/culture/theatre/3664627/People-have-no-shame-these-days.html.

Epigraph 1: Ñāṇavīra (1987), p. 403.

Epigraph 2: ibid., p. 466.

1.  Given the monastic rule that forbids a *bhikkhu* to speak of his attainments to lay people, it is surprising that Ñāṇavīra would have mentioned any of this to Maugham and Maddock.

## A Secular Buddhism

First epigraph below ("Birth is *dukkha* . . ."): This and all further quotations from the Buddha's first discourse are in my own translation, which can be found in Batchelor (2015), pp. 334–35. Cf. *Mahāvagga* 1.6 (Horner [1951], pp. 15–17), and *Saṃyutta Nikāya* 56:11 (Bodhi [2000], pp. 1843–47).

1.  Cupitt (2011), p. 100.

2.  Norman (2003), p. 223.

3.  The texts literally say, "Does the Tathāgata exist after death or not . . ." My reasons for replacing "Tathāgata" with "one" are given in Batchelor (2010), p. 263.

4.  Vattimo (2011), p. 77. Vattimo adds the qualification, "Not all metaphy-

sicians have been violent, but I would say that almost all large-scale perpetrators of violence have been metaphysicians."

5. Theravāda orthodoxy falls back on the metaphysics of *kamma* and re-birth to explain this point: *bhava* is divided into *kammabhava* (acts that give rise to becoming) and *upapattibhava* (the re-becoming that results from those acts).

6. Cf. Gombrich (2009), chapter 3.

7. Rig Veda 10.129, translation by John Peacock.

8. *Brhadāranyaka Upaniṣad* 4. 4.5–6, Radhakrishnan (1994), p. 282.

9. This discourse is called the *Kalahāvivādā Sutta* (*Discourse on Quarrels and Disputes*). The translated passages are from Norman (2001), pp. 113–15.

10. Horner (1951), p. 54.

11. *Saṃyutta Nikāya* 12:15, my translation. Cf. Bodhi (2000), p. 544.

12. *Mūlamadhyamakakārikā* 15: 6–7, Cf. Garfield (1995), p. 40.

13. E.g., *Majjhima Nikāya* 79, Ñāṇamoli and Bodhi (1995), p. 655.

14. *Saṃyutta Nikāya* 12:65. Cf. Bodhi (2000), pp. 601–4.

15. *The City* presents the Four in conjunction with *ten* links of conditioned arising. This ten-link model occurs only twice in the canon (cf. the *Mahāpadāna Sutta* in the *Dīgha Nikāya*). It is the same as the twelve-link model except that the first two links of ignorance (*avijjā*) and inclinations (*sankhāra*) are omitted. It appears to be an intermediate version, which occurred during the evolution of the theory from six to twelve links.

16. That the Buddha saw the practice he taught as similar to childbirth is suggested by a curious passage in the *Saccavibhanga Sutta* (*Exposition of the Truths*), *Majjhima Nikāya* 141. In this discourse, the Buddha returns to Isipatana, where he delivered *The First Discourse*, in the company of his two principal disciples Sāriputta and Moggallāna. He encourages his audience to cultivate the friendship of these two in their practice of the path with the words: "Sāriputta is like a pregnant woman (*janetā*); Moggallāna is like a midwife (*jātassa āpādetā*)." Although this *sutta* is said to be an exposition of the four noble truths, when Sāriputta is invited by the Buddha to explain them, his presentation covers the definition of the Four but ignores the concluding sections of *The First Discourse*, which describe them as four tasks to be recognized, performed, and accomplished.

17. *Saṃyutta Nikāya* 24:1. See Bodhi (2000), pp. 991–92.
18. *Saṃyutta Nikāya* 55:5. See Bodhi (2000), p. 1792.
19. *Saṃyutta Nikāya* 55:2. See Bodhi (2000), p. 1789.
20. For example, *Sutta-Nipāta.* 231. See Norman (2001), p. 29.
21. *Saṃyutta Nikāya* 22:83. See Bodhi (2000), pp. 928–29.
22. *Majjhima Nikāya* 73. See Ñāṇamoli and Bodhi (1995), p. 597.
23. *Saṃyutta Nikāya* 55:24. See Bodhi (2000), pp. 1813–16.
24. *Saṃyutta Nikāya* 56:35. See Bodhi (2000), p. 1860.
25. *Saṃyutta Nikāya* 22:60. See Bodhi (2000), p. 903.
26. *Saṃyutta Nikāya* 35:13, abridged. See Bodhi (2000), pp. 1136–37.
27. Cf. Introduction, section 4, above.
28. *Majjhima Nikāya* 22. See Ñāṇamoli and Bodhi (1995), pp. 228–29.

### Rebirth: A Case for Buddhist Agnosticism

1. Jackson and Morgan (1990), p. 156.
2. Mackenzie (1989), p. 90.
3. Ibid., p. 96.
4. Ibid., p. 101.
5. The *Kālāma Sutta* is found among the *Numerical Discourses of the Buddha: Aṅguttara Nikāya* 3.65. See Bodhi (2012), pp. 279–83.
6. Pabongka Rinpoche (1991), p. 323.
7. Udāna 5.5. See Ireland (1997), p. 74.
8. Śāntideva, *Bodhicaryāvatāra* 8:98.

### Creating Sangha

This is a revised version of an essay entitled "Monks, Laity and Sangha," which appeared in the *Middle Way,* the journal of the Buddhist Society, London (vol. 58, no. 1), in 1983, written while I was a monk in South Korea.

1. When this article was published (in 1995), fifty years ago would have been 1945. While Buddhism suffered badly at the hands of Communist regimes in Asia in the decades that followed, it has recovered significantly since then. To a considerable extent its resurgence has been realized through the rebuilding of monasteries and the ordination of new generations of monks and nuns, thereby weakening my argument.

## THE AGNOSTIC BUDDHIST

This essay is an edited version of a talk given at the symposium "American Buddhism Today" to celebrate the thirtieth anniversary of the Rochester Zen Center, Rochester, New York, June 22, 1996.

1. Huxley (1904) in the essay "Agnosticism," pp. 245–46.
2. Recent research by Brian Bocking, Alicia Turner, and Laurence Cox has shown that the first European to become a *bhikkhu* was an itinerant Irishman called Laurence Carroll (or O'Rourke), who was ordained in Burma and received the ordination name Dhammaloka. See Batchelor (2015), pp. 316–19. Also: https://dhammalokaproject .wordpress.com/u-dhammaloka/.
3. The magazine was *Buddhism: An Illustrated Review,* no. 2, edited by Bennett and published in Rangoon in October 1905. See Batchelor (1997), pp. 119–20.
4. *Majjhima Nikāya* 63. See Ñāṇamoli and Bodhi (1995), pp. 534–35.
5. I do not recall the source for this translation. Cf. Yamada (2004), case 41.

## THE OTHER ENLIGHTENMENT PROJECT

1. See Tuck (1990).
2. Lyotard (1986), p. xxiv. I have translated Lyotard's *grands récits* as "grand narratives" rather than as "metanarratives," as found in this English translation.
3. Strawson (1996), pp. 21–22.
4. In 2010 the FWBO changed its name to the Triratna Buddhist Community.
5. For further information on these organizations, see Batchelor (1994).
6. See, for example, Hookham (1991).

## WHAT'S WRONG WITH CONVERSION?

1. See Bodhi (2012), pp. 279–83.

## A SECULAR BUDDHIST

This paper was written as my part in a dialogue with the theologian Don Cupitt on the topic "The Future of Religion," which was held at the Friends Meeting House, Euston Road, London, on May 20, 2012. For his part, Don Cupitt wrote a paper entitled "A Secular Christian," which is available here: http://www.londoninsight.org/images/up loads/DC_A_Secular_Christian.pdf.

1. See Ling (1973).
2. See Cupitt (1995).
3. *Saṃyutta Nikāya* 45:49. See Bodhi (2000), p. 1543.

## A MINDFUL NATION?

1. This article is available online: http://secularbuddhism.org.nz/ resources/documents/facing-the-great-divide/.
2. Dalai Lama (2011), pp. xiii–xv.
3. This report can be read online: http://www.themindfulnessinitiative .org.uk/images/reports/Mindfulness-APPG-Report_Mindful-Nation -UK_Oct2015.pdf.
4. *Satipaṭṭhāna Sutta, Majjhima Nikāya* 10. See Ñāṇamoli and Bodhi (1995), p. 145. In their translation, the term *ekāyano* is translated as "the direct path."

## STUDY AND PRACTICE

1. *Dīgha Nikāya* 33. See Walshe (1995), p. 486.

## AFTER BUDDHISM

1. *Majjhima Nikāya* 89. See Ñāṇamoli and Bodhi (1995), pp. 728–33.
2. *Saṃyutta Nikāya* 22:94. See Bodhi (2000), p. 949.
3. *Cūḷamālunkya Sutta, Majjhima Nikāya* 63. See Ñāṇamoli and Bodhi (1995), pp. 533–41.
4. For a translation of the *Aṭṭhakavagga*, see Norman (2001), pp. 323–94.
5. *Saṃyutta Nikāya* 12:15. See Bodhi (2000), p. 544.
6. Batchelor (2000), p. 47.

## A CONVENIENT FICTION

1. Dalai Lama (1990), p. 290.

## A DEMOCRACY OF THE IMAGINATION

1. Cleary (1984), p. 55.
2. Sullivan (1964), p. 37.
3. Ibid., p. 63.
4. Aitken (1986), p. 119.

5. From the poem "Preludes," Eliot (1974), p. 25.
6. *Henri Cartier-Bresson* (1978), p. 5.
7. Ibid., p. 3.

## SEEING THE LIGHT

1. *Henri Cartier-Bresson* (1978), p. 3.

## A COSMOS OF FOUND OBJECTS

1. Wittgenstein (1977), p. 7.
2. David Batchelor (2014), p. 60.
3. From *The Marriage of Heaven and Hell,* see Blake (1994).
4. This fragment of Heraclitus is no. DK B124. www.heraclitusfragments .com.

## AN AESTHETICS OF EMPTINESS

This essay served as the keynote address for a symposium on dharma and art at the Barre Center for Buddhist Studies, April 28 to May 1, 2016.

1. Quoted in Holmes (1998), p. 130.
2. Quoted in Gittings (1966), pp. 40–41.
3. *Mūlamadhyamakakārikā* 18.1. This translation is from Batchelor (2000), p. 114. For a more literal translation, see Garfield (1995), p. 48.
4. With the exception of *Trikāya* 1.3, which is made of 324 pieces.
5. On the cosmological scale of multiple lifetimes, the three *kāya*s reflect the process of death, the intermediate state (Tibetan: *bar do*), and rebirth.
6. Rhys Davids and Stede (1979), p. 188.
7. *Saṃyutta Nikāya* 22:79. Cf. Bodhi (2000), p. 915. The primacy of white, yellow, blue, and red is here shown by the Buddha's answer to the rhetorical question: "What is perceived by perception (*saññā*)?" He says: "We perceive white, we perceive yellow, we perceive blue, we perceive red." These four are consistently grouped together in the *suttas* whenever color is described. Many centuries later, they reappear as such in the first lesson of Tibetan Geluk monastic education, *Ka dog dkar dmar* ("color theory").
8. *Saṃyutta Nikāya* 12:15. Cf. Bodhi (2000), p. 544.
9. *Majjhima Nikāya* 121. Cf. Ñāṇamoli and Bodhi (1995), pp. 965–70.

# BIBLIOGRAPHY

AITKEN, ROBERT. *A Zen Wave: Bashō's Haiku and Zen.* New York: Weatherhill, 1996.

ANDERSON, CAROL S. *Pain and Its Ending: The Four Noble Truths in the Theravāda Buddhist Canon.* Delhi: Motilal Banarsidass, 2001.

AUGUSTINE. (Trans. R. S. Pine-Coffin.) *Confessions.* Harmondsworth: Penguin, 1961.

BAAS, JACQUELYNN, and Mary Jane Jacob (Eds.). *Buddha Mind in Contemporary Art.* Berkeley: University of California Press, 2004.

BATCHELOR, DAVID. *Chromophobia.* London: Reaktion Books, 2000.

———. *The Luminous and the Grey.* London: Reaktion Books, 2014.

BATCHELOR, MARTINE. Photography by Stephen Batchelor. *Meditation for Life.* London: Frances Lincoln, 2001 (reissued by Echo Point Press, 2016).

BATCHELOR, STEPHEN. *After Buddhism: Rethinking the Dharma for a Secular Age.* New Haven: Yale University Press, 2015.

———. *Alone with Others: An Existential Approach to Buddhism.* New York: Grove, 1983.

———. *Buddhism without Beliefs: A Contemporary Guide to Awakening.* New York: Riverhead, 1997.

————. *The Faith to Doubt: Glimpses of Buddhist Uncertainty.* Berkeley: Counterpoint, 2015 (first published 1990).

————. *Living with the Devil: A Meditation on Good and Evil.* New York: Riverhead, 2004.

————. *Verses from the Center: A Buddhist Vision of the Sublime.* New York: Riverhead, 2000.

BLAKE, WILLIAM. *The Marriage of Heaven and Hell.* London: Dover, 1994 (first published 1790).

BODHI, BHIKKHU (Trans.). *The Connected Discourses of the Buddha: A New Translation of the Saṃyutta Nikāya.* Somerville, MA: Wisdom Publications, 2000.

———— (Trans. and ed.). *In the Buddha's Words: An Anthology of Discourses from the Pali Canon.* Somerville, MA: Wisdom Publications, 2005.

———— (Trans.). *The Numerical Discourses of the Buddha: A Translation of the Aṅguttara Nikāya.* Somerville, MA: Wisdom Publications, 2012.

BRONKHORST, JOHANNES. *Buddhism in the Shadow of Brahmanism.* Leiden: Brill, 2011.

———— . *Greater Magadha: Studies in the Culture of Early India.* Leiden: Brill, 2007.

CH'EN, KENNETH. *Buddhism in China: A Historical Survey.* Princeton: Princeton University Press, 1964.

CLEARY, THOMAS (Trans.). *The Flower Ornament Scripture: A Translation of the Avatamsaka Sutra.* Vol. 1. Boulder: Shambhala Publications, 1984.

CUPITT, DON. *Emptiness and Brightness.* Santa Rosa: Polebridge Press, 2001.

————. *Solar Ethics.* London: SCM Press, 1995.

————. *Turns of Phrase: Radical Theology from A to Z.* London: SCM Press, 2011.

DALAI LAMA. *Beyond Religion: Ethics for a Whole World.* New York: Houghton Mifflin Harcourt, 2011.

———. *Freedom in Exile: The Autobiography of His Holiness the Dalai Lama of Tibet.* London: Hodder and Stoughton, 1990.

EVOLA, JULIUS. *Le Chemin du Cinabre.* Milan: Arché-Arktos, 1982.

———. (Trans. Harold Musson.) *The Doctrine of Awakening: A Study on the Buddhist Ascesis.* London: Luzac, 1951.

FEUERBACH, LUDWIG. (Ed. and abridged by E. Graham Waring and F. W. Strothmann.) *The Essence of Christianity.* New York: Frederick Ungar, 1957.

GARFIELD, JAY L. (Trans.). *The Fundamental Wisdom of the Middle Way: Nāgārjuna's* Mūlamadhyamakakārikā. New York: Oxford University Press, 1995.

GITTINGS, ROBERT (Ed.). *Selected Poems and Letters of John Keats.* London: Heineman, 1966.

GOMBRICH, RICHARD F. *How Buddhism Began: The Conditioned Genesis of the Early Teachings.* London: Athlone, 1996.

———. *What the Buddha Thought.* London: Equinox, 2009.

HADOT, PIERRE. (Trans. Michael Chase. Ed. and with an Introduction by Arnold I. Davidson.) *Philosophy as a Way of Life: Spiritual Exercises from Socrates to Foucault.* Oxford: Blackwell, 1995.

*Henri Cartier-Bresson: His Archive of 390 Photographs from the Victoria and Albert Museum. With an Essay by Sir Ernst Gombrich.* Exhibition catalogue. Edinburgh: Scottish Arts Council, 1978.

HOLMES, RICHARD. *Coleridge: Darker Reflections.* London: Harper-Collins, 1998.

HOOKHAM, S. K. *The Buddha Within: Tathagatagarbha Doctrine According to the Shentong Interpretation of the Ratnagotravibhaga.* Albany: State University of New York Press, 1991.

HORNER, I. B. (Trans.) *The Book of Discipline*. Vol. 4, *Mahāvagga*. Oxford: Pali Text Society, 1951.

HUXLEY, T. H. *Science and the Christian Tradition*. London: Macmillan, 1904.

IRELAND, JOHN D. (Trans.). *The Udāna and the Itivuttaka*. Kandy: Buddhist Publication Society, 1997.

JACKSON, PETER, and David Morgan. *The Mission of Friar William of Rubruck*. London: Hakluyt Society, 1990.

KING, URSULA (Ed.). *Faith and Praxis in a Postmodern Age*. London: Cassell, 1998.

KUSAN SUNIM. *The Way of Korean Zen*. Boston: Weatherhill, 2009 (first published 1985).

LING, TREVOR. *The Buddha: Buddhist Civilisation in India and Ceylon*. London: Temple Smith, 1973.

LYOTARD, JEAN-FRANÇOIS. (Trans. Geoff Bennington and Brian Massumi.) *The Postmodern Condition: A Report on Knowledge*. Manchester, UK: Manchester University Press, 1986.

MACKENZIE, VICKI. *Reincarnation: The Boy Lama*. London: Bloomsbury, 1989.

MAUGHAM, ROBIN. *Search for Nirvana*. London: W. H. Allen, 1975.

———. *The Second Window*. London: Heinemann, 1968.

MAUGHAM, W. SOMERSET. *The Razor's Edge*. London: Mandarin, 1990 (first published 1944).

ÑĀṆAMOLI, BHIKKHU. *The Life of the Buddha*. Kandy: Buddhist Publication Society, 1978.

ÑĀṆAMOLI, BHIKKHU, and Bhikkhu Bodhi (Trans.). *The Middle Length Discourses of the Buddha: A Translation of the Majjhima Nikāya*. Boston: Wisdom Publications, 1995.

ÑĀṆASUCI, BHIKKHU HIRIKO. *The Hermit of Būndala: Biography of Ñāṇavīra Thera and Reflections on His Life and Work*. Path Press Publications, 2014.

ÑĀṆAVĪRA THERA. (Ed. Sāmaṇera Bodhesako.) *Clearing the Path, 1960–1965.* Colombo: Path Press, 1987 (revised edition, Path Press Publications, 2010).

NORMAN, K. R. *Collected Papers.* Vol. 2. Oxford: Pali Text Society, 2003.

——— (Trans.). *The Group of Discourses (Sutta-Nipāta).* Oxford: Pali Text Society, 2001.

PABONGKA RINPOCHE. (Ed. Trijang Rinpoche. Trans. Michael Richards). *Liberation in the Palm of your Hand: A Concise Discourse on the Path to Enlightenment.* Boston: Wisdom Publications, 1991.

PARKIN, SARA. *The Life and Death of Petra Kelly.* London: Harper-Collins, 1994.

RADHAKRISHNAN, S. *The Principal Upaniṣads.* Delhi: HarperCollins, 1994.

RHYS DAVIDS, T. W., and William Stede. *The Pali Text Society's Pali-English Dictionary.* London: Pali Text Society, 1979 (first published 1921–25).

RORTY, RICHARD. *Contingency, Irony and Solidarity.* New York: Cambridge University Press, 1989.

ŚĀNTIDEVA. (1) Trans. from Sanskrit by Kate Crosby and Andrew Skilton. *The Bodhicaryāvatāra.* Oxford: Oxford University Press, 1996. (2) Trans. from Tibetan by Stephen Batchelor. *A Guide to the Bodhisattva's Way of Life.* Dharamsala: Library of Tibetan Works and Archives, 1979.

SCHOPEN, GREGORY. *Bones, Stones, and Buddhist Monks: Collected Papers on the Archaeology, Epigraphy, and Texts of Monastic Buddhism in India.* Honolulu: University of Hawai'i Press, 1997.

SCHUMANN, H. W. *The Historical Buddha: The Times, Life and Teachings of the Founder of Buddhism.* London: Arkana, 1989.

SKORUPSKI, TADEUSZ (Ed.). *The Buddhist Forum.* Vol. 4. London: School of Oriental and African Studies, 1996.

STRAWSON, GALEN. "The Sense of Self." *London Review of Books,* April 18, 1996.

SULLIVAN, J. W. N. *Beethoven: His Spiritual Development.* London: Unwin Books, 1964 (first published 1927).

TSONG-KHA-PA. (Trans. The Lamrim Chenmo Translation Committee.) 3 volumes. *The Great Treatise on the Stages of the Path to Enlightenment.* Ithaca, NY: Snow Lion, 2000, 2002, 2004.

————. *rTsa she tik chen rigs pa'i rgya mtsho.* Sarnath: Pleasure of Elegant Sayings Printing Press, 1973.

TUCK, ANDREW P. *Comparative Philosophy and the Philosophy of Scholarship: On the Western Interpretation of Nāgārjuna.* New York/Oxford: Oxford University Press, 1990.

VATTIMO, GIANNI. *A Farewell to Truth.* New York: Columbia University Press, 2011.

WALSHE, MAURICE (Trans.). *The Long Discourses of the Buddha: A Translation of the Dīgha Nikāya.* Boston: Wisdom Publications, 1995.

WATERFIELD, R. "Baron Julius Evola and the Hermetic Tradition." *Gnosis,* no. 14 (Winter 1989–90).

WETTIMUNY, R. G. de S. *The Buddha's Teaching: Its Essential Meaning.* Sri Lanka: Private edition, 1990 (first published 1969).

WILLSON, MARTIN. *Rebirth and the Western Buddhist.* London: Wisdom Publications, 1984.

WITTGENSTEIN, LUDWIG. (Trans. G. E. M. Anscombe.) *Philosophical Investigations.* Oxford: Basil Blackwell, 1958.

————. (Ed. G. E. M. Anscombe. Trans. L. L. McAlister and M. Schättle.) *Remarks on Colour.* Oxford: Basil Blackwell, 1977.

WYNNE, ALEXANDER. *The Origin of Buddhist Meditation*. London: Routledge, 2007.

YAMADA, KŌUN (Trans.). *The Gateless Gate: The Classic Book of Zen Kōans*. Somerville, MA: Wisdom Publications, 2004.

ZOLLA, E. "The Evolution of Julius Evola's Thought." *Gnosis*, no. 14 (Winter 1989–90).

# Acknowledgments

"Existence, Enlightenment, and Suicide" first appeared in Tadeusz Skorupski, ed., *The Buddhist Forum*, vol. 4 (1996).

"A Secular Buddhism" first appeared in the *Journal of Global Buddhism* 13 (2012).

"Rebirth: A Case for Buddhist Agnosticism" first appeared in *Tricycle* 2, no. 1 (Fall 1992).

"Creating Sangha" first appeared in *Tricycle* 5, no. 2 (Winter 1995).

"The Agnostic Buddhist" first appeared in the newsletter of the Rochester Zen Center (1996).

"The Other Enlightenment Project: Buddhism, Agnosticism and Postmodernity" first appeared in Ursula King, ed., *Faith and Praxis in a Postmodern Age* (1998).

"What's Wrong with Conversion?" first appeared in the *Independent* (London), May 29, 1999.

"Limits of Agnosticism" first appeared as a blog on the *Tricycle* website, April 12, 2006.

"A Secular Buddhist" first appeared in *Tricycle* 22, no. 1 (Fall 2012).

"A Mindful Nation?" appeared in an edited form in the *Times* (London), February 6, 2016.

"The Eclectic Cleric" first appeared in *Tricycle* 13, no. 1 (Fall 2003).

"Study and Practice" first appeared in the *Sati Journal* 1 (2011).

"After Buddhism" first appeared in the *Insight Journal* (2015).

"A Convenient Fiction" first appeared in *Resurgence*, no. 156 (1993).

"A Democracy of the Imagination" first appeared in *Tricycle* 4, no. 2 (Winter 1994).

"Seeing the Light" first appeared in Martine Batchelor, *Meditation for Life* (2001), and Baas and Jacob, eds., *Buddha Mind in Contemporary Art* (2004).

"A Cosmos of Found Objects" first appeared in the *International New York Times*, January 2, 2015.

"In Search of a Voice," "A Much Younger Man, but No Less Charming," and "An Aesthetics of Emptiness" are published here for the first time.

I am grateful to Peter Maddock and Don Cupitt for permission to use their words in my interviews with them; to Bhikkhu Hiriko and Path Press for permission to reprint passages from Ñāṇavīra Thera's *Clearing the Path;* to the Sati Center and Jeff Hardin for permission to reprint "Study and Practice"; and to the Barre Center for Buddhist Studies and Chris Talbott for permission to reprint "After Buddhism." Chris Talbott created the original figure "Four noble truths or four great tasks?" to illustrate a point I was making.

I would like to thank Jan Willis, Mick Brown, Marshall Glickmann, and Winton Higgins, all of whom played a role in making this book possible.

I am indebted to my agent Anne Edelstein and my editor Jennifer Banks for steering this project to completion.

# INDEX

imagination, 227–28; language for, 192, 205–6; postmodern perspective in, 145–50; psychological dimension of, 192–93; stereotypes of, 52; transmission process in, 143–44. *See also* Musson, Harold Edward (Ñāṇavīra Thera); secular Buddhism

"wheel of dharma," 221

Wheeler, Roger Ash, 113

Wijesekera, O. H. de A., 51

William of Rubruck, 111, 113

Willson, Martin, 120

Wittgenstein, Ludwig, 205

Wolf, Hannelore (Vajira), 42–43

*Work No. 227* (Creed), 249–50

*World, the Flesh and Myself, The* (Davidson), 69

Yeshe, Lama Thubten, 111–12, 114, 122

Zen Buddhism, 25, 37, 79, 117, 125, 140, 165

Zhiyi, 222

Zopa, Lama Thubten, 112, 113, 122